SUFFOLK RECORDS SOCIETY

SUFFOLK CHARTERS

Founding Editor
the late Professor R. Allen Brown

XVI

DODNASH PRIORY CHARTERS

Dodnash Priory was one of numerous Augustinian priories founded in East Anglia in the twelfth and early thirteenth centuries. Its history has hitherto been totally obscure. The two hundred original charters edited here demonstrate that it was founded by Wimer the chaplain, sheriff of Norfolk and Suffolk and a prominent servant of Henry II, and that the community, although always small, played a disproportionate role in the economic and social life of south-east Suffolk for the next three centuries. The early charters include the first known references to Flatford Mill at East Bergholt; later documents relate to serious flooding at the end of the thirteenth century, and soon thereafter to the leasing of estates in order to adapt to new economic conditions. As always in such collections, the charters provide much information about local lay society as well as the canons themselves.

CHRISTOPHER HARPER-BILL, a former pupil of R. Allen Brown who founded the Suffolk Charters series, is general editor of two Boydell & Brewer series, Suffolk Charters and Studies in the History of Medieval Religion. He has published several editions of medieval ecclesiastical records and articles on medieval East Anglia. He is now Professor of English History at UEA, Norwich.

SUFFOLK RECORDS SOCIETY

SUFFOLK CHARTERS

ISSN 0261–9938

General Editor
Professor Christopher Harper-Bill

External Advisors

Professor G.W.S. Barrow	Dr Marjorie Chibnall
Dr Pierre Chaplais	Miss Kathleen Major

Details of previously published volumes of Suffolk Charters
are available from the publishers.

DODNASH PRIORY CHARTERS

Edited by Christopher Harper-Bill

The Boydell Press

Suffolk Records Society

First published 1998

Published for the Suffolk Records Society
by The Boydell Press
an imprint of Boydell & Brewer Ltd
PO Box 9, Woodbridge, Suffolk IP12 3DF, UK
and of Boydell & Brewer Inc.
PO Box 41026, Rochester, NY 14604–4126, USA

ISBN 0 85115 372 0

A catalogue record for this book is available
from the British Library

This publication is printed on acid-free paper

Printed in Great Britain by
St Edmundsbury Press Ltd, Bury St Edmunds, Suffolk

CONTENTS

FOR NORMAN SCARFE

IN RECOGNITION OF HIS CONTRIBUTION TO
THE HISTORY OF SUFFOLK
AND WITH THANKS FOR HIS KINDNESS

This volume is published with the assistance
of a grant from Isobel Thornley's Bequest to
the University of London.

PREFACE

The present volume is an edition of the surviving original charters of the small community of Augustinian canons at Dodnash, found in various repositories. Thanks are due to the authorities of the Suffolk Record Office, the Public Record Office, the British Library and the Bodleian Library, Oxford, for permission to publish documents in their custody, and most especially to Lord Tollemache for allowing access to and granting leave to publish charters from his family archive at Helmingham Hall.

I have incurred many debts in the preparation of this volume, which I happily acknowledge. Much of the work was accomplished during two periods of sabbatical leave, generously funded by the Leverhulme Trust and by another sympathetic charitable foundation. Mr William Serjeant provided me with photostats of the Helmingham Hall documents, and arranged for their temporary deposit for checking at Ipswich. Dr David Jones, of the Suffolk Record Office, allowed the 'cartulary' to be temporarily lodged at Kingston, and Dr David Robinson, County Archivist of Surrey, kindly received it there for my use. Mr Sandy Heslop gave me much help when confronted by my amateurish description of seals. Dr Sandra Raban analysed for me the complex process under the provisions of mortmain legislation by which the manor of Dodnash was acquired. Professor Jane Sayers discussed with me the suspicious bull of Pope Honorius III. None of them, of course, is responsible for the errors and infelicities which doubtless remain. I am grateful, also, to Mrs Vivien Brown for reading the proofs, to Mr Donald Desborough, Professor Mark Ormrod and Miss Caroline Palmer for various kindnesses, and to my wife, Dr Ruth Harvey, for her unfailing support and patience. Special thanks are due to my colleagues, who have made my translation to Norwich such a happy experience.

As general editor of the series, I wish to record my thanks, and that of the Society, to the Trustees of Miss Isobel Thornley's Bequest to the University of London for yet another grant in aid of publication, and to Dr Richard Barber and the staff of Boydell and Brewer for their customary care and for their patience with an editor who persists in using an antique manual typewriter.

Most of all, I wish to acknowledge my gratitude to Norman Scarfe. From his vast store of knowledge he has helped me immeasurably on several difficult problems of topography, and in other practical ways. The dedication of this volume is an expression of my personal debt to him, and also a recognition of his status as doyen of the modern historians of Suffolk.

School of History   *Christopher Harper-Bill*
UEA, Norwich

Possessions of Dodnash Priory (underlined)

ABBREVIATIONS

BAR	British Archaeological Reports, British Series
Battle Chronicle	*The Chronicle of Battle Abbey*, ed. E. Searle, Oxford 1980
Birch, *Cat.* BM Seals	W. de Gray Birch, *Catalogue of Seals in the Dept. of MSS, British Museum*, i, London 1887
Bk Fees	*Liber Feodorum: The Book of Fees commonly called Testa de Nevill*, ed. H.C. Maxwell-Lyte, 3 vols, London 1920–31
BL	British Library
Bodl.	Bodleian Library, Oxford
C Ch R	*Calendar of Charter Rolls*, 6 vols, London 1903 etc.
CCR	*Calendar of Close Rolls*, 67 vols, London 1902 etc.
CIPM	*Calendar of Inquisitions Post Mortem*, 16 vols, London 1917 etc.
C Inq Misc	*Calendar of Inquisitions Miscellaneous*, 7 vols, London 1916 etc.
Copinger, *Manors*	W.A. Copinger, *Manors of Suffolk: Notes on their History and Devolution*, 7 vols, London 1905–11
Copinger, *Materials*	W.A. Copinger, *Materials for the History of Suffolk*, 6 vols, London 1904–7
CPR	*Calendar of Patent Rolls*, 60 vols, London 1901 etc.
CRR	*Curia Regis Rolls*, 16 vols, London 1923 etc.
CYS	Canterbury and York Society
DB	*Liber censualis vocatus Domesday Book*, ed. A. Farley, 2 vols, Record Commission, London 1783
EEA vi	*English Episcopal Acta vi: Norwich 1070–1214*, ed. C. Harper-Bill, London 1990
EHR	*English Historical Review*
Eye Cartulary	*Eye Priory Cartulary and Charters*, ed. V. Brown, 2 vols, Suffolk Charters xii–xiii, Woodbridge 1992–94
Farrer, *Honours and Knights' Fees*	W. Farrer, *Honours and Knights' Fees*, 3 vols, London 1923–25
Fasti	*John le Neve, Fasti Ecclesiae Anglicanae, 1066–1300*, ed. D.E. Greenway, London 1968 etc.
Fines ii	*Feet of Fines for the County of Norfolk, 1202–15, and of Suffolk, 1199–1214*, ed. B. Dodwell, PRS ns xxxii, 1958
Foedera	*Foedera, conventiones, litterae et cuiuscunque generis acta publica*, ed. T. Rymer, 20 vols, London 1727–35
GEC	*The Complete Peerage of England . . .*, ed. V. Gibbs *et al.*, 13 vols, London 1913 etc.

Abbreviations

HBC	*Handbook of British Chronology*, ed. E.B. Fryde *et al.*, 3rd edn, London 1986
HMCR	*Reports of the Historical Manuscripts Commission*
Hospitaller Cartulary	*The Cartulary of the Knights of St John of Jerusalem in England: Secunda Camera, Essex*, ed. M. Gervers, British Academy Records of Social and Economic History ns vi, 1982
HR	*Rotuli Hundredorum temp. Henry III et Edward I*, ed. W. Illingworth, 2 vols, Record Commission, London, 1812–18.
JL	P. Jaffé, ed., *Regesta pontificum Romanorum . . . ad annum 1198*, 2nd edn, ed. S. Loewenfeld *et al.*, 2 vols, Leipzig 1885–8
Leiston Cartulary	*The Leiston Cartulary and Butley Charters*, ed. R. Mortimer, Suffolk Charters i, Woodbridge 1979
Loyd, *Anglo-Norman Families*	L.C. Loyd, *The Origins of Some Anglo-Norman Families* Harleian Society ciii, 1951
LPFD	*Letters and Papers, Foreign and Domestic, Henry VIII*, ed. J.S. Brewer, J. Gairdner and R.H. Brodie, 22 vols, London 1864–1932
Monasticon	*Monasticon Anglicanum* of William Dugdale, ed. J. Caley *et al.*, 6 vols in 8 parts, London 1817–30
MRH	D. Knowles and R.N. Hadcock, *Medieval Religious Houses, England and Wales*, 2nd edn, London 1971
NRO	Norfolk Record Office
ns	new series
PBKJ	*Pleas before the King and his Justices, 1198–1212*, ed. D.M. Stenton, 4 vols, Selden Society, London 1948 etc.
PR	Pipe Roll
PRO	Public Record Office
PRS	Pipe Roll Society
PSIA	*Proceedings of the Suffolk Institute of Archaeology*
Red Bk Exchq.	*The Red Book of the Exchequer*, ed. H. Hall, 3 vols, Rolls Series xcix, London 1897
Reg. Butley	*The Register or Chronicle of Butley Priory, Suffolk, 1510–1535* ed. A.G. Dickens, Winchester 1951
Rot. Litt. Claus.	*Rotuli Litterarum Clausarum*, ed. T.D. Hardy, 2 vols, Record Commission, London 1833
Rye, *Fines*	W. Rye, *A Calendar of the Feet of Fines for Suffolk*, Ipswich 1900
SCH	*Studies in Church History*
Shotley Parish Records	S.H.A. Hervey, *Shotley Parish Records*, Suffolk Green Books xvi (2), Bury St Edmunds 1912
Sibton Cartularies	*Sibton Abbey Cartularies and Charters*, ed. P. Brown, 4 vols, Suffolk Charters vii–x, Woodbridge 1985–8
SRO	Suffolk Record Office
Sudbury Charters	*Charters of St Bartholomew's Priory, Sudbury*, ed. R. Mortimer, Suffolk Charters xv, Woodbridge 1996

Taxatio	*Taxatio Ecclesiastica Angliae et Walliae auctoritate* P. *Nicholai IV,* Record Commission, London 1802
Tout, *Chapters*	T.F. Tout, *Chapters in the Administrative History of Mediaeval England,* 6 vols, Manchester 1920–33
VN	*The Valuation of Norwich,* ed. W.E. Lunt, Oxford 1926
X	'Decretales', in *Corpus Iuris Canonici,* ed. E. Friedberg, 2 vols, Leipzig 1879–81

CONCORDANCE OF MANUSCRIPTS WITH NUMBERS IN THIS EDITION

Note: The numbers given in brackets in the caption to each charter are given for the convenience of those using the handlist in the Institute of Historical Research, London, and possibly elsewhere. They are now obsolete and should not be used.

Helmingham Hall

MS no.	Edn no.	MS no.	Edn no.	MS no.	Edn no.
T/Hel/		98/12	142	98/27	169
44/1 (Tollemache		98/13	143	98/28	171
cartulary), no. 6		98/14	145	98/29	170
	24A	98/15	146	98/30	155
98/1	47	98/16	148	98/31	172
98/2	109	98/17	152	98/32	200
98/3	130A	98/18	153	98/33	201
98/4	43	98/19	212	98/34	174
98/5	179	98/20	154	98/35	204
98/6	110	98/21	67	98/36	176
98/7	74	98/22	65	98/37	192
98/8	162	98/23	214	98/38	112
98/9	163	98/24	159	98/39	193
98/10	196	98/25	187	98/40	208
98/11	141	98/26	207	98/41	178A
(S)/10/54	15A				

Ipswich, SRO, HD 1538/202/1 (Dodnash 'cartulary')

MS no.	Edn no.	MS no.	Edn no.	MS no.	Edn no.
1	8	13	74	25	58
2	1	14	75	26	59
3	3	15	72	27	15, 19, 49
4	53	16	71	28	111
5	29	17	7	29	32
6	29	18	7	30	77
7	10	19	114	31	16
8	9	20	114	32	17
9	54	21	2	33	35
10	7	22	6	34	36
11	55	23	13	35	33
12	56	24	128	36	93

MS no.	Edn no.	MS no.	Edn no.	MS no.	Edn no.
37	35	78	76	117/2	184
38	87	79	18	118	140
39	108	80	105	119	144
40	92	81	21	120	147
41	91	82	23	121	197
42	79	83	130	122	149
43	78	84	24	123	150
44	131	85	83	124	210
45	132	86	89	125	211
46	134	87	25	126	151
47	101	88	20	127	123
48	81	89/1	106	128	124
49	102	89/2	100	129	199
50	103	90	161	130	125
51	80	91	161	131	198
52	82	92	46	132	164
53	95	93	45	133	165
54	60	94	26	134	156
55	61	95	122	135	180
56	94	96	129	136	66
57	30	97	84	137	157
58	88	98	34	138	213
59	115	99	160	139	166
60	97	100	85	140	167
61	98	101	183	141	186
62	96	102	86	142	188
63	31	103	63	143	168
64	33	104	51	144	116
65	121	105	42	145	189
66	14	106	48	146	181
67	133	107	208	147	69
68	135	108 *vacat*		148	203
69	104	109	206	149	215
70	90	110	27	150	117
71	40	111	65	151	175
72	50	112 *vacat*		152	191
73	41	113	73	153	191
74	39	114	127	154	177
75	44	115	195	155	178
76	136	116	28	156	158
77	99	117/1	126		

Ipswich, SRO, HD 1538/204

1	22	5	68
3	148	6	190
4	185		

Concordance of Charters

Ipswich, SRO, HD 1538/278

MS no.	Edn no.	MS no.	Edn no.
1	118	3	194
2	119	4	120

Ipswich, SRO, q s 271 (Fitch's Monasticon Suffolciense, vol. ii)

at p. 166	5	at p. 178	182, 202
at p. 167	70	at p. 186	57, 107

London, British Library

Additional charter 9551	170A
Additional charter 9602	152A

London, Public Record Office

CP25/1 (Feet of Fines)

/212/1/20	12	/213/10/78	38
/213/7/14	62	/215/38/29	64

E210 (Ancient Deeds)

/376	4

Oxford, Bodleian Library

Suffolk charter 196	173

CHRONOLOGICAL LIST OF CHARTERS

Before 25 Sept. 1188: 1–3
25 Sept. 1188: 4
13 Nov. 1188 × 6 July 1189: 5
Late 1188 × late 1189: 6
Before 14 Nov. 1196: 7–10
14 Nov. 1196: 12
Late 12th century: 11
Late 12th – early 13th century: 13, 29,
   53–6, 58, 71–2, 74–5, 113, 128
Early 13th century: 31, 43, 77, 87
Shortly after 21 March 1215: 15
17 Jan. 1218: 111
Before 2 Aug. 1221: 14, 114
28 Oct. 1223 × 27 Oct. 1224: 16
28 Oct. 1224 × 27 Oct. 1225: 17
1226: 35
13 Oct. 1228: 62
Before Easter 1232: 88, 118
16 May 1232: 19
20 Nov. 1234: 38
1220s–1230s: 109
Early–mid 13th century: 18, 30, 32–3,
   36–7, 44, 60–1, 70, 76, 78–82, 90–8,
   102–5, 108, 110, 115, 119–20, 131–4
6 Nov. 1243: 23
May 1250: 25
28 Oct. 1252 × Michaelmas 1257: 42
Before 1253: 89
11 June 1257: 63
Before Michaelmas 1257: 24A
Mid 13th century: 20–2, 24, 39–40, 57,
   59, 83–4, 100, 115A, 129, 135–6,
   160–1, 194
Mid–late 13th century: 34, 41
Probably 1272–73: 45
Shortly after 1272–73: 46
14 May 1276: 48
23 Dec. 1279: 209
Shortly after 1279: 130
c. 1279 × 1304: 26
1270s–1280s: 85–6, 107
1 Aug. 1282: 49
Michaelmas 1284: 206
Probably before 1285: 99

12 March 1285: 27
1 Dec. 1286: 64
Probably 1287: 50
1 May 1297: 73
Late 13th century: 47, 51, 122, 183
Early 14th century: 179
Early–mid 14th century: 165
1301: 126–7
1307: 28
1309: 162
1316: 163
1321: 196
1326: 184
1327: 52
1331: 137–40
1332: 141–4
1333: 145–50, 197, 210
1334: 211
1335: 123, 151
1336: 124, 152–3
1337: 125, 199
1338: 212
1341: 198
1342: 154
1343: 164, 185
1348: 156
1350: 65, 180
1351: 66–7, 157–8
1352: 68, 213
1355: 214
1356: 166–7
1358: 159
1361: 186
1362: 168, 187–8, 207
1363: 169–71
1366: 155
1368: 116, 189
1369: 172
1370: 181
1371: 200
1372: 69, 201
1373: 182, 202
1375: 190, 203
1377: 173

PRIORS OF DODNASH

ALAN   first prior, occurs 25 August 1188 (4)

JORDAN   occurs Michaelmas 1228 (*CRR* xiii, no. 1202); 13 October 1228 (62); 12 November 1234 (38)

RICHARD   mid thirteenth century (160, 194); probably, but not certainly, before Robert

ROBERT   28 October 1252 × Michaelmas 1257 (42); mid thirteenth century (21, 24A, 161)

JOHN   occurs 16 December 1279 (209)

RALPH   occurs 12 March 1285 (27); 1 December 1286 (64); 1 May 1297 (73): 29 September 1301 (127)

[EDMUND OF STONE elected 1304, before 13 April, when right of appointment devolved upon bishop because of 'ineptitude and sin' of election, and his own unsuitability (NRO, NER 1/1, fo. 5v)]

HENRY OF FRAMLINGHAM   canon of Dodnash, appointed by bishop, 13 April 1304 (NRO, NER 1/1, fo. 5v)

JOHN   occurs from 25 October 1304 (195) to 2 February 1316 (163)

JOHN OF GUSFORD   canon of Dodnash, election and examination confirmed 26 March 1317 (NRO, NER 1/1, fo. 69v); last dated occurrence 9 November 1343 (164); resigned by 10 May 1346 (NRO, NER 2/4, fo. 54r)

ADAM (LE) NEWMAN   canon of Dodnash; election quashed because of 'ineptitude of matter and form', but appointed by bishop on 10 May 1346 because of his merits and the unanimous election of canons (NRO, NER 2/4, fo. 54r); still prior on 25 November 1348 (156)

HENRY OF BENACRE   canon of Dodnash; election quashed because of 'ineptitude of matter and form', but appointed by bishop on 19 June 1349 (NRO, NER 2/4, fo. 85v); last occurs on 11 June 1362 (168)

ROGER   occurs from 24 September 1363 to 15 December 1382 (169, 215)

THOMAS OF THORNHAM   resigned by 10 July 1383, when appointed prior of Holy Trinity, Ipswich (NRO, NER 3/6, fo. 90v)

WALTER BAA   canon of Butley, unanimously postulated by canons of Dodnash; postulation quashed because of 'ineptitude', but appointed by bishop, 12 April 1384 (NRO, NER 3/6, fo. 98v); still prior on 5 April 1397 (174)

JOHN CAPEL   canon of Dodnash, appointed by bishop, on whom collation had devolved, 15 June 1406 (NRO, NER 3/6, fo. 332r); still prior on 13 December 1411 (175)

ROBERT NEWBORNE   prior by 8 September 1427 (176); resigned by 27 November 1438 (NRO, NER 5/10, fo. 19v)

MICHAEL OF COLCHESTER   canon of St Osyth; appointed by vicar-general, since collation had devolved upon ordinary, 27 November 1438 (NRO, NER 5/10, fo. 19v); resigned by 17 August 1444 (ibid., fo. 55v)

RICHARD WHITING   canon of Buckenham, appointed by bishop, on whom collation had devolved, 17 August 1444 (NRO, NER 5/10, fo. 55r; still prior on 1 September 1472 (112)

ROBERT CARRE   occurs 12 December 1492, 8 May 1493 (178, 193)

JOHN BRYDGEWATER   occurs 30 June 1497, 20 March 1523 (178A, 208)

WILLIAM MELFORD   formerly canon (1514) and cellarer (1520) of Butley; occurs late May 1524 (*Reg. Butley*, 44)

THOMAS   occurs 1 February 1525, at dissolution (*LPFD* iv(i), no. 1137 (vi)); but *Reg. Butley*, 47, still has Melford as prior at dissolution which it dates on 25 January 1525

INTRODUCTION

The history of the small priory of Augustinian canons at Dodnash has long remained particularly obscure. Only two of its charters have hitherto been published (4, 12), and the episcopal confirmation of 1188 has been misinterpreted, so
that the foundation has been attributed to Baldwin de Tosni and his mother Ada,
from whom, in fact, the real founder, Wimer the chaplain, acquired land for the
fulfilment of his intention.[1] The only reference to the house in the records of the
chapters of the English Augustinian canons is its inclusion in lists of communities.[2] More strangely, there is no record of visitation by the bishops of Norwich in
1492, 1514 or 1520, although the priory was not exempt from episcopal jurisdic-
tion.[3] In the context of recent historiography, Dodnash receives no mention in the
comprehensive study of the geography of Augustinian settlement, despite providing an interesting example of a site change.[4] The reason for modern neglect is
certainly that the vast majority of the more than two hundred charters here
printed or calendared either are, or until recently were, in private hands, and their
existence was not widely known.

This edition of documents, drawn largely from the collection formerly of the
Earl of Iveagh, now deposited at the Suffolk Record Office at Ipswich, and from
the archives of Lord Tollemache at Helmingham Hall, certainly does not represent the entire documentary record of the priory. Most notably, there is practically
nothing relating to the canons' most valuable estate at Falkenham. The collection
does, however, amplify in many ways the history of a small community which,
while it was of absolutely no national significance, did obviously play an important part in the life of its own locality, even within the crowded religious land-
scape of south-eastern Suffolk.

---

1   *MRH*, 156. *Monasticon* vi (i), 50, following T. Tanner, *Notitia Monastica*, Suffolk xvi, states that
    Dodnash was founded by one Wymarus, or by the ancestors of the dukes of Norfolk.
2   *Chapters of the Augustinian Canons*, ed. H.E. Salter, CYS xxix, 1922, 270, 275, 277.
3   *Visitations of the Diocese of Norwich, A.D. 1492–1532*, ed. A. Jessopp, Camden Society ns xliii,
    1888. The priory was visited by the commissary of the archbishop of Canterbury during the va-
    cancy of the see of Norwich in June 1336 (NRO, DCN 42/1/16), but not in similar circumstances
    in 1499 (*Register of John Morton, Archbishop of Canterbury, 1486–1500*, ed. C. Harper-Bill, 3
    vols 1987 etc., CYS, iii, forthcoming).
4   D.M. Robinson, *The Geography of Augustinian Settlement in Medieval England and Wales*, BAR,
    British Series lxxx, 2 vols, Oxford 1980.

1

THE FOUNDER

The text of Bishop John of Oxford's confirmation charter (4) and the endorsement 'fundator' on one of his own charters (6) make it quite clear that the founder of the community of Augustinian canons established originally in the aldergrove at East Bergholt and soon afterwards at Dodnash was Wimer the chaplain.[5] It will be suggested below that he was of the same family as the descendants of Hervey of Dodnash who provided, usually for a price, so much of the early endowment of the priory. Wimer first appears in royal records in 1165–66 as a servant of the king active in East Anglia; he accounted for the castles of Eye and Orford, where the king's great building programme was just beginning.[6] In 1169 he was with Henry II on the continent, and with Walter of Grimsby brought to England the constitutions designed to strengthen royal control over the English church and to thwart Thomas Becket's initiatives. After the archbishop's return to England, Wimer was excommunicated, along with several other royal servants, but was apparently absolved, without papal or archiepiscopal consent, by William, bishop of Norwich.[7] In spring 1170, following the Inquest of Sheriffs, he became sheriff of Norfolk and Suffolk, and his returns to the Exchequer at Michaelmas 1170 still include the abbey of St Benet of Holme and the honour of Eye, which he had previously administered.[8] He acted as itinerant justice in Norfolk and Suffolk, Cambridgeshire and Huntingdonshire in 1172–73, and the next year in Essex and Hertfordshire.[9] His activities as sheriff are recorded annually on the Pipe Rolls until his resignation is entered in the roll of 34 Henry II, that is, before Michaelmas 1188; this coincides almost exactly with the foundation of his priory. He paid the king 200 marks in quittance of any claims which might be made against himself or his servants for actions committed in the execution of their duties.[10]

In Becket's notification of his excommunication, Wimar is referred to as a protegé (*alumnus*) of Hugh Bigod, earl of Norfolk, and it is notable that, twenty and more years later, the tenants of Roger Bigod occur among the benefactors of Dodnash and the witnesses of charters in its favour. Earl Hugh's participation in the great rebellion of 1173–74 against Henry II caused a clash of interests, but Wimer remained firmly loyal to the king, and as sheriff was probably closely involved in the demolition of the defeated earl's castles. During the war, or in its aftermath, Wimer allegedly attempted to eject Thomas, a clerk of Earl Hugh, from his church of Holy Cross, Bungay, and inflicted damage on the property of

---

5 For a short biography, see *Decretales ineditae saeculi xii*, ed. S. Chodorow and C. Duggan, *Monumenta Iuris Canonici* series B, vol. iv, Vatican City 1982, 84–5.

6 *PR 12 Henry II*, 17.

7 D. Knowles, A.J. Duggan and C.N.L. Brooke, 'Henry II's Supplement to the Constitutions of Clarendon', *EHR* lxxxvii, 1972, 757–71, esp. 765; *Materials for the History of Thomas Becket*, ed. J.C. Robertson, 7 vols, Roll Series LXVII, London 1875–85, vi, Ep. 507, p. 603; *Decretales Ineditae*, no. 51.

8 *PR 16 Henry II*, 1, 3, 13.

9 *PR 19 Henry II*, 19, 159.

10 *PR 34 Henry II*, 58.

that church. In one of the four mandates to papal judges-delegate elicited by Thomas's complaints in the years 1174–76, it was ordered that the excommunication of 1169, never canonically lifted, should be reimposed, and a subsequent papal letter suggests that Wimer was attempting to manipulate the course of justice by suppression of the truth.[11] His eye for profit is illustrated, too, by the marriage of his niece to Reginald of Layham, which he alleged was done 'per dominum regem',[12] while in the year ending Michaelmas 1185 he was amerced £200 for disseising Geoffrey 'Gloriosus'.[13]

After a career of at least a quarter of a century in the service of the Angevin monarchy Wimer, like all those who implemented Henry II's policies and gained great status and profit in the process, must have done much for which at the end of his term of office he felt the need to atone. His foundation stands alongside those of Ranulf de Glanvil at Butley (1171) and Leiston (1183), of Herbert Walter at West Dereham (1188), and John of Oxford's revival of Holy Trinity, Ipswich, as witness to the compulsion felt by the king's ministers to make reparation, and also to their commitment to the canonical rather than to the monastic life.[14]

THE SITE

The known site, of which there is only one stone, about a foot high, standing, is just north of the stream which serves as the parish boundary between East Bergholt and Bentley, on the Bentley side and to the south of Dodnash wood. Nearby is a man-made pond, and a number of ramparts and earthworks.[15] This was, almost certainly, the second and permanent site. That there was a site-change is clearly indicated by a mid thirteenth-century grant by Prior Richard and the canons to John son of Andrew of a parcel of land in Dodnash, on which the house of St Mary of Dodnash was once located (160).

It is clear from the charters of Ada de Tosny and Baldwin her son that the land which they granted to Wimer the chaplain was intended to be the site of a religious house (2–3), and from the episcopal confirmation that the canons were first established on this land in East Bergholt (4). Strangely, East Bergholt, despite its obvious importance as revealed in Domesday Book,[16] did not have parochial status, and spiritual ministrations in the vill were conducted at a chapel which was a dependency of Brantham church, which by a grant of King William Rufus

---

11 *Decretales Ineditae*, nos 46, 51–3.
12 PRS os xxxv (*Rot. de dominabus*), xxiv, 48.
13 *PR 31 Henry II*, xxxii, 41.
14 For Glanvil especially, see R. Mortimer, 'Religious and Secular Motives for some English Monastic Foundations', *SCH* xv, 77–86.
15 S. Podd, *Earthwork Reconnaissance in Suffolk: Rapid Identification Survey*, Archaeological Section, Suffolk County Council, 1995, at map 5A, notes: 'Two dams (? to create fishponds) in Dodnash wood . . . These dams appear to be old features, and given their proximity to the site of Dodnash Priory . . . it seems likely that they are, in fact, part of the Priory complex.'
16 *DB* ii, 287.

pertained to Battle abbey, the rights of which were safeguarded at the foundation of Wimer's priory.[17] It is, indeed, probable that this first site was in Dodnash, since, although Dodnash is both in Domesday Book and in thirteenth-century charters considered to be in Bentley, one mid thirteenth-century deed refers to a grant from one layman to another of a field and meadow in the parish of Brantham and in the hamlet of Dodnash;[18] so the location of the first site of the priory on the fringes of the vill of East Bergholt, within Brantham parish, and in the hamlet of Dodnash, is perfectly feasible.

Shortly before the bishop dedicated the cemetery on 25 September 1188, however, Wimer had acquired land at Dodnash from William and Maurice, sons of Hervey (4). Part of this, certainly, was that land which William son of Hervey had formally sold to Wimer in the court of Aubrey de Vere, earl of Oxford (1).[19] Within a few months of the bishop's charter, Maurice issued a notification of an agreement made between him and Wimer in the court of Henry II (5). This document can be dated 13 November 1188 x 6 July 1189, and the agreement, for which Maurice paid a fine to the king, was made in the year ending Michaelmas 1188. The land to which reference is here made was held of Simon of Thunderley; it was certainly in Bentley, for Simon is some years later recorded as holding one fee of the honour of Brittany or Richmond, to which in 1086 two manors were ascribed there.[20] This land had, again, been sold to Wimer by Maurice's brother William, and it was now agreed that Wimer might found thereupon whatever religious community he might wish. At about this time, after the establishment of the community in the aldergrove at East Bergholt, Wimer granted to the canons there all the tenement which he held in Dodnash of the fee of Simon of Thunderley and other tenements, of whatsoever fee they might be held (6).

There was, however, further conflict and litigation in the royal court between Maurice and Wimer, resolved only in November 1196 by a final concord whereby Maurice quitclaimed to Wimer and to the religious men *there* serving God and St Mary all right and claim in William son of Hervey's land in Dodnash (12). Whereas the earliest grants to the house were made to the canons *sancte Marie de Alneto in Bercholte* (4, 6–10), henceforth charters which may be dated to the very last years of the twelfth century or the early thirteenth century were in

---

17 The episcopal actum of 1188 (4) refers to East Bergholt as a parish church, but the Battle Abbey chronicle has it as a dependent chapel of Brantham when that church was granted to the monks by William Rufus (*Battle Chronicle*, 98). Bentley was also at that time a dependent chapel of Brantham, although it had attained parochial status by 1216 at the latest (15; cf. *VN*, 463). East Bergholt was again stated to be a chapel of Brantham in 1254 (*VN*, 463); it is not listed in the *Taxatio* of 1291, and was again, despite the impressive size of the building, listed as a dependent chapel in the *Valor Ecclesiasticus* (Record Commission, 6 vols, 1810–34, iii, 428).

18 BL Add. ch. 9470, a grant by Geoffrey son of Maurice of Dodnash to Geoffrey son of Thomas of Dodnash of the field called 'Cumbwalle' in the parish of Brantham and the hamlet of Dodnash.

19 Late fourteenth-century inquisitions post mortem record one knight's fee in Hintlesham and Dodnash held of the earl of Oxford by the abbot of Walden (*CIPM* x, no. 638, p. 520; xiii, no. 125, p. 99).

20 For Simon, see *Red Bk Exchq.*, 480 (1210 x 12); for the estate of the honour of Brittany or Richmond, *DB* ii, 295b.

favour of the canons of Dodnash. That the new site was indeed within the parish of Bentley is corroborated by the agreement made in 1216 before papal judges-delegate between the canons of Dodnash and of Holy Trinity, Ipswich, the patrons of Bentley church. It stipulated that the hired servants of Dodnash priory should attend Bentley parish church at the three great festivals of the liturgical year (15). In the course of a further dispute between the same parties in 1232, it was specifically stated that Dodnash priory was situated on land in Bentley which William son of Hervey had granted to the canons (19).

It is impossible to determine the exact course of events, but it is possible that the original intention was to establish the community on the land at Dodnash acquired from William son of Hervey, but that the claims of Maurice his brother put obstacles in the way of the immediate fulfilment of this plan; and that because of this the initial foundation was made on the land obtained from Ada de Tosny on the borders of the vill of East Bergholt, but also in Dodnash hamlet. It would not be surprising that such a transient occupation has left no physical traces.

The issue is complicated by a strange memorandum, written in English in a hand which appears to be of the late fifteenth or early sixteenth century (15A), which is in effect a commentary on the verdict of papal judges-delegate commissioned by Pope Innocent III in 1215 (15). In short, it was argued that the judgement should be of no effect, because it made reference to the canons of Dodnash rather than of 'Seynt Maryes of the Altercar (*or* Altcarre) in Bergholt', and it is well known both from papal bulls and from the founder's charter(s) that they were founded and set within the parish of Bergholt, and are so called. The founder's extant charter (6) and other early charters do indeed refer to the community in this manner, and so too may have papal bulls of Clement III (1187–91) or Celestine III (1191–98) ratifying the foundation, which are now lost. The bull of Pope Honorious III of 1218 (111), however, although itself suspect, refers to the prior and canons of Dodnash, and the community itself, in documents issued from the mid thirteenth to the early sixteenth centuries, names itself as 'of St Mary of Dodnash'. The priory is similarly known as Dodnash in the Norwich episcopal registers from the early fourteenth century and in the very few documents emanating from the royal chancery and the provincial chapter of the Augustinian canons.

The 'memorandum' goes on to state that the canons possess a lordship called Dodnash after a knight named Sir Hugh of Dodnash, situated in the parish of Bentley, and that after it was granted to the priory, one of the current prior's predecessors dismantled the manor-house and out-buildings, and set them up again in the aldercarr, or aldergrove. He then converted the site into a vineyard, which he fenced and ditched, as is still evident on the ground, but in time this vineyard was abandoned, as the soil was not suitable, and the land was turned over to forestry, so that the wood around it increased in size. The prior of Ipswich, it is alleged here, mistakes river (*vivarii, sic*) for vineyard (*vinarii*). In fact *vivarium* can mean an enclosure for animals, but more often means fishpond.[21] The original of the judges'-delegate decision is not extant, but the

---

[21] See above, n. 15.

thirteenth-century transcript has, quite clearly, *vivari*. There is no other reference, among the extant charters, to a vineyard in Dodnash, although the existence of such is not inherently improbable.[22] In other ways, however, the 'memorandum' is garbled. The pope is recorded as either Innocent I or II, rather than Innocent III; and although two Hughs of Dodnash, sons of Maurice and Thomas, do attest charters, they were minor members of the family, do not occur in the extant charters as donors, and were never described as '*dominus*' or '*miles*'.[23] There may be a confusion between William and Maurice, sons of Hervey of Dodnash, from whom Wimer obtained much of the original endowment, and Sir Hugh Tollemache, who confirmed to the canons the grant made by Geoffrey son of Maurice of Dodnash, saving the relief payable at the death or removal of any prior (24).

This strange memorandum may be an original composition of *c.* 1500, or it may be a translation of a thirteenth-century Latin document, produced at the time of litigation between 1229 and 1232 (19) or in 1282 (49). In any case, it suggests continuing tension between Dodnash and Holy Trinity, Ipswich, only a few years before their dissolution. On the dorse of the document is copied the important decretal of Pope Alexander III relating to the payment of tithes by religious, *Ex parte*.[24] The 'memorandum' may have been the instructions drafted for the proctor of Dodnash in a case relating to the claim by Holy Trinity, Ipswich, for payment of tithes from the Dodnash priory estate in the parish of Bentley, most likely in the court of Rome itself, where the precise geography of south-eastern Suffolk would not be so well known as it would be in the Norwich diocesan court, and *suppressio veri* or *suggestio falsi* might be hoped to win the day, or at least long delay a verdict unfavourable to Dodnash. There is certainly no other evidence that the canons were re-established in East Bergholt, or outside Bentley, after the end of the twelfth century.

THE EARLIEST BENEFACTORS

a. The Tosny Family

The Tosny family rose to prominence in the duchy of Normandy in the eleventh century. The centre of their honour there, which in 1177 comprised more than fifty fees, was Conches. Ralph I succeeded his father as standard-bearer of Normandy, and apparently discharged this duty at Hastings. His estate, as recorded in Domesday Book, comprised lands in Hertfordshire, Berkshire, Essex and Norfolk, and had its *caput* at Flamstead, Herts. By the death of Roger III in

---

[22] Four Suffolk vineyards are recorded in DB; see H.C. Darby, *The Domesday Geography of Eastern England*, Cambridge 1971, 203.

[23] See index, *s.v.* Dodnash.

[24] *X*, III, 30, 10; *JL* 14117. For discussion, see G. Constable, *Monastic Tithes from their Origins to the Twelfth Century*, Cambridge 1964, 298 ff.

1264, the honour comprised fifty-two fees and the centre of gravity had shifted towards the Welsh march.[25]

When Roger I de Tosny, who died 1157 × 62, married Ida, daughter of Baldwin, count of Hainault, he was granted by Henry I £20 worth of land at East Bergholt.[26] Roger and Ida had four sons, Ralph III (who succeeded to the honour of Flamstead), Roger and Baldwin, all knights, and Geoffrey, who became a clerk. Baldwin was brought up at the court of Hainault and died in 1170.[27] It was not therefore him, nor his mother Ida, who made grants to Wimer and to the newly established canons in and after 1188. Ada, or Alda, must rather have been the widow, and this Baldwin the son, of Roger, the younger son of Roger I, who apparently succeeded to the estate at East Bergholt, which was given to Ada as her *maritagium*. This explains why East Bergholt does not occur in the records of the lands of the main branch of the Tosny family as recorded in the Beauchamp cartulary.[28] Both Ada and Baldwin were still alive after Michaelmas 1201.[29]

It is clearly stated in their charters (2–3) that the original site of the priory was given by Ada and Baldwin to Wimer in free alms, for the salvation of the soul of Roger de Tosny. It is not necessary to read *'perquisitione'* in the episcopal confirmation (4) as purchase, for 'by the endeavour' or 'at the entreaty' would be a reasonable translation; but it is possible that money did change hands, and certainly a subsequent grant by Ada to the canons entailed an annual rent to her of 3s, as well as an entry-fine of 20s (7). In 1228 Roger de Akeni brought a case against the canons relating to the lands which they had been granted by Ada (60), and it is very probable that the claim of Robert de Pavilly and Alice his wife also concerned this land (62).

b. The Dodnash Family

While the involvement of the Tosnys was confined to the initial foundation of the priory, that of the Dodnash family extended over four generations at least, from the late twelfth to the early fourteenth centuries. It is highly likely, though nowhere stated, that Wimer the Chaplain was himself a member of the family, as the name Wimer, which is not common and is of uncertain origin,[30] occurs in at least two generations. It is possible that Wimer, chaplain and sheriff, is identical to Wimer son of Hervey of Dodnash, who in association with his brother Maurice made a grant to the canons (13), and to whom reference is made retrospectively

---

25 For the family, see GEC xii pt i, 753–75; I.J. Sanders, *English Baronies: a Study of their Origin and Descent*, Oxford 1960, 117–18; *The Beauchamp Cartulary Charters, 1100–1268*, ed. E. Mason, PRS ns xliii, 1980, pp. xliii–xliv, where the genealogical table at p. lx understandably omits Ada the wife and Baldwin the son of Roger son of Roger I. For the continental background, see L. Musset, 'Aux Origines d'une classe dirigeante: les Tosny, grands barons normands du xe au xiiie siècle', *Francia* v, 1978 for 1977, 45–80.

26 *Bk Fees*, 134.

27 GEC xii pt i, 764, citing *Receuil de l'Histoire de France* xiii, 553, 571.

28 *Beauchamp Cartulary*, xliv–xlv.

29 *PR 4 John*, 115.

30 See PRS ns. xxxii, subject index, Names, personal, where it is stated to be Old English Wigmaer or Continental Germanic.

in two later charters (18–19); but nowhere is the chaplain referred to as the brother of William and Maurice, sons of Hervey (1–2, 12), and it much more likely that he belonged to the previous generation, and was perhaps the brother of Hervey of Dodnash.

The episcopal confirmation of 1188 states that Wimer the chaplain had acquired lands from the two sons of Hervey (4). A notification by Aubrey de Vere, earl of Oxford, records that William came to his court to obtain ratification of his sale to Wimer of all his land and inheritance in Dodnash for payment of 20 marks (1).[31] This is probably that William son of Hervey who, it is recorded in 1212, had held Shelley (*Selflegam*), an outlying grange of the manor of East Bergholt, in chief of the king for 52s *p.a.*, which rent Henry II had given in alms to Butley priory.[32] Soon after William's appearance before the earl, his brother Maurice confirmed the agreement made in the king's court between him and Wimer that the former sheriff might found upon land acquired from William (by then probably dead) whatever religious house he might wish, according to the charter obtained from Simon of Thunderley, capital lord of the fee (5).[33] There was further litigation in the *curia regis* between Maurice and Wimer over this land in 1196; Maurice quitclaimed to Wimer and to the religious now established there all claim on William son of Hervey's land in Dodnash, but Wimer paid heavily for this renunciation (12). Shortly afterwards, Maurice and Wimer sons of Hervey granted to the canons that part of their land at Dodnash held of Roger Bigod, earl of Norfolk (13).[34] At about this time, too, the brothers also made a grant to Thomas of Dodnash, their uncle, of various lands in Dodnash held of the Bigod fee,[35] which was to lead to subsequent confusion.

In the next generation, Maurice son of Maurice before 1221 made a grant to the canons, for a price, of all the land which had come to him by hereditary right from his father (14). Together with his brother Thomas, he also quitclaimed to the priory any right in all possessions acquired by the canons from the time of their foundation; these renunciations were made in the mid 1220s (16–17). Not all grants made in the previous generation had, however, taken effect; Maurice and Thomas entered into an agreement with the prior that they would attempt to acquire, at the best possible price, all the lands which had been held by Maurice and Wimer sons of Hervey, some of which had previously been granted to the canons, and to divide them between them (18).[36]

Geoffrey son of Maurice occurs towards the middle of the thirteenth century. He was almost certainly the son of Maurice son of Maurice, rather than his

---

[31] For de Vere holdings in the immediate locality, see below, no. 1 n.

[32] *Bk Fees*, 134; cf. *DB* ii, 287.

[33] See above n. 20, and below no. 5 n.

[34] In 1242–43 Hugh Bigod is recorded as holding half a knight's fee of the king in Bentley and Copdock (*Bk Fees*, 916).

[35] Helmingham, T/Hel/49/6.

[36] Maurice granted to Thomas his brother, for his homage and service, for 17s entry fine and for an annual rent of 12d, plus scutage, sheriff's aid and castleguard, all his land called 'Steicheresland' in Bentley, probably before 1202, because witnessed by Eustace of Brantham (Ipswich, SRO, HD 1047/1/67). Maurice also granted to Thomas the whole of 'Langelond', held of Morell's fee, for half a mark entry fine and annual rent of 10d, in exchange for land at 'Scarbotswelle' of the fee of Holy Trinity, Ipswich. Hubert of Braiseworth also granted to Thomas land of Morell's fee in the

younger brother, although in one charter (21) he refers to his brother Maurice, who had presumably died shortly after their father; he quitclaimed to the canons all lands in Bentley, Brantham and Tattingstone ever held by his brother by hereditary right or by his mother Mary as her dower. In another charter, now mutilated, he also quitclaimed any right in land granted by another brother, Hervey, and made a small gift himself (22). In 1243 he accepted 4 marks from the prior for acquittance from all debts owed to him, reserving to himself and his wife the daily corrodies due to them (23). Seven years later, they surrendered all corrodies in return for a lump sum of £19 6s 8d (25)

Geoffrey son of Maurice was probably dead by 1257, when Hugh Tollemache confirmed to the canons all land which Geoffrey had granted to them of his fee (24–A). His widow Isabelle survived until 1285, when she quitclaimed to the priory all right in her dower land in the three vills, in return for a twice-yearly corrody of grain, peas and beans (27). A Geoffrey of Dodnash attests several times after 1257, but one of the documents which he witnesses is Isabelle's quitclaim, and it is probable that all these attestations are by Geoffrey son of Thomas of Dodnash, to whom his cousin Geoffrey son of Maurice had granted the field called 'Cumbwelle', previously given to the canons.[37] Geoffrey son of Thomas had a brother Hugh, who also held lands in the vicinity.[38]

In the Hundred Rolls of 1279 it was recorded that the prior of Dodnash has the land of Maurice of Dodnash, whereby the crown has lost the reliefs due to the soke of Chelmondiston; and also that Geoffrey of Dodnash had subtracted one suit due to the court of Chelmondiston, and Hugh Tollemache and the prior of Dodnash had withdrawn another suit of the same court, which used to be that of Thomas and Maurice of Dodnash.[39]

Probably around the time of the widow Isabelle's quitclaim in 1285, Geoffrey son of Maurice's son William also made a quitclaim, for an unspecified sum of money, of all the land held by his father in Bentley (26), and a further quitclaim was made by him in 1307 for payment of £4 (28). Another quitclaim, not to the priory, reveals that he had taken the name 'Waldoune' – William de Waldoune of Bentley, son and heir of the late Geoffrey son of Maurice of Dodnash,[40] and Waldounes occur in these charters until the late fifteenth century (26 (endorsement), 112, 116–18, 193).

vill of Bentley, held of Maurice (Bodl., Suff. ch. 195, a–c). Thomas was also granted land at Buxton (*Buggesdon*) by the abbot and convent of Tilty, who held it of Hugh Tollemache (Helmingham, T/Hel/49/1).

37 BL Add. ch. 9470; for the earlier grant of 'Cumbwalle' by Maurice son of Maurice to the canons, see no. 14 below. Geoffrey son of Thomas had a holding in Tattingstone, for which he was in 1268–9 sued by John de Luvetot (Rye, *Fines*, 69, no. 64).

38 Hugh son of Thomas of Dodnash received a grant from Baldwin Brawod of land in the field of 'Smerisfeld', probably in the 1230s (BL Add. ch. 9468); he was still alive well into the second half of the thirteenth century, when he made a grant to Ralph the clerk (BL Add. ch. 9514); in the last quarter of the century his widow Sybil quitclaimed certain lands which had been held by him in Bentley (BL Add. ch. 9494). A third brother, another son of Thomas son of Maurice, was William, since Thomas son of William of Dodnash in 1256 quitclaimed a messuage to Geoffrey son of Thomas of Dodnash his uncle (BL Add. ch. 9480; cf. 9467, 9486).

39 *HR* ii, 177b, 190.

40 BL Add. ch. 9579, to Sir Edward Charles, of all rights in certain lands in Bentley, Tattingstone and Dodnash; see below, pp. 20–23.

9

CONJECTURAL GENEALOGY OF THE DODNASH FAMILY

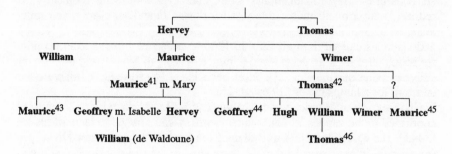

PATRONAGE

The large sum paid by the canons in 1250 to Geoffrey son of Maurice of Dodnash for the renunciation of corrodies due to him and his wife (25) suggests that these obligations were so substantial that they were likely to be rendered only to a patron. The relief payable on the death or resignation of a prior to Hugh Tollemache, acknowledged at about the same time (24–A), does not reflect patronal rights, but merely the assumption by the canons of the customary obligations on the lands previously held of Tollemache by the Dodnash family.

By the beginning of the fourteenth century, however, patronage was vested in the Bigod earls of Norfolk, as unambiguously stated in the inquisition taken after the death of Earl Roger in December 1306.[47] The relationship with Bigod's successor, Thomas of Brotherton, fifth son of Edward I, was chequered. At some date before April 1337 the canons had sued him for the advowson of the church of 'Sterstone in Norfolk' – probably Starston (125). There appears to have been considerable confusion over which church was at issue, and the litigation probably occurred before the earl conceded in June 1335 that his predecessors had unjustly deprived the priory of 'Stirstone' church, almost certainly Kirton in Colneis hundred, Suffolk (123), for which concession the canons in April 1336 agreed to maintain a chantry of two priests for the souls of the earl and his kindred (124). Since Dodnash did not, apparently, subsequently enjoy the rectorial portion of

---

41 Occurs probably before 1202 (SRO, HD 1047/1/72); probably dead by 1236–37 (HD1047/2/55).
42 Probably before 1202, still alive in 1236–37 (HD 1047/1/72; /2/55); he was the uncle of Geoffrey son of Maurice (HD 1047/1/59, 71).
43 Occurs only once in this collection (20).
44 Hugh and Geoffrey sons of Thomas were brothers (HD 1047/1/15, 75).
45 Wimer and Maurice were nephews of Maurice and Thomas of Dodnash (90).
46 Thomas son of William, who occurs in 1250 (BL Add. ch. 9480), is in 1268 described as nephew of Geoffrey of Dodnash (SRO, HD 1047/1/46).
47 *CIPM* iv, no. 434 (p. 302).

Kirton church, it must be doubted if these masses were ever celebrated.[48] The priory seal was, however, changed to incorporate the Brotherton leopards (175). On 12 March 1339, after Brotherton's death, the king's escheator was ordered to restore the advowson of the priory, valued at £20, to John Lord Segrave and Margaret his wife, eldest daughter and co-heir of the earl.[49]

On 1 August 1472 John de Mowbray, duke of Norfolk, consented to the annexation of the priory, founded as he claimed by his ancestors, to the recently established Magdalen College, Oxford, for the purpose of offering prayers for himself, his wife and others.[50] Apparently in autumn 1459 Bishop William Waynflete of Winchester, the founder of Magdalen, had sent an agent to enquire into the value of its lands, said to be about £40, and had acquired the advowson from the duke's father, although there is no evidence of any payment,[51] and both the transfer of the patronage and the annexation were ineffective. Certainly the duke of Norfolk was still considered to be the patron of the priory at the time of its dissolution in 1525, and it was recorded that he had released his title as founder by fine.[52]

DISPUTES WITH HOLY TRINITY, IPSWICH

In 1188, when the canons were established in East Bergholt, the fear expressed in the episcopal confirmation charter was of potential conflict with Battle Abbey, in whose parish of Brantham East Bergholt lay (4). A monk of Battle was present at the dedication, and it was stipulated that any dispute should be settled by negotiation between the canons, the monks of Battle and the incumbent of East Bergholt, and if that failed, by the arbitration of the diocesan, without recourse to superior authority.

The removal of the priory to its new site in the parish of Bentley resulted in a series of disputes during the thirteenth century with the canons of Holy Trinity, Ipswich, patrons and proprietors of that church. Twice in the first half of the century cases were taken to the papal curia. In 1215 Holy Trinity complained to Pope Innocent III that Dodnash had misappropriated tithes due to the parish church; the compromise reached before papal judges-delegate appears to have been largely in favour of the canons of Ipswich (15). Fourteen years later, in 1229, Holy Trinity alleged that the canons of Dodnash had refused due obedience – this is the only indication that Dodnash was a daughter house of Holy Trinity, and perhaps indicates that Alan, the first prior, had been drawn from there – and also that they had usurped various lands, including the site of the priory, and rents and tithes in Bentley. Eventually, again before papal judges-delegate and with the

---

48 For discussion of the complex matter of the identity of 'Stirstone' church, see no. 123 n., also nos 4, 111.
49 *CCR 1339–41*, 38.
50 *HMCR 4th Report*, 1874, 462.
51 V. Davis, *William Waynflete, Bishop and Educationalist*, Woodbridge 1993, 129–30.
52 *LPFD* iv (i), no. 3538 (ii).

consent of the diocesan, the canons of Holy Trinity withdrew their suit in return for the payment of annual rent of 20d (19).

Trouble flared up again in 1282, when Holy Trinity once more alleged subtraction of tithes due to Bentley church (49). A compromise was now reached before the Official of Norwich diocese. The canons of Dodnash claimed privileges granted to the order of Augustinian canons in general and to their own house in particular regarding their exemption from payment of tithes of produce from land cultivated by their own hands. The canons of Ipswich eventually acknowledged the validity of these privileges – which elsewhere would be to their own advantage – but reserved the right to claim the tithes should Dodnash ever in the future alienate the curtilage and the dovecote at the centre of this dispute. The late medieval 'memorandum' concerning tithes, cited above in relation to the site of the priory, even if a translation of a briefing in this 1282 case, suggests that tension between the two houses over tithes in Bentley long remained a live issue.

INTERNAL LIFE

It is only from the early fourteenth century that there are any indications of life within the community, and they remain sparse. In 1306 the convent consisted of a prior and three canons,[53] in 1381 the total was five,[54] and in 1492 there was only the prior and two canons (178). Any decline in numbers cannot, therefore, be attributed to the consequences of the Black Death. It is the tiny size of the community, rather than any incompetence or wrong-doing, which led to the frequent quashing by the bishop of the elections of a new prior and his appointment of a superior, normally the man uncanonically chosen by the canons.[55]

Of the priors, two certainly were from local families: John of Gusford (1317–c.1346), from the family which held the manor of that name in Stoke by Ipswich, and Adam le Newman (1346–c.1349), of a family of local landholders which occurs several times in the charters. Of others, Walter Baa was introduced in 1384 and William Melford before 1524 from Butley, Michael of Colchester in 1438 from St Osyth's and Richard Whiting in 1444 from Buckenham. The only recorded move in the opposite direction was Prior Thomas of Thornham's translation to the headship of Holy Trinity, Ipswich, in 1383.

There is sporadic evidence of corrodies provided by the canons. Geoffrey son of Maurice of Dodnash and his wife had in the mid thirteenth century a daily corrody with other benefits, which they quitclaimed in 1250 for a considerable sum of money (25). Thirty-five years later, however, the canons granted to Isabelle, Geoffrey's widow, now a very old lady, a corrody of grain, peas and beans in return for the quitclaim of her dower lands (27). There is no implication that Geoffrey or Isabelle actually lived in the priory. Far more detail is provided for

---

53 *CIPM* iv, no. 434 (p. 302).
54 *MRH*, 156.
55 See list of priors, pp. xix–xx.

the residential corrody granted in 1343, for a cash payment, to John of Stanton, and transferred five years later at his request to John de Lewalle, chaplain of Tattingstone (156); for them complete provision in every respect was to be made within the priory. John Beneyt's quitclaim of the priory's debt to him, in 1382, implies the provision by the canons in return of his livelihood as well as the means of his salvation (215).

The canons' debt to Beneyt is only the last of a series recorded from 1334 onwards (157, 211–13). The largest of these, £100 owed to William le Newman, rector of Erwarton and kinsman (probably brother) of the late prior Adam le Newman, was recompensed in 1351 by the establishment of a chantry (157). It was contracted that each day one of the canons should offer mass for the souls of William and those nominated by him; their anniversary should be celebrated on the first Monday of Lent, when a pittance should be provided for the canons and a distribution made to the poor; while the names of the beneficiaries should be entered on the mortuary roll circulated among all the Augustinian houses of England. Over a century and a half later Thomas Fincham, gentleman, distant heir of William le Newman, on discovering in 1506 that the canons were failing to fulfil their spiritual contract, attorned John Tollemache to distrain upon all the priory's lands until satisfaction was made, according to the terms of the original indenture (157–8). It is doubtful if the chantry ordained in April 1336 for the soul of Thomas of Brotherton, earl of Norfolk, which would have entailed the service of two canons, was ever established, since the canons apparently never exercised the advowson of 'Stirstone' church, in return for which liturgical commemoration was conceded.[56]

There is no record of any indulgence granted in favour of the priory itself, but in 1472 the prior, as patron of the parish church of Falkenham, together with the vicar and the wardens of the confraternity of St Mary Magdalen, appointed a questor to expound the indulgences of the guild throughout the county of Essex (112).

SALVATION AND PROFIT

There was much competition for the alms of the faithful in the area of Ipswich at the turn of the twelfth and thirteenth centuries. A second house of Augustinian canons, St Peter and St Paul, was established in the town late in Henry II's reign. Smaller Augustinian communities were founded at Woodbridge *c.* 1193 and Alnesbourn *c.* 1200. There were very many other convents not far distant, not to mention the wide net cast by the great Benedictine monasteries at Bury St Edmunds and Colchester. Dodnash did, however, succeed in attracting a fairly large number of benefactions, usually very modest, from its neighbours, ranging from members of the knightly class down to very small landholders. It should be

---

56 For the identification of 'Stirstone' with Kirton, and the confusion with a Norfolk church, probably Starston, see no. 123 n.

emphasised that, in this very localised context, the hope of salvation and the appeals for the prayers of the canons were as heartfelt and genuine as the aspirations towards eternity expressed in charters recording grants to the great Burgundian abbey of Cluny or the venerable English and Norman Benedictine houses. It is notable, however, that the number of grants diminishes considerably after the mid thirteenth century, and this is almost certainly connected with the various orders of friars established at Ipswich, Sudbury and Clare.

From 1188 to *c.* 1250 forty-four grants or confirmations state that they were made for the salvation of the donor and of those whom he wished to be remembered. In a few cases this was restricted to wife (129) or parents (63, 68), but normally the desire for commemoration and redemptive prayer extended across the generations, embracing both ancestors and successors. It is notable that grants stated to be made in the quest for salvation did not normally entail payment either of an entry-fine (as the purchase price) or of annual rent to the grantor. A notable exception to this rule is the acquiescence by Maurice son of Hervey of his brother William's sale of land to Wimer the chaplain; he made this concession with the consent of his heirs, for their salvation and that of their predecessors and successors, although there had been contention which culminated in the royal court (5); and certainly in 1196 Maurice before the same tribunal secured the considerable sum of 40 marks (12).

Very few of the early charters specify what exactly was expected in return for the gift. One exception is Geoffrey son of William of Boyton's grant of himself, at the end of this life, to the priory, that is, deathbed reception as a canon was the condition of his gift (10). Bishop John of Oxford in 1188 authorised the burial of members of the priory's confraternity alongside the canons themselves in the cemetery (4), and despite the doubt surrounding the bull of Honorious III in its present form there is no reason to be suspicious of his utterly conventional concession in 1216 that the canons might admit laymen into their community (111). When as late as 1286 John de la Mare in the *curia regis* received in return for his quitclaim receipt into the spiritual benefits of the priory, this was merely a formal statement of what was expected by all benefactors (64). One donor, however, was more specific in her requirements; in the mid thirteenth century Agnes, widow of William of Pebmarsh, in return for a grant at Wenham, required the canons to keep a candle burning before the image of Our Lady by the high altar, with provision for distraint on the land should they fail in this obligation (136). This foreshadows the detailed provision for the maintenance of chantries in the next century.

Although very many grants were made in return only for spiritual services, the acquisition of land by the canons could also be a matter of precise financial calculation on both sides. Late twelfth and thirteenth-century charters relating to properties in various vills of the hundred of Samford indicate that there was a very active land-market, in which the priory too operated.[57] The record of Wimer's acquisition of the canons' original endowment is incomplete, but for the land he

---

[57] A large number of charters relating to secular tenants in the vills of Samford hundred are distributed between the archive of Lord Tollemache at Helmingham Hall, Ipswich SRO, HD 1047, and

purchased from William son of Hervey he paid 20 marks, and in addition 5 marks to the earl of Oxford for confirmation (1), and some years later twice the original price for a quitclaim (12), while for twelve acres at Flatford he paid to Edward son of Wlfard half a mark and contracted to pay an annual rent of 2s (11).

In the first century of the community's existence, apart from the payment to Geoffrey son of Maurice of Dodnash and his wife of the large sum of £19 6s 8d for the renunciation of corrodies due to them (25), the canons also paid a total of £58 7s 4d in forty-two separate transactions either as entry-fines or as payment for confirmations by lords or for quitclaims by the heirs of donors or by rival claimants to land or rent. Such payments range from 2s (and fifteen were less than 10s) to the 10 marks paid to Maurice and Wimer sons of Hervey of Dodnash early in the thirteenth century (13) and to William of Waldingfield a few years later (97). Twenty-eight grants to the canons in this period also entailed payment of an annual rent to the grantor.

THE ESTATE

The Development of the Priory Estate to 1291

A summary account of the priory's estates and their value can be abstracted from the *Taxatio Ecclesiastica* of 1291, although this probably represents an under-valuation of ecclesiastical revenues.[58] Near to the house itself, in Samford hundred, the canons were credited with land and rent in Bentley, assessed at £1 17s 8d; rent, land, a mill and customs in East Bergholt, value £2 6s 8d; rent, land and a mill in Capel St Mary, value £2 16s 4d; land at Copdock, value 5s 6d; and rent of 18s 1d at Brantham.[59] By far the most valuable holding was at Falkenham in Colneis hundred, which was assessed at £10 16s 11½d, with 1s 4d at nearby Kirton. There were town rents in Ipswich, 3d in the parish of St Mary at Tower and 1½d in that of St Nicholas; and other rents at Monewden in Loes hundred (6d), Framsden in Thredling hundred (2s), Clopton in Carleford hundred (2s), Ship-meadow and Mettingham in Wangford hundred (3s 4d and 5s),[60] and also in

---

Additional charters in BL. There is ample material here for a study of the land-market from the late twelfth to the early fourteenth centuries.

58 For discussion, see R. Graham, 'The Taxation of Pope Nicholas IV', in her *English Ecclesiastical Studies*, London 1929, 271–301, especially for temporalities 290–7; her analysis suggests that the assessment 'was calculated on the rental – and that probably a minimum – at which manors and granges might be let, although the bishops and the religious then farmed the greater part of their own lands at a profit' (p. 294). With regard to the value of ecclesiastical benefices, the most recent work has suggested that the *Taxatio* presents as near to a true valuation as was realistically possible – but this hardly affects Dodnash, which for an Augustinian community had remarkably little income from spiritualities (J.H. Denton, 'The Valuation of the Ecclesiastical Benefices of England and Wales in 1291–2', *Historical Research* lxvi, 1993, 231).

59 *Taxatio*, 128b–29.

60 *Taxatio*, 124–8 *passim*.

Gillingham, in Clavering hundred in Norfolk (3s 8d).[61] The total valuation is £19 19s 5d.[62]

(a) The hundred of Samford

Bentley The land purchased from William and Maurice sons of Hervey by Wimer the chaplain for the eventual site of his foundation at Dodnash is discussed above (pp. 4–5, 8). Soon after the site change, Maurice and Wimer sons of Hervey sold to the canons part of their land at Dodnash held of Earl Roger Bigod (13), and in the next generation Maurice son of Maurice made a further substantial sale of land held of Earl Roger and of Ermeiot of Wenham (14). In the early 1220s this Maurice and his brother Thomas both quitclaimed to the priory all possessions acquired from its foundation to date (16–17). That the process of acquisition had not been straightforward or uncontested is indicated by an agreement between these brothers and the prior to attempt to obtain possession of all the lands once held by Maurice I and Wimer, which included some which had previously been granted to the canons (18). In the mid thirteenth century Geoffrey son of Maurice quitclaimed to the priory all the land which his brother Maurice had held by hereditary right or his mother Mary by right of dower in Bentley, Brantham and Tattingstone (21), and also confirmed the lands of his brother Hervey while making another small grant himself (22).

In the earliest years of the thirteenth century the canons consolidated their holding in Hulney wood, straddling the parish boundaries of Bergholt and Capel St Mary, by a series of purchases from the Norman abbey of Aumale (29), Robert son of Richard of Boyton (87) and Robert of Hulney (30).

Around this time, too, a grant was made by the three daughters of Richard de Brueria (that is, Heath), of their heathland in Bentley, held of the fee of Hugh Tollemache (31). Two of the daughters, with their husbands, made further grants from the same heath (33, 37), and one of them, Edith, with her husband Ranulf the smith of Coddenham, made another small sale (36) and conceded a lease (35), but also entered with another sister, Avice, and her (probably second) husband into litigation against the canons (38). Adam, son of William Flanke and of the third sister, Matilda, quitclaimed and confirmed to Dodnash all the land in the field called 'Bruere' (which implies heathland now brought into cultivation) which he had inherited from his mother (39–41).

Probably in the 1220s William son of William of 'Kenebroc' (Kembroke in Bucklesham) made a small grant of land which he had recently acquired (44). Late in the century there is a group of four quitclaims (45–8) and a grant of a small parcel of land (51). The total valuation of land and rent in Bentley in 1291 was £1 17s 8d.[63]

---

61 *Taxatio*, 103b, 114b.
62 *VN* adds portions in the churches of Kirton, 4s 8d, and Holbrook, 12d (*VN*, 458, 464).
63 *Taxatio*, 128b.

East Bergholt Here the total 1291 valuation was £2 6s 8d.[64] The initial grant had been made by Ada de Tosny and Baldwin her son of the land on which the priory was initially and temporarily sited, close to the Bentley parish boundary (2–3, and above pp. 3–4). Further grants were made, for a price, by Ada (7, 57), who also confirmed a grant, before 1196, by Richard of Bramford (8), whose son William made the first of the grants to the priory in Hulney wood (9), and subsequently further grants of land and men held of Roger Bigod (58). The earl also confirmed to the canons the grant by Edward de Alneto, son of Wlfard, of his mill at Flatford (55–6), where Edward had previously sold land to Wimer, presumably destined for the religious (11). In the mid thirteenth century Edward's heir, Nicholas de Alneto, held the mill of the canons for the substantial annual rent of 11s 7d (57). Another early grant was made by Alexander son of Christiana, and this was replicated by his son John (58–9).

Two grants were made, probably in the late 1220s, by Roger de Akeni, one apparently in free alms, the other for a substantial rent (60–1), but it is highly likely that, rather than being new gifts, these represent a recognition of the priory's existing rights in the land granted by Ada de Tosny. The Akeni family were tenants of the Tosnys in Normandy and in Cambridgeshire and Oxfordshire, and held the manor in East Bergholt which became known as Spencer's. At Michaelmas 1228 Roger brought actions in the *curia regis* against the prior and others relating to the Tosny estate in East Bergholt,[65] and his charters probably represent the resolution of that conflict. A claim by Robert de Pavilly against the canons was almost certainly in respect of the same lands, and the prior paid for his quitclaim in October 1228 (62). There was a further dispute over this estate in 1286 between the prior and John de la Mare, successor of the Akenis, who claimed suit of court against the tenor of their charter (64).

Brantham[66] The *Taxatio* records here rent valued at 18s 1d *p.a.*[67] The earliest recorded grant is of a salthouse, donated by Eustace of Brantham, a prominent member of Roger Bigod's household who occurs in closely datable documents only until 1202 (71–2). Around the same time Hugh son of Alan of Brantham granted land and meadow, which was confirmed by Hubert de Montchesney (74–5), and not long afterwards William (son of) Helte gave land adjacent to the small castle (*castello*) of Hamo Petit (77).

Probably in the 1220s John de la Mare granted land and rent (79–80) and Hugh Maupetit conceded the homage and service of John himself (78). One of John's tenants, John Godswein, granted a rent (81). A rather different, but surely valuable concession, was the liberty granted by Ranulf of Braham of crossing his water between Cattawade and 'Stutteflet' and lading and unlading their boats,

---

[64] *Taxatio*, 129.
[65] *CRR* xiii, no. 1201.
[66] There were four manors in Brantham. One of these came to be known as Brantham Hall, another as Braham Hall, near the hamlet of Cattawade (Copinger, *Manors* vi, 22–3). The vill of Brantham is always rendered in the charters as 'Braham', and in most cases it is impossible to know if the vill of Brantham or the manor of Braham is intended.
[67] *Taxatio*, 129.

free from any toll (82). Further small grants in free alms were made in mid-century by Osbert son of John Henry (84) and some years later by John Attebroc (85–6).

Capel St Mary (Boyton)[68]   In the *Taxatio* the canons are recorded as having here land, rent and a mill valued at £2 16s 4d.[69] There is no record among the surviving charters of the mill, nor indeed is it listed in the dissolution valuation. In the early thirteenth century Richard of Boyton granted his pasture below Hulney wood in free alms (87) and sold the canons four acres in 'Michelefeld' for a money rent, subsequently reduced by his son to a token pair of gloves (88–9). Alan Bruning's grant of three acres in 'Furlong' (surely a field name as well as a description of measurement) was made at about the same time (91–2). Probably in the 1220s William of Boyton made a grant of heathland (90) and Matilda daughter of Gilbert and Geoffrey the clerk made small grants of land held of the fee of William son of Robert of Raydon (95–6), who himself gave a small parcel of land called 'Wdelee' (93–4). More substantial grants were made at this time by Sir William of Waldingfield (97, 99), and around the middle of the century Hervey Glanvill made a grant of land (100).

Copdock   The *Taxatio* valued the priory's land here at 5s 6d.[70] This comprised two tenements, both granted in the early to mid thirteenth century. 'Hunemannes-lond' was given by Alan Bernard of Tattingstone for 5s entry-fine and an annual rent of 9d; it was held by his wife Wimarc of the fee of Hugh Tollemache (101); another charter of Alan grants what is probably the same land for the reduced rent of 1d *p.a.*, for payment of a further £2 (102). Other parcels in 'Hunemanne-slond' were given by Robert Predican (103) and by Denise daughter of Fulkelove, confirmed by her husband (104–5). Quitclaims in the mid thirteenth century by Robert and Roger, sons of Ivo of Copdock (106) and late in the century by Roger son of Robert Yve (107) probably relate to yet another parcel in this field.

The other property in Copdock was 'Pinell's land', where Sewal son of Richer granted an annual rent which he used to receive from Denise's husband, Simon of Bury, and from Alan Bernard (108). Wimarc, Alan's widow, subsequently granted all her part of this land (109), and Hugh Husbonde also granted an annual rent here (110).

Holbrook   There is no revenue listed here in the *Taxatio*, although the earlier *Valuation of Norwich* records a portion of 12d in the church.[71] In an isolated charter for this vill, Hugh, a younger son of Eustace of Brantham, granted four acres of land here (115).

---

[68] Most DB entries for Capel St Mary appear under Boyton, a part thereof; cf. the modern Boynton Hall; under this heading are listed three manors (*DB* ii, 296, 378, 445b; also Copinger, *Manors* vi, 28).

[69] *Taxatio*, 128b.

[70] *Taxatio*, 129.

[71] *VN*, 464,

Stratford St Mary There is no mention in the *Taxatio*, and the grant of rent for the meadow of 'Hauckesmedwe' by Ralph Locun and the quitclaim by William of Bramford (121–2) are obviously there included under East Bergholt (cf. 60).

Tattingstone Again, no revenue here is listed in the *Taxatio*. Yet around 1200 William the clerk gave three small parcels of land here (128), and in the mid thirteenth century Michael of Freston granted 6d annual rent (129). A more substantial holding here is indicated by Adam de Gardino's recognition of his obligation to render an annual rent of 14d to the canons and 10d to the court of Chelmondiston for a tenement once held by Maurice of Dodnash in Tattingstone (130, cf. 14). This was probably included in the *Taxatio*'s assessment for Bentley.

Great Wenham Although nothing is listed here in the *Taxatio*, the canons held the land called 'Aspelond'; William of Bramford granted them three acres and a rood there, his son Richard and Matthew son of Warin Testard remitted the rents due to them (132–4), and Vinnais de Alno confirmed this remission (135). In the mid thirteenth century another parcel of land here was granted by Agnes, widow of William of Pebmarsh (136).

(b) *Land outside Samford hundred*

Few charters are extant for the outlying properties whose value is detailed in the *Taxatio* (see above). The most serious loss is for Falkenham, in Colneis hundred across the Orwell estuary, where the canons held one of the two manors, the proceeds of which were valued at £10 16s 11½d.[72] They also held the advowson of the church (111–12), but even after its appropriation at some unknown date, they can have drawn little profit from it after the maintenance of a vicar, since its total 1291 valuation was £8.[73]

Of the other properties, charters have been found relating only to Framsden and Shipmeadow. The Framsden rents had been acquired before 1221 by grants from Warin son of Philip of Framsden and William son of William of Cretingham (113–14). In Shipmeadow, rents totalling 10s *p.a.* had been given early in the thirteenth century by Bartholomew of Shipmeadow from lands held of Thomas son of Gilbert of Ilketshall (118–20). It is possible that this rent is listed (and undervalued) in the *Taxatio* under Mettingham, as there is no other reference to Dodnash property there.[74]

---

[72] *Taxatio*, 124b, The manor of Falkenham Dodnash was that in DB held of Bigod by Ralph de Tur-
lavilla (*DB* ii, 339, 340b, 341). Another Ralph de Turleville was a Bigod tenant in 1166 (*Bk Fees*,
396); see also Copinger, *Manors* iii, 40–1.

[73] *Taxatio*, 119b. The total valuation of the priory's spiritualities at the dissolution was only £2 13s
4d (below, p. 26).

[74] *Taxatio*, 126.

Fourteenth-century Acquisitions

By the late thirteenth century the number of grants to the canons of Dodnash, as apparently to all houses of monks and canons, had markedly declined. They did not, however, cease altogether. In 1301 Ralph del Breggs (*de Ponte*) gave his tenement in Stutton (126–7), and in the mid fourteenth century the canons acquired further land in East Bergholt which had been held by the Buk family of the Hospitallers, who had the manor known subsequently as 'Commandry's' or St John's, which had been granted by Peter de Liscamp in the reign of Henry II to the Templars.[75] In January 1350 the Master of the Hospital granted to Dodnash for a hundred years the tenement of Alan le Buk, which after his death (perhaps of the plague) had reverted to the Hospital by escheat (65). Eighteen months later Henry de Brokes granted an annual rent of 20d which he had recently purchased from John le Buk and Alexander Vivien (66), and further land purchased by William le Buk was acquired in the same year (67–8).

In the meantime, however, the priory had in the 1330s secured a major asset, the manor of Dodnash with its appurtenances in various neighbouring vills, which had been held since 1275 by various members of the Charles family, descendants of Charles of the Wardrobe, or Charles son of Charles, who died before 13 May 1241, holding lands in Yorkshire and Norfolk.[76] His son, William Charles, had a distinguished career in the royal service in the later years of Henry III; he was granted extensive lands in East Anglia by the Lord Edward on his marriage in 1262 to Joan de Valle Viridi, lady-in-waiting to the prince's wife.[77] William's son Edward followed him into the royal service, serving as admiral in 1306.[78]

In 1275 John Carbonel, a sergeant-at-arms in the royal household,[79] successfully brought a case against Hugh Tollemache for a tenement in Dodnash, Tattingstone and Bentley.[80] On 14 December 1275 Carbonel and Alice his wife bound themselves in the sum of £5 to deliver seisin of these lands to Charles son of Charles of Sisland, Norf.,[81] almost certainly the brother of the late William

---

[75] *Bk Fees*, 134; Copinger, *Manors* v, 20–1.

[76] *Bk Fees*, 1005; *Close Rolls 1237–42*, 299.

[77] *CPR 1258–66*, 212–13. In July 1264, in the aftermath of the battle of Lewes, he was sent as the king's personal emissary to Louis IX of France (*Close Rolls 1261–64*, 391, 394; cf. F.M. Powicke, *Henry III and the Lord Edward*, Oxford 1947, 474–5); in the wake of the eventual royal victory, in March 1267 he was placed in command of the expedition launched from Lynn to subdue those of the disinherited who had taken refuge in the Isle of Ely (*CPR 1266–72*, 44–5, 113). From November 1271 he served as steward of the royal household (ibid., 493), but was dead by 20 January 1271 (ibid., 509).

[78] M.C. Prestwich, *War, Politics and Finance under Edward I*, London 1972, 57; N. Denholm-Young, *History and Heraldry, 1254–1310*, Oxford 1965, 36–7.

[79] Tout, *Chapters* ii, 163. A Gilbert Carbonel attests no. 1 in this edition; a Geoffrey Carbonel held one and a half fees of the earl of Oxford in Great Waldingfield in 1242–43 (*Bk Fees*, 920). Sir John Carbonel attested two charters for St Bartholomew's, Sudbury, with Sir Hugh Tollemache, c. 1303 (*Sudbury Charters*, nos 85–6).

[80] PRO, C66 (Patent Rolls)/94, m. 20d.

[81] BL Add. ch. 9516.

20

Charles and himself described in 1272 as 'king's yeoman',[82] and on 13 June 1276 they granted these lands to him for an annual rent of a penny.[83] All this was done within the milieu of the royal court: the bond was attested by the mayor of London and the queen's treasurer and seneschal, the grant by Bishop Robert Burnell and three justices of the bench. Hereafter, the descent of the manor through the branches and generations of the Charles family is not entirely clear. In February 1292 William son of Edward Charles had a grant of free warren in his demesne lands of Dodnash, Bentley and Tattingstone.[84] On 10 April 1301 Edward Charles, son of Sir William Charles, granted to Edward Charles his son all his lands in the three vills, except the land called 'Manesford'.[85] On 7 July 1309 William, son of the lord Edward Charles, quitclaimed to his father the manor of Dodnash with its appurtenances,[86] but Edward was dead by July 1325, when William of 'Echebrugge' quitclaimed a moiety of the manor to his widow Agnes and a moiety to their son William, who was to have the remainder on his mother's death.[87]

At some time between July 1325 and February 1331 this William, after the death of his mother, sold the manor to Edmund Gauge (138), possibly because of debt to the financier Richard de la Pole (144).[88] Edmund was the son of the Sudbury burgess Geoffrey Gauge,[89] whose widow, Sarah, Edmund's mother, on 7 February 1331 conceded to John of Goldingham, clerk,[90] Roger of Gusford[91] and Nicholas Bonde[92] the manor of Dodnash and all the lands which had been held by William Charles in Bentley, Capel St Mary, Tattingstone and Brantham.[93] It

---

82 *C Ch R, 1257–1300*, 182, 184.

83 BL Add. ch. 9517.

84 *C Ch R, 1257–1300*, 418. The father can hardly have been Edward the admiral, who on the death of his mother Joan in 1305 was stated to be about thirty-six years old (*CIPM* iv, no. 299), and certainly cannot have been more than thirty in 1292, his parents having married in 1262. It is possible that this William is the grandson of Charles son of Charles, and his father another Edward, cousin of the admiral.

85 BL Add. ch. 9498, 9548.

86 BL Add. ch. 9567.

87 BL Add. ch. 9585–6.

88 Richard was the eldest of three sons of William de la Pole, merchant of Hull; he was born *c.* 1281 and died 1345. He was alderman of London, 1330–40, and knighted in 1340. He was a prominent financier to the royal government, and was king's butler from 1327 to 1331, and restored to that office in 1333 (Tout, *Chapters* ii, 22, 121; iv, 85–8; S.L. Thrupp, *The Merchant Class of Medieval London*, Michigan 1948, 361).

89 Geoffrey Gauge was still alive in 1313–14 (Rye, *Fines*, 129, no. 4); for the family, see also *Sudbury Charters*, 17).

90 Goldingham, in the parish of Bulmer, Essex. The family held lands there, and in Kersey and Belstead, Suffolk; see the family cartulary, Chelmsford, Essex RO, D/D EX M 25. John was probably a clerk of Thomas of Brotherton, earl of Norfolk, whose charters he attests (123–4). Since he does not appear as a defendant in June 1333 (147), he was probably dead by then.

91 Godlesford, now Gusford Hall, was a manor of St Mary Stoke (by Ipswich), by the fourteenth century held by Canonsleigh abbey, Devon (Copinger, *Manors* iv, 128–9).

92 Nicholas Bonde is termed 'of Freston' in charters of SS Peter and Paul, Ipswich, for which he acted as a feoffee (PRO, E40/3424, 3970, 7111). He was knight of the shire for Suffolk in 1339, served as attorney for the earl of Suffolk, and was royal custodian of Eye priory; his main residence was at Halstead (*CPR 1334–38*, 9, 96, 167, 275). He held land in several vills (Rye, *Fines*, 147 no. 18; 180, no. 11; 181, no. 28).

93 BL Add. ch. 9592.

appears that Edmund Gauge had purchased the Charles lands for his mother, and that she subsequently sold them – John of Goldingham stated seventeen months later that he had purchased them from her (143). Edmund Gauge himself quitclaimed and confirmed the estate to Goldingham and his associates a week later, on 14 February 1331. Potentially competing claims on the manor were abandoned in quitclaims by Robert of 'Stanmere' to Edmund Gauge and his mother on 4 February 1331[94] and by Richard of 'Echebrugge' to John of Goldingham on 10 April.[95] The annual rent of £20 payable to the canons, to which Edmund bound himself and his heirs (138), cannot be adequately explained, but was probably an additional charge on the lands which was retained by Edmund when the sale was planned; it seems to have been the matter of a separate quitclaim by William Charles to the priory in September 1333 (149). In 1331 the canons would have wished to ensure that the rent charge should continue to be paid should the land pass to a third party, and they may even have been alerted to the possibility of acquiring the manor themselves during negotiations over this matter.

The royal licence to acquire land to the value of £10 taken out in January 1331 (137) might indicate that the priory already had in view the acquisition of the Charles lands, now held by the Gauges, but it could equally be that the licence was purchased with no specific acquisition in view, and that its rapid implementation through the appearance of this estate on the market was fortuitous. John of Goldingham was clearly the priory's principal agent in the complicated process of securing the lands.[96] The fact that he was a clerk is normal in such transactions, as was the conveyance for a term of years (140). It is, however, rather strange that this lease on 5 May 1331 follows, rather than precedes, the royal licence to Goldingham granted on 2 April (139). That the term in no. 140 is not specified demonstrates that this is not a *bona fide* lease, but the licence should have eliminated the need for such manoeuvres. It is possible that the canons were attempting to safeguard themselves against any possible contingency, and it may be that Goldingham had leased the estate to the priory as soon as he and his associates had acquired it, and before the April licence to him.

The quitclaims by Nicholas Bonde and Roger of Gusford – the latter obviously a kinsman of the current prior – are a renunciation of any possible claim arising from their association with Goldingham in the acquisition of the lands from Sarah Gauge (141–2), which led in 1333 to their citation as co- defendants with the prior in the case brought by John Tollemache (147). There is a strong indication, however, that this action was not a genuine attempt by Tollemache to recover the lands allegedly disseised by John Carbonel in 1275 since, unless dated by a feast of St Dunstan observed only at Christ Church, Canterbury,[97]

---

94 BL Add. ch. 9591. On 6 November 1330 William Charles had made a grant of the manor of Dodnash, with the lands and tenements formerly of Edward Charles in Bentley, Tattingstone, Brantham and Capel St Mary to Robert of 'Stanmere' (Helmingham, T/Hel/49/57).

95 BL Add. ch. 9595.

96 For the whole process, see S. Raban, *Mortmain Legislation and the English Church, 1279–1500*, Cambridge 1982, esp. ch. 4, 'Manipulation of the Statute'.

97 No. 145 is dated the day after the feast of St Dunstan, which is 19 May. The feasts of the translation, 7 September, and ordination, 21 October, are contained only in Canterbury calendars (C.R.

Tollemache's quitclaim (146) preceded the opening stages of the litigation, although it is stated in the record that it was made after the prior and his associates had presented their case. This appears, therefore, to be a collusive action, designed to establish the priory's claim beyond any doubt.

The quitclaims by William Charles (148, 148A, 151) and by his uncles Edward and Edmund (152, 152A) are clearly designed as further guarantees against any claim on the manor from that family. The bond (150) appears to be an inducement by the canons to encourage William to discharge his debt to Richard de la Pole, which if not paid would be a claim on the estate. No. 153 suggests that the canons paid Edmund Charles for his quitclaim. The sequence is completed by the quitclaim in 1342 by the widow of Edmund Gauge (154).

A second royal licence, to acquire lands to the annual value of £10 in mortmain, was obtained in July 1366 (155). The only surviving evidence of its implementation is the grant by William Marigon of a messuage and seven acres in East Bergholt (69), and another in 1368 by Thomas Bonde and his sister of a messuage in the parish of St Nicholas in Ipswich (116).

On 6 November 1379 an inquisition *ad quod damnum* was taken relating to the projected grant by Roger of Woolverstone of East Bergholt, William Andrewe of Stoke and Andrew, parson of Horham, to the canons of land and rent in fifteen vills, but there is no indication that this was implemented.[98]

A last view of the extent of the priory's estate is provided by an inquisition taken by the king's escheator in Suffolk following the dissolution of the community.[99] The priory had held the manors of Dodnash and Falkenham; three water mills in Bentley, East Bergholt and Tattingstone; and forty messuages, a thousand acres of land, an hundred acres each of meadow and woodland, forty acres of pasture, two hundred acres of marshland and £5 worth of rent in Dodnash, Falkenham, East Bergholt, Capel St Mary, Bentley, Tattingstone, Stutton, Holbrook, Brantham, Wenham, Copdock, Stratford St Mary, Raydon, Framsden and Ipswich. The estate was valued in total at more than forty marks.

Grants from the Priory's Fee

The first recorded grants of land to be held in perpetuity of the priory date from the middle of the thirteenth century. The most interesting of these has been discussed above (p. 3) – the grant to John son of Andrew and his heirs of the former

Cheney, *Handbook of Dates for Students of English History*, Royal Historical Society, London 1970, 49).

98 A messuage, land and rent in Hemingstone, Coddenham, Barham, Ashbocking, Baylham, Great and Little Blakenham, Hintlesham, Raydon, Wenham, Chattisham, Aldham, Burstall, Bramford and Sproughton; they were to retain land in East Bergholt, Sproughton and Culpho (PRO, C143/396/24).

99 PRO, C142/76/42. C142/77/48, very badly stained and almost illegible, apparently contains the same information. A post-dissolution rental is abstracted in *Monasticon* vi (i), 590; East Bergholt, land and rent, £2 19s 6d; Capel St Mary, land and rent, £1 8s 0½d; Bentley, rent, £4 11s 10d; Tattingstone, land and rent, £5 9s 1d; Stutton, rent, £1 1s 5d; Brantham, farm of the land, 14s 4d; Wenham, land, 5s; Holbrook, land, 1s; Falkenham, land etc., £9 0s 6½d; total: £26 10s 9d.

site of the priory, with the stipulation that they might not build thereupon without the canons' consent (160). At about the same time, another prior granted to Robert of Falkenham, clerk, and his successors in perpetuity a parcel of land in Bentley for an annual rent of half a pound of wax (161). There are also late thirteenth-century grants of small pieces of land in East Bergholt (179), Brantham (183) and Shipmeadow (194). Thereafter, there is a group of grants by the prior and convent, or recognitions by tenants of service due, relating to lands in East Bergholt, Brantham, Stutton and Tattingstone, and dating from 1309–75 (162–3, 165–9, 171–2, 181, 185, 197–8, 203). Most such grants were made to the recipients, their heirs and assigns, thus allowing free disposition of the lands providing that the due service was rendered to the priory. A grant in Stutton in 1333, however, stipulated that the land should revert to the canons in the event of the failure of direct heirs (197), and a grant in Tattingstone in 1375 was restricted to legitimate heirs of the body. One grant in Bentley was made to a widow until her son should come of age (165), another to a man who was presumably the guardian until the heir should attain his majority (166). From 1316 onwards a distraint clause became common form in such grants (166–7, 169, 171–2, 181, 203).

The Leasing of the Demesne

The earliest lease, of all the priory's estate in Wenham to William Treysgos is surprisingly early, a term of twelve years from Michaelmas 1284 (206). In 1304 the canons leased to Roger Argent and his wife, for their lifetimes, the tenement lately granted to the priory by Ralph de le Brege (195). Particularly interesting is the recognition by the lessee in 1326 of his obligation to pay 18d and half a measure of refined salt each year for a lifetime lease of the salthouse at Brantham, which had been· granted to the priory a century and a quarter before (184, cf. 75–7). In 1343 a lease of pasture in Bentley was made to William Schereve, his wife and their son, a minor, for the lifetime of all three (164).

Leases became more frequent in the wake of the plague. In June 1350 the priory leased a piece of land in East Bergholt to Richard Ade and his heirs for an hundred years (180). Thereafter, documentation is extant for twenty-one leases over the century and a half from 1361–1522. Apart from the five-year lease granted in 1493 for £10 *p.a.* of all the priory's extensive estate at Falkenham made to Richard and Roger Martyn of Long Melford (193), these were all of lands very near to the priory, in Bentley (170, 173–8), East Bergholt (182), Capel St Mary (186, 188–92), Tattingstone (200–5) and Great Wenham (207–8).

It is difficult to establish any clear pattern for leases after 1350. The length varies from three years (178, in 1492) to a hundred years (180, in 1362; 175, in 1411); the average term of the fifteen leases stipulating a fixed time-scale is 31½ years, but this conceals great variations, and it is likely that the real average would be raised by leases granted for a lifetime (190, in 1375; 177, in 1460), two lifetimes (188, in 1362; 201, in 1372), or several lifetimes covering two generations of a family (200, in 1371; 202, in 1373). There seems to be no chronological development in thè length of leases. In 1362, for example, one lease at Great

Wenham was granted for twelve years at 3s 6d *p.a.* (207), another at Capel St Mary for 3s *p.a.* for two lifetimes (188); and in 1492 a lease in Bentley was granted for three years (178), four years later one in Great Wenham for 41 years (208). A particularly interesting lease is that in 1397 of a tile-kiln in Bentley for a term of five years, for a rent of 8000 tiles *p.a.*, which indicates that work was in progress at the priory (174).

Most of the leases appear to have been granted in return for a reasonable rent. The total, low, valuation of the priory's possessions in Bentley in 1291 had been £1 17s 8d. The lease of a fulling-mill and some land there granted in 1427 was for £3 2s, and at this time another lease was still in effect for an annual return of 10s 4d *p.a.* (175–6). In 1493 all the priory's possessions in Falkenham, valued in 1291 at £10 16s 11½d, were leased for £10 *p.a.* (193). The notable exception was the lease of land in Capel St Mary in 1436 to Gilbert Debenham, esquire, and his heirs for an hundred years for the annual rent of a red rose, should it be demanded – but since he was a member of the affinity of the duke of Norfolk, it may in these difficult times have been prudent to win his favour (191).

THE DISSOLUTION

Dodnash was one of the many small houses founded in East Anglia in the twelfth and early thirteenth centuries with a perilously small endowment, barely viable even before the economic down-turn of the early fourteenth century. The monastery's income could, indeed, support the minuscule community which lived therein, but that community was insufficient to maintain a proper liturgical round. From the middle of the fifteenth century the resources of several small convents in the diocese of Norwich were transferred to other religious uses, either by consolidation with a larger community or by diversion to educational (although, of course, still ecclesiastical) purposes.[100] As for Dodnash, incorporation into the endowment at Magdalen College, Oxford, had been seriously considered between 1459 and 1472 (above, p. 11). The end, however, was deferred until the priory fell into the net cast in the 1520s by Cardinal Wolsey in his search for endowment for his new college at Oxford and its projected sister institution at Ipswich, which enterprise triggered the dissolution of twenty religious houses.[101] On 1 February 1525 Dodnash priory was surrendered to a commission headed

---

100 J.C. Dickinson, 'Early Suppressions of English Houses of Austin Canons', in *Medieval Studies presented to Rose Graham*, ed. V. Ruffer and A.J. Taylor, Oxford 1950, 54–77. Houses in the diocese of Norwich which were dissolved or lost their independence include Great Bricett and Kersey, to King's College, Cambridge, 1444; Peterstone, Norf., amalgamated with Walsingham, 1449; Spinney, Cambs., and Molycourt, Norf., to Ely, 1449–50; Alnesbourne, amalgamated with Woodbridge, ? *c.* 1466; Chipley, to Stoke-by-Clare college, 1468; Wormegay, Norf., to Pentney priory, 1468; Great Massingham, Norf., to Westacre priory, 1476; Creake Abbey, Norf., to Christ's College, Cambridge, 1506.

101 On 3 April 1524 Pope Clement VII authorised the conversion of St Frideswide's, Oxford, into a college; on 11 September he permitted the dissolution for its endowment of religious houses with annual revenue to the value of 3,000 ducats. Twenty houses, including Dodnash and Snape, were

by Dr John Allen.[102] On the following 21 September, its estate was granted to Cardinal College, Oxford.[103] The valuation, taken in 1527, was £40 5s 4½d in temporalities and £2 13s 4d in spiritualities, a total of £42 18s 8½d.[104] On 1 December 1528 the Dodnash estate was granted by the dean of Cardinal College to Wolsey's college at Ipswich, established by authority of a papal bull issued the previous May.[105] After Wolsey's fall, however, and the failure of his scheme, the site and lands of Dodnash priory were assigned on 1 April 1531 to Lionel Tollemache and his heirs and assigns.[106]

THE CHARTERS

William Stevenson Fitch (1792–1859), chemist and, from 1837, Postmaster of Ipswich, formed a remarkable collection of manuscripts relating to the history of Suffolk which, probably because he fell upon hard times, were sold in four auctions between 1853 and 1859.[107]

In 1844 Fitch had 156 charters relating to Dodnash priory bound together into a fine volume, conventionally known as the Dodnash cartulary. It is certain that these documents were obtained by some means (possibly dubious) from the library of the Tollemache family at Helmingham Hall, where there are still some fifty deeds concerning the priory among a splendid collection of documents relating to the family and the estates acquired by it from the end of the twelfth century.[108] Apart from the 'cartulary', Fitch possessed a few other priory deeds, and some of these he included in his compilation *Monasticon Suffolciense* in four volumes, largely notes and transcripts, but including a few original documents.[109]

dissolved for this purpose, with a total annual value of £1,913 0s 3½d (Rymer's *Foedera* xiv, 23–5; *LPFD* iv (i), no. 1499; iv (ii), no. 3538). For a short account of the whole process, see M.D. Knowles, *The Religious Orders in England* iii, Cambridge 1971, ch. 12.

102 *LPFD* iv (i), no. 1137 (vi). For Allen, subsequently archbishop of Dublin, see A.B. Emden, *A Biographical Register of the University of Oxford to A.D. 1500*, 3 vols, Oxford 1957–59, 20–1. *Reg. Butley*, 46–7, which gives the date of dissolution as 21 January 1525, states that there was the prior and one other canon, and also indicates the resentment caused by the suppressions, for which see further D. MacCulloch, *Suffolk and the Tudors*, Oxford 1986, 151–2.

103 *LPFD* iv (i), no. 1833.

104 *LPFD* iv (ii), no. 3538 (iii). The valuation is notably higher than that of the rental (see above, n. 97), probably because it includes the priory complex and its contents.

105 For papal authorisation of the conversion of SS Peter and Paul, Ipswich, into a college, see *Foedera* xiv, 421–2, and for the diversion of the Dodnash revenues thereto, ibid., 247–8; see also *LPFD* iv (ii), nos 4576, 4578. The dissolution of the priories of Blythburgh and Mountjoy, Norf., was also now projected, but did not take effect because of Wolsey's fall (*Foedera* xiv, 240–1).

106 *LPFD* v, no. 220 (iv), grant to fifteen feoffees for the use of Lionel Tollemache and his heirs and assigns. Tollemache, as a lawyer, was in the service of the duke of Norfolk (MacCullough, *Suffolk and the Tudors*, 65).

107 For a biography, see A.H. Denney, 'William Stevenson Fitch, 1792–1859', *PSIA* xxviii, 1958–60, 109–35; J.I. Freeman, *The Postmaster of Ipswich*, London 1997.

108 A future volume in this series, edited by W.R. Serjeant, will contain the medieval charters relating to the Tollemache family.

109 Ipswich, SRO, q s 271.

and some of these he included in his compilation *Monasticon Suffolciense* in four volumes, largely notes and transcripts, but including a few original documents.[109]

The 'cartulary' is a morocco-bound volume with dentelle borders and gilt edges, measuring approx. 375 × 280 × 80 mm. The charters have been mounted on the paper leaves, the seals removed, and very often the fold-up at the lower margin cut off; of most of the detached seals there are fine watercolour facsimile drawings beneath the relevant charter. The title page is illustrated at the four corners by the arms of de Vere, Bigod, Brotherton and Tollemache, and at the base by two versions of the priory seal and that of Wimer the chaplain. Included in the volume are three engravings of various churches mentioned in the charters.

The 'cartulary' and seals were purchased at the second of the auctions, conducted by Messrs Puttick and Simpson on 2 July 1855, by Sir Thomas Phillips, who paid £100, by far the highest price in the sale.[110] It became Phillips MS 16732. At the same time many charters relating to the hundred of Samford were purchased by the Department of Manuscripts of the British Museum (see, for example, the annotation to this effect on the dorse of BL Add. ch. 9602, no. 152A in this edition). On the dispersal of the Phillips collection the 'cartulary' was purchased by the earl of Iveagh and remained at Elveden Hall until 1987, when it came with many other Elveden manuscripts to the Suffolk Record Office at Ipswich, where it is now HD 1538/202/1, and the seals HD 1538/202/2.

Endorsements

Many, but far from all, of the charters have either contemporary or later medieval descriptive endorsements. These range from the very terse, such as *carta comitis* (1) and *Mauricius filius Hervei* (5), to an almost full repetition of the dispositive clause of the charter (e.g. 66, 69, 127, 200–6). Only occasionally does an endorsement provide information not included in the text, for example, the enigmatic *comes Rogerus, non demonstretur* (54), the note that a tenement had reverted to the canons through default of legitimate heirs of the body (197), and the interesting provision relating to a rent charge on the Charles estate (168). Occasionally a later endorsement indicates the current tenant of the land to which the charter relates (39, 59, 84–6).

A few of the endorsements suggest how far from complete is this collection, even for the properties of the priory within Samford hundred. The four extant charters of Ada de Tosny are numbered ii, iii, v and viii (2, 7–8, 53), indicating that at least four of her charters have been lost. The one extant charter of Wimer the chaplain in endorsed *Wimarus capellanus et fundator*, iiii (6), and one of Alan Bernard's charters, of which only two survive, is endorsed v (102).

Apart from these numbers identifying the different charters of individual donors, there is another set of numerical endorsements, apparently written by a single hand, which may indicate the arrangement of the priory's archive. Most grants to the priory have such a number, although there are eleven exceptions; on and a few with medieval numeration have no other endorsement. It is impossible, however, to determine the system of numeration which is being used. For example, xii is used both for three charters relating to a grant by Hugh son of Alan in Brantham (74–6), and also for two deeds concerning a grant by Richard son of Warin of Raydon in Capel St Mary (93–4); xvi is used for six charters relating to 'Hunemaneslond' in Copdock (191–2, 104–7), but also for a grant in Brantham (77). The deeds relating to the acquisition of the Charles estate centring on the manor of Dodnash bear numbers from xxiii to xxxii (138–52), but the number xxvi, used on nos. 143 and 145, is also used on a grant by Avice widow of Walter Tibi in East Bergholt (33).

The Seals

One of the features of the Dodnash 'cartulary' is the fine series of drawings of seals, removed from the charters in order to facilitate the binding of the compilation volume and preserved separately. Over the years between 1844 and their arrival at the Suffolk Record Office many of these seals suffered considerable further deterioration, so that the drawings often give a better idea of the design than the surviving seals themselves.

Notable among the seals are an example of the great seal of King Edward III (155), and a fine example of a lead *bulla* of Pope Honorius III, still attached to the highly suspicious privilege of that pope (111). Appended to the two versions of no. 29 were fine specimens of the seal of the abbot and convent of Aumale and of the abbatial seal of Abbot Martin. There is a specimen of the seal of the founder, Wimer the chaplain and former sheriff: an eagle displayed on a small round shield (6). There are military equestrian seals of Aubrey de Vere (1), Baldwin de Tosny (attached by green and white cords, 3), Geoffrey son of William of Boyton (10), and Thomas son of Gilbert of Ilketshall (120); armorial seals of Thomas of Brotherton, earl of Norfolk (123), Richard de la Pole, the king's butler (144) and Edmund Charles (152A); and other less elaborate armorial seals (61, 114, 116, 192, 204, 211). There are several seals which feature living creatures: a bull (115), a squirrel (197), a porpoise (154) and perhaps a dragonfly (128); among birds (41, 87, 199, 207) are several other examples of an eagle displayed (27, 34, 172, 181, 203). Most interesting, perhaps, is the wolf on the seal of Edward son of Wlfard (55). The seal of Margery, widow of Roger Argent, shows one human figure kneeling at the feet of another (210), and that of Alan Bernard shows a star nestling in a crescent moon, a device popularised by Richard the Lionheart and widely used by his agents and adherents.[111] One strange device is apparently a human figure with arms and legs outstretched (149). The most common designs, however, are a fleur-de-lys (80, 84, 93, 95, 100, 129–31, 136) and radiating petals which may represent a flower (20, 26, 28, 31, 39, 51, 77, 86, 94, 106, 113, 126). The vast majority of seals were originally attached by parchment

---

[111] Ex info. T.A. Heslop. On 29 January 1199 a grant of immunity from tallages was made to an Ellis Bernard (PRS ns xiii, no. 557).

tags, although there is one example of a tongue cut from the parchment (159) and three seals are attached by cords – royal, papal and Baldwin de Tosny (3, 111, 155).

There are at least three types of the priory seal.[112] The earliest, of which an impression is apparently no longer extant, is illustrated not under any charter, but on the title page of the 'cartulary'. It measures approx. 58 × 42 mm. and shows the Virgin cradling the Christ child on her right knee. It has the legend . . .ANTE M. . .IE DE ALNETO DE BERGH, and the style of the figures also suggests a date around the end of the twelfth century.

The next priory seal, of which a small fragment was in 1844 still appended to a mid thirteenth century charter (161) was apparently still in use in 1361 (186). It, too, is illustrated on the title-page of the 'cartulary'. It is vessica shaped and smaller than the previous seal, measuring approx. 35 × 26 mm. The seated Virgin now holds the Christ child cradled on her left knee.

Sometime after 1361 and before 1411, the date of the charter to which it was affixed (175), the priory seal was redesigned to incorporate the Brotherton arms. This was presumably done before 1399, when Margaret, elder daughter of Earl Thomas, died. This was probably the same seal as was attached in 1460 to no. 154. The earlier impression, which has the right and left-hand sides of the vessica missing, shows a crowned Madonna cradling the Christ child in her right arm, at the base a shield of arms with the three leopards of Brotherton. The later impression, from which the base is broken off so that no shield can be seen, shows the same image of the Madonna and Child between columns. If this is indeed the same seal, its measurements can be reconstructed as approx. 68 × 44 mm.

Another seal, probably that of Prior Adam le Newman rather than of the prior and convent, was attached to a charter of 1348 (156). It shows a small figure in a habit, with a crozier in his right hand and a halo (probably St Augustine), standing before a seated Madonna with Child cradled in the left arm.

EDITORIAL METHOD

The editorial method is essentially that employed in earlier volumes of this series. With the exception of a very few transcripts on single sheets, all the charters are originals. Those before *c.* 1250 are printed in full, with spelling and punctuation modernised. All documents are on parchment and in Latin, unless otherwise stated. With regard to measurement, from most of the charters bound in the 'cartulary' the turn-up has been cut off, so dimensions are given in the form 156 × 86+ mm. Medieval endorsements are given, unless exceptionally long and merely reiterating material in the charter, when 'descriptive endorsement' has been thought to suffice. Post-medieval endorsements are not given unless of

---

112 J.J. Howard, 'Seal and Charters of the Priory of Dodnash, Suffolk', *Proceedings of the Society of Antiquaries* iv, 1857–59, 172, 211, merely records the exhibition of two seals from Fitch's collection, without any description.

especial interest. Post-1250 charters are calendared, unless, as no. 50, the content is of particular significance. An attempt to avoid reproducing the repetitiousness of late medieval deeds has been balanced by an effort to retain, as far as is possible, the diplomatic forms. Witness lists in calendared texts are given in the form of the manuscript, and the original forms of modern placenames are given in brackets. Minor placenames are normally given in the form of the charter, within inverted commas. Dating has been modernised.

The main problem has been the organisation of the charters in this edition, and in the attempt the editor has acquired even greater respect for those medieval archivists who compiled cartularies for their communities. Without such a guide, any decision made as to arrangement is necessarily arbitrary. In the end, it was determined to print first the earliest charters in favour of Wimer the founder and the canons of St Mary de Alneto in East Bergholt; then those relating to the lands and interests of the Dodnash family, the main early benefactors; then, alphabetically by vill, other grants and confirmations to the canons of Dodnash. There follow grants and leases by the prior and convent, and finally miscellaneous obligations and acquittances. Some charters refer to land in various vills – these have been placed under the first and probably main location (normally Bentley), but may be located through the index.

CHARTERS

GRANTS IN FAVOUR OF THE CANONS

1–159

GRANTS TO WIMER THE CHAPLAIN AND
TO ST MARY DE ALNETO

1. Notification by Aubrey [de Vere], earl of Oxford, that William son of Hervey of Dodnash came to his court so that he might sell to Wimer the chaplain all his land and inheritance in Dodnash for twenty marks of silver, and this he returned to the earl by token of a rod as freely and quit as he ever held it, and entirely renounced it, for himself and his heirs, to Wimer and to whomsoever he might constitute his heir. The earl has conceded this purchase and sale, and at William's petition has granted the land to Wimer and his received for it his oath of fealty. Wimer shall hold this land of the earl as long as the said earl shall retain it in his own hands, saving service, and as long as the earl does not bestow it upon an heir. If it should happen that the earl does grant the land to an heir and cannot with that heir's consent retain Wimer's service, he will make the heir receive Wimer's homage without any payment, saving the service pertaining thereto. If the land should remain in the earl's demesne, he concedes that it shall be held by Wimer and the heir whom he constitutes. For this concession Wimer has paid five marks of silver.   [Before 25 September 1188]

Cartulary no. 2; approx. 202 × 140 + 35 mm; endorsed: Carta comitis; seal, round, approx. 65 mm, brown wax, equestrian military figure facing right.

Alb(ericus) comes Oxeneford omnibus hominibus et amicis suis, clericis et laicis, tam presentibus quam futuris, salutem. Sciatis universi quod Willelmus filius Hervei de Dodenes venit in curiam meam coram me et baronibus meis in eadem curia, quod vendiderit Wimero capellano totam terram suam et hereditatem in Dodenes pro .xx. marcis argenti, et michi reddidit per unum baculum sicut illam unquam habuit liberam et quietam in manu sua, et penitus eam abfidavit de se et heredibus suis Wimero et illi quem heredem constitueret. Ego vero comes Alb(ericus) emptionem illam et vendicationem concessi, et petitione Willelmi et concessu reddidi illam terram predicto Wimero, et inde est meus affidatus. Et hanc predictam terram tenebit de me quamdiu eam tenuero in manu mea, salvo servitio terre, et quamdiu eam heredi non reddidero. Et si forte contigerit quod heredi predictam terram reddiderim, et non possim eius voluntati retinere servitium Wimeri de terra illa, faciam predictum heredem sine appositione pecunie sue capere homagium predicti Wimeri de eadem terra, salvo servitio quod pertinet ad eandem terram. Et si illa terra resideret in dominicum meum, tunc concedo de me et heredibus meis eam tenendam Wimero et heredi quod constituerit. Et pro hac donatione et concessu dedit michi Wimerus .v. marcas argenti. Quare volo et firmiter precipio ut hanc terram habeat et teneat bene et in pace, libere et quiete et hereditarie, sicut hec presens confirmat carta et testatur. Hiis testibus: Roberto de Cockefeld, Simone de Cantelu, Rogero de Bellocampo, Eustacio de Braham, Gilberto Carbunel, Fulcone dapifero, Thoma de Benetleia, Waltero de Midelt(on), Pag(ano) clerico, Galfrido Arsic, Willelmo de Criketot.

Before John of Oxford's confirmation (4). This land is presumably that on which the priory was eventually sited. The Veres held various lands in the locality. In 1086 Aubrey de Vere held a socman of Bergholt, having 4 acres worth 12d (*DB* ii, 287b). In 1242–43 it is recorded that Richard of Brantham held half a knight's fee of the earl of Oxford in Boyton, that is, Capel St Mary (*Bk Fees*, 916). In 1360 and 1371 inquisitions *post mortem* on the death of earls listed one knight's fee in Hintlesham and Dodnash held of them by the abbot of Walden (*CIPM* x, no. 638, p. 520; xiii, no. 125, p. 99).

2. Notification by Ada de Tosny that, at the petition of Baldwin her son and for the soul of Roger de Tosny her husband, her own and those of her ancestors, she has granted to Wimer the chaplain in pure and perpetual alms, free from all secular obligation, all her land in [East] Bergholt, that is, the land between 'Sagrimmesleia' and that of Godwin Luvegos, as it is embanked before the gate of Adam de Bussuin and Richard Hauec, as far as the aldergrove of Godwin Luvegos and even to the water which divides Bergholt from Dodnash, for the establishment of a religious house.   [Before 25 September 1188]

Cartulary no. 21; approx. 156 × 86+ mm; endorsed: ii, Ada de Tonei.; seal missing.

Ada de Tonei omnibus hominibus suis et amicis presentibus et futuris salutem. Sciatis me, petitione et assensu Baldewini de Toeni filii mei, dedisse et conces-sisse Wimero capellano in puram et perpetuam elemosinam, tam pro salute Rogeri de Toeni viri mei quam pro salute anime mee et omnium antecessorum meorum, totam terram inter Sagrimmesleiam et terram Godwini Luvegos, sicut fossatum cingit iam dictam terram, que iacet ante ianuam Ade de Bussuin' et Ricardi Hauec, usque ad alnetum Godwini Luvegos, maxime usque ad aquam que dividit Bercholt de Dodenes, ad religionem constituendam. Unde volo et firmiter precipio quod predictus Wimerus et religio illa in quam iam dictam terram transferre voluerit teneant predictam [terram] cum omnibus pertinentiis et pratis et alnetis liberam [et] ab omni exactione seculari absolutam. Hanc itaque concessionem carte mee confirmatione et sigilli mei munimine confirmavi. Hiis testibus: Ricardo de Bramford, Ada de Kanavilla, Amauri fratre eius, Roberto Quareme, Willelmo Talamasche, Seward', Gerardo Luvegos.

For the Tosny tenure at East Bergholt, see p. 7.

3. Notification by Baldwin de Tosny that he has granted to Wimer the chaplain, in pure and perpetual alms for the souls of Roger de Tosny his father, his mother and all his ancestors, his land at [East] Bergholt as described in no. 3, for the

establishment of a religious house. Wimer and this house shall hold the land with appurtenances free from all secular exactions.   [Before 25 September 1188]

Cartulary no. 3; approx. 217 × 85 + 15 mm; endorsed: Baldewinus de Toeni, i.; seal, round, approx. 55 mm, natural wax varnished brown; equestrian military figure facing to right, drawn sword in left hand, SIGILL. BALWI DE TOONE.; originally attached by green and white cords.

Baldewinus de Toeni universis matris ecclesie filiis et omnibus hominibus et amicis suis, presentibus et futuris, salutem. Noverit universitas vestra me dedisse et concessisse Wimero capellano in puram et perpetuam elemosinam, pro salute anime Rogeri de Toeni patris mei et matris mee et omnium predecessorum meorum, totam terram in Bercholt que continetur infra Sagrimesleiam et terram Godwin(i) Luvegos, sicut fossatum cingit iam dictam terram, que iacet ante ianuam Ade de Buissun et Ricardi Haueic, usque ad alnetum Godwini Luvegos, maxime usque ad aquam que dividit Bercholt de Dodenes, ad religionem constituendam. Unde volo et firmiter precipio quod predictus Wimerus et religio illa in quam iam dictam terram conferre voluerit teneant predictam terram et habeant cum omnibus pertinentiis et pratis et alnetis liberam [et] ab omni exactione seculari absolutam. Hanc itaque concessionem carte mee confirmatione et sigilli mei munimine confirmavi. Hiis testibus: domina Ada matre mea, Roberto de Chaumunt, Gilberto filio Wimeri, Huctred, Roberto de Forest', Radulfo Bule, Willelmo Ducat, Reginaldo capellano, Edwardo de Bercholt et David.

4. Notification by John [of Oxford], bishop of Norwich, that Baldwin de Tosni and Alda his mother have granted to Prior Adam and the canons of the aldergrove in [East] Bergholt this same place called the aldergrove, at the instance of Wimer the chaplain, founder of the place, who has assigned to the canons his land at Dodnash, which he acquired from William and Maurice, sons of Hervey, and also the church of Thurston [in Kirton] by the grant of the advocates. The canons have sworn upon the Gospels that they will not infringe the rights of the parish church, which pertains to the abbot and convent of Battle. Licence has been granted that they may bury in their own cemetery canons, members of their confraternity and others who, with the consent of their parish priest and having indemnified their parish church, choose to be buried there. Any dispute shall be settled by the common counsel of the churches of the aldergrove and Battle and the incumbent of [East] Bergholt, and if this should fail, by the arbitration of the bishop of Norwich, without recourse to any superior judge. This was done at the dedication of the cemetery and the foundation of the church.   25 September 1188

PRO, E210/376; approx. 168 × 190 + 20 mm; chirograph, indented at top margin; endorsed: De ecclesia de Burcholt; tags and seal missing.

Copies: London, Lincoln's Inn ms. Hale 87 (Battle cartulary), fo. 32r–v (lacks last twelve witnesses); San Marino, Huntingdon Library, Battle Abbey Papers vol. 29 (Battle cartulary), fo. 95r–v (84r–v).

Pd, PRS o.s. x, no. 53; *EEA* vi, no. 211.

Universis Cristi fidelibus ad quos presens scriptum pervenerit Iohannes Dei gratia Norwicensis episcopus salutem in Domino. Ea que usibus virorum relligiosorum collata sunt necesse est ut eis possint perpetua pace constare. Proinde notum omnibus esse volumus quod nobilis vir Baldwinus de Toeni et domina Alda mater sua Deo et sancte Marie et Ade priori et canonicis de alneto in Burcholt ibidem Deo et sancte Marie famulantibus et in perpetuum servituris eundem locum de alneto in Burch' sicut certis limitibus distinctum est et in scriptis redactum, liberum et quietum ab omni servitio, dominatione et exactione sicut liberam et puram elemosinam coram nobis et in manu nostra, pietatis et relligionis intuitu, concesserunt et dederunt, obtentu et perquisitione Wimari capellani eiusdem loci fundatoris, qui eidem loco assignavit et canonicis ibidem in perpetuum Deo servientibus terram suam de Dodenes, quam adquisierat a Willelmo et Mauricio filiis Hervei eiusdem terre patronis, et ecclesiam de Terston' concessione advocatorum Roberti de Bosco et Hervei clerici et Ricardi parcarii et Bartholomei filii sui de Everols. Et quia predictum locum esse constat infra terminos parochie ecclesie de Burch', que ecclesia ad venerabilem virum abbatem et conventum de Bello pertinet, ut omnis occasio turbationis auferatur et ut indempnitas eiusdem ecclesie, quantum in ipsis canonicis est, in omnibus et per omnia conservetur in posterum, idem canonici pro se et successoribus suis in perpetuum tactis sacrosanctis evangeliis iuraverunt et fide in manu nostra corporaliter prestita firmaverunt quod neque per se neque per aliquem iura ecclesie de Burch' occupabunt, diminuent vel subtrahent, sive in parochianis sive in sepulturis sive in decimis sive in oblationibus sive in obventionibus vel alio aliquo, eisdem canonicis data licentia proprios in suo cimiterio sepelire canonicos et fratres eorum sibi redditos et alios cuiuscumque parochie sint qui in eorum cimiterio cum assensu persone sue et indempnitate ecclesie sibi sepulturam elegerint. Si vero ab eisdem canonicis contra ecclesiam de Burch' in aliquo fuerit excessum, querela illa communi consilio ecclesie de Bello et ecclesie de alneto et persone de Burch' amicabiliter terminabitur. Si quidem per eorum consilium sopire non poterit, arbitrio et iudicio domini Norwicensis episcopi absque diffugio appelationis ad maiorem iudicem finem accipiet. Hoc autem est factum coram nobis anno ab incarnatione Domini m°c° lxxx°viii°, vii kalendas Octobris, in dedicatione cimiterii et fundatione loci de alneto in Burch', presentibus Alano priore sancte Trinitatis de Gipeswic' et Iohanne canonico suo et Willelmo de Brisete et Iordano canonicis sancti Petri de Gip' et Willelmo monacho de Bello, Galfrido capellano episcopi et officiali archidiaconatus de Gip', et magistro Roberto de Wacstun', magistro Rogero, magistro Lamberto, Roberto de Gipeswic', Willelmo de Redehal', Hugone de Ilketesh', Roberto notario decanis, et Alano de Bellafago et multis aliis clericis et laicis et multitudine alia virorum et mulierum.

The church confirmed cannot be Thurston, in Thedwardestre hundred, as incorrectly identified by the present editor in *EEA* vi, no. 211, as the monks of Bury paid a pension of 13s 4d *p.a.* to the bishop of Norwich for this church (*Register of John Morton, Archbishop of Canterbury, 1486–1500* iii, no. 193). It is almost certain that this church was Kirton, in Colneis hundred, of which parish 'Sterston' or Strewston (DB *Struustuna*) was certainly a hamlet, and the distinct

'Terston' or Thurston (DB *Turstanestuna*) possibly so. See also no. 111, and for full discussion no. 123n.

This actum refers to East Bergholt as a parish church, but other sources from the twelfth to the early sixteenth century have it as a chapel within the parish of Brantham; see Introduction, p. 4, n. 17.

5. Notification by Maurice son of Hervey that he has confirmed the agreement made in the court of King Henry II between himself and Wimer the chaplain, concerning the land which William, Maurice's brother, sold to Wimer. It was agreed that Wimer might found thereon whatever religious community he might wish, according to the charter which he has obtained from Simon of Thunderley, capital lord of the fee. This concession Maurice has made with the assent of his heirs, for their salvation and that of their ancestors and predecessors.

[13 November 1188 × 6 July 1189]

Ipswich, SRO, q s 271 (Fitch's *Monasticon*), vol. ii, at p. 166; approx. 251 × 58 + 10 mm; endorsed: Mauricius filius Hervei; tag and seal missing.

Universis Cristi fidelibus presentibus et futuris Mauricius filius Hervei salutem. Sciatis me concessisse firmiter et ratam habuisse conventionem factam in curia domini regis H(enrici) secundi inter me et Wimerum capellanum de terra illa de Dodenes quam Willelmus frater meus eidem Wimero vendiderat, scilicet quod liceat prefato Wimero pie devotionis intuitu religionem quamcumque voluerit in eadem terra fundare, liberam et quietam ab omni exactione seculari, quousque ad aliquam laicam personam spectare possit. Concedo similariter quod eadem facta sit secundum tenorem carte quam idem Wimerus a Simone de Tunderleg' capitali domino eiusdem fundi eadem devotione impetravit. Hanc quidem concessionem feci assensu heredum meorum pro nostra propria salute et pro animabus antecessorum nostrorum et successorum. Et ut hec nostra concessio rata sit et firma, eam presentis carte confirmatione et sigilli mei appositione corroboravi. Hiis testibus: domino Norwicensi Iohanne episcopo, Thoma et Galfrido archidiaconis, magistro Alano de Bellofago, magistro Hugone de Freseton', Willelmo Talamasch, Osberto filio Ervei, Huberto de Brisewurth, Roberto Quadrag', Galfrido de Boiton, Roberto et Radulfo et Reginaldo capellanis, Willelmo de Barham[a] et Ruold et Ernald Bastun clericis, Radulfo de Frivill' et Stephano de Caldecote et Rogero de Frivill' et Reginaldo Carpenter et quampluribus aliis.

[a] reading uncertain

The final concord was made in the *curia regis* in the year ending Michaelmas 1188, when account was rendered for a fine of two and a half marks paid by Maurice to the crown (*PR 34 Henry II*, 59). The notification is after 13 November 1188, when Geoffrey was not yet archdeacon (*EEA* vi, no. 272), but before the death of King Henry II.

Simon of Thunderley held one fee of the honour of Brittany in 1210–12 (*Red Bk Exchq.*, 480); to this honour there pertained in 1086 two manors in Bentley (*DB* ii, 295b). Probably before 1202 Simon confirmed a grant to SS Peter and Paul,

Ipswich, by Roger Bigod of nine acres of his fee at Hintlesham (Ipswich, SRO, HD 226, fo. 20r).

6. Notification by Wimer the chaplain that, through the promptings of charity and for his own soul and those of his predecessors and successors, he has granted in pure and perpetual alms to the church founded in honour of the Blessed Virgin Mary in the aldergrove at [East] Bergholt, and to the canons there serving God under the Rule of St Augustine, all the tenement which he holds in Dodnash of the fee of Simon of Thunderley, and all other tenements which he has acquired in Dodnash and its environs, of whosesoever fee, so that they may be set to their use in the best way possible, free from all human service and labour and all secular exaction. [Late 1188 × late 1189]

Cartulary no. 22; approx. 178 × 105 + 20 mm; endorsed: Wimarus capellanus et fundator, iiii.; fragment of seal, round, approx. 25 mm, natural wax varnished red-brown, an eagle displayed, S. . . . . .ELLI+.

Universis sancte matris ecclesie filiis et fidelibus presentibus et futuris Wimarus capellanus salutem. Universitati vestre notum fieri volo me, bone et pie devotionis intuitu et salutis anime proprie et predecessorum et successorum meorum optentu, dedisse et contulisse in puram et perpetuam elemosinam Deo et ecclesie in honore beate Marie in alneto aput Bircholt' fundate et canonicis ibidem sub regula beati Augustini inperpetuum servituris totum tenementum quod habui in Dodenes de feudo Symonis de Tunderl', simul et omnia alia tenementa sine aliquo retenemento que in eadem villa de Dodenes et in confinia eiusdem perquisivi, cum edificiis, boscis, molendinis, vivariis, stagnis, pasturis et cum universis eorundem tenementorum proventibus et exitibus, de cuiuscumque fuerunt feodo, prout commodius in usus illorum converti poterint. Quare volo et firmiter precipio quod idem canonici habeant et teneant supradicta tenementa cum integritate omnium ad eadam tenementa pertinentium, in puram sicut supradicitur elemosinam ab omni humano servitio, labore et exactione seculari exempta. Testibus: Iohanne Norwicensi episcopo, Walkelino archidiacono, Galfrido archidiacono, Thoma archidiacono, Rogero comite Norfolch(ie), Roberto decano de Gypesw(ico), Alano decano, magistro Samuel, Radulfo et Rogero capellanis, Symone de Tunderl', Eustachio de Braham, Clerenbaldo de Alno, Roberto Quareme, Osberto filio Hervei, Huberto de Brisew', Edwardo de Alneto, Ricardo de Bromford, David de Bircholt, Rogero.

The witness list to this charter raises two main problems. Geoffrey succeeded the ancient Walkelin as archdn of Suffolk sometime shortly after 13 Nov. 1188; they cannot properly occur together as archdns (*EEA* vi, pp. lxxxvi-vii; *Fasti 1066–1300* ii, 67). Roger Bigod was not created earl of Norfolk until 25 Nov. 1189 (*HBC*, 473). This charter records a grant made before, or at least at, the consecration of the cemetery by bp John of Oxford (4); it is otherwise unobjectionable, and was probably written after Geoffrey's promotion and the earl's creation, describing a grant made some months before.

7. Grant by Ada de Tosny to the canons in perpetuity of all the land which was held by Brithwald on the day of his death, that is, the messuage before the gate of Ralph del Huls with the cultivable land, meadow and alderwood, and the field before Hugh's gate, and 'le Heifeld' with the path which leads from the mound of the canons' garden, and the land which was held by Godric le Goc from the mound called 'le Wolfe'; she has also conceded to them common pasturage on the heath. For all this they shall render to her and her heirs three shillings a year, and they have given her twenty shillings as entry find[Before 14 November 1196]

A1 = Cartulary no. 18; approx. 188 × 95+ mm; endorsed: Ada de Toeni, v; seal, oval-shaped, approx. 40 × 54 mm, natural wax varnished brown, device indecipherable, + SECRETUM A. . D. THOENI .

A2 = Cartulary no. 17; approx. 195 × 81 + 17 mm; no medieval endorsement.

Ada de Thoeni[a] omnibus hominibus et amicis suis Francis et Anglicis tam futuris quam presentibus salutem. Sciatis me dedisse et concessisse et hac carta mea confirmasse priori sancte Marie de Alneto in Bercholtia[b] et canonicis ecclesie sancte Marie ibidem Deo servientibus totam terram que fuit Brithwaldi[c] in die qua fuit vivus et mortuus, scilicet mesuagium ante portam Radulfi del Huls cum terra wainabili et cum prato et cum alneto, et campum ante portam Hugonis et le Heifeld[d] cum chemino quod iacet a monte gardini eorundem canonicorum,[d] et terram que fuit Godrici le Goc a monte de Wolfe;[e] et preterea concessi eis communem pasturam de bruario. Istas prenominatas terras concessi illis in bosco, in plano, in pratis, in pasturis, in viis et in semitis et in aquis et in exutis et in omnibus aliis pertinentibus, tenendas libere et quiete et perpetue, reddendo mihi et heredibus meis tres solidos de censu per annum pro omnibus secularibus servitiis ad quatuor[f] terminos, scilicet ad festum sancte Marie in quadragesima[g] .ix. d. et ad festum sancti Iohannis Baptiste[h] .ix. d. et ad festum sancti Michaelis .ix. d. et ad festum sancti Andree .ix. d. Et pro hac donatione et concessione dedit mihi predictus prior et conventus viginti solidos de gersuma.[j] Isti sunt testes:[k] Eustachius de Braham, Rogerus filius eius, Radulfus de Bromford, Simon de Tunderle, Willelmus de Bromfort, Galfridus et Ricardus fratres eius, Robertus Quareme, David de Bercholte, Galfridus de Boitun', Ricardus de Cattiwade, Rogerus filius Godwini, Willelmus clericus de Tatingest(on), Willelmus Argent, Mauricius de Framesdene, Gaufridus clericus de Capella et multi alii.

[a] Touni A2   [b] Bercoltia A2   [c] Britwoldi A2   [d...d] omitted A1   [e] Holfe A2   [f] .iiii. A2   [g] quadragesuma A2   [h] Baptiste *om.* A2   [j] .xx. solidos de gersumia A2   [k] *There follows a variant witness list in A2*: Rogerus de Braham, Simon de Tunderle, Ricardus de Bramford et Galfridus filius eius, Willelmus de Bromford et Ricardus frater eius, Robertus Quareme, David de Bercholtia, Ricardus de Catiwade, Rogerus filius Godwini, Robertus de Boit(on), Willelmus Argent', Mauricius de Framesdene, Galfridus clericus de Capella.

8. Confirmation by Ada de Tosny of the pledge made to them by Richard of Bramford, that is, the land of Hauec which he held of her, saving the service due to her, as the charters of Richard and William his son bear witness.

[Before 14 November 1196]

Cartulary no. 1; approx. 151 × 48 mm; endorsed: viii.

Ada de Toneio omnibus hominibus suis Francis et Anglicis, vicinis et amicis, salutem. Noverit universitas vestra me concessisse et hac mea carta confirmasse priori et canonicis sancte Marie de Alneto de Bercholte vadium quod fecit Ricardus de Bromford predicto priori et canonicis, scilicet terram Hauec quam predictus R(icardus) de Bromford de me tenet, salvo servitio meo, sicut carta sepedicti R(icardi) de Bromford et carta Willelmi de Bromford filii eius testatur. Hiis testibus: Edwardo de Alneto, David de Bercholte, Gerardo de Locebroc, Willelmo Anglico, Rogero de Witesford, Girardo Lovegos, Roberto de Hemingestun, Rogero de Sachesdune.

While the canons were still in East Bergholt.

9. Confirmation by William of Bramford to the canons in pure and perpetual alms of the grant made to them by Geoffrey son of William of Boyton of all the wood of his fee in 'Hulney' and all the land between the road from the bridge of 'Walne' and the elm-wood to the east, with appurtenances, as is detailed in Geoffrey's charter (no. 10), which they have.   [Before 14 November 1196]

Cartulary no. 8; approx. 160 × 118+ mm; endorsed: Willelmus de Brumford, i.

Universis Cristi fidelibus presentibus et futuris Willelmus de Bromford salutem. Noveritis me concessisse et paratum habuisse et hac presenti carta mea confirmasse Deo et ecclesie beate Marie de Bercholt et canonicis ibidem Deo servientibus donationem quam Galfridus filius Willelmi de Boit(un) fecit eisdem canonicis de toto bosco quod est de feodo eiusdem Galfridi in Hulney et de tota terra que est inter viam que iacet a ponte de Walne usque ad hulnetum versus orientem cum pertinentiis suis, prout in carta ipsius Galfridi quam ab eo obtinuerunt continetur, in puram et perpetuam elemosinam. Hiis testibus: domino Wimero capellano, R. decano de Gip(ewico), Roberto Quareme, Willelmo de Maneton, Mauricio de Framed'. Henrico Bloman, Willelmo clerico de Tatinhest', Waltero fratre eius, Roberto clerico, David de Bercholt et pluribus.

> While the canons were still in East Bergholt. William of Bramford occurs in 1202, 1211 (*Fines* ii, nos. 345, 543), and was probably still alive in 1228 (*CRR* xiii, no. 1201). For the confirmation by Earl Roger Bigod of another grant by him, see no. 54; and for further quitclaim and grant, nos 121, 133.

> The endorsement of no. 10 locates Hulney wood on the borders of Dodnash (in the parish of Bentley) and Capel St Mary. For other grants to the priory there, see nos 29–30, 87; and for leases of adjacent land, nos 187–90.

10. Grant by Geoffrey son of William of Boyton to the canons, in free and perpetual alms, for his own salvation and that of his wife, ancestors and successors, of all the wood of his own fee in 'Hylneia' and all his land between the road from the bridge of 'Hwolne' up to the elm-grove to the east and to Dodnash wood, with all appurtenances, for which they shall render to him and his heirs two shillings a

year for all services, saving scutage of six pence in the mark, and *pro rata*. He has granted himself at the end of his life to the house[Before 14 November 1196]

> Cartulary no. 7; approx. 230 × 126+ mm; endorsed: Dodenes, Capel, Galfridus de Boitune; fragment of seal, round, approx. 34 mm, natural wax varnished brown, equestrian military figure facing to right, legend missing.

Sciant presentes et futuri quod ego Galfridus filius Willelmi de Boiton' dedi et concessi ecclesie sancte Marie de Alneto in Bercholt et canonicis Deo et sancte Marie ibidem servientibus totum boschum meum quod est de feudo meo in Hylneia, et totam terram meam que est inter viam que iacet a ponte de Hwolne usque ad holneiam versus orientem cum pertinentiis, usque ad boschum de Dodenes, in liberam et perpetuam elemosinam, reddendo annuatim mihi et heredibus meis duos solidos, scilicet ad Pascha .vi. denarios et ad festum sancti Iohannis Baptiste .vi. d. et ad festum sancti Michaelis .vi. d. et ad festum sancti Andree .vi. d. pro omni servitio, salvo servitio domini regis, scilicet ad marcam scutagii .v. d. et ad plus plus et ad minus minus. Et hoc feci pro salute mea et uxoris mee et antecessorum et successorum meorum. Et ego reddidi me eidem domui in fine vite mee. Testes: Willelmus prior de West Acra, Iwein canonicus eius, Wimerus capellanus, Radulfus capellanus, magister Saoier, Herveius de Doden', Radulfus Bule, Wimerus frater eius, Robertus Quadrag', Constant(inus) clericus, Willelmus Plucat, Clemens, Iohannes de Ponte, Walterus.

> While the canons were still at East Bergholt. For confirmation, see no. 9.

11. Grant by Edward son of Wlfard to Wimer the chaplain, in fee and heredity, of twelve acres of land in Flatford, to be held by the service of two shillings a year. For this grant Wimer gave him half a mark as entry-fine, and for this tenement he is bound by fealty.   [Late twelfth century]

> Cartulary no. 10; approx. 182 × 56+ mm; no endorsement.

Sciant tam presentes quam futuri quod ego Aedwardus filius Wlfard' de Bercholt dedi et concessi et hac carta mea confirmavi Wimero capellano .xii. acras terre in Flotford tenendas de me et heredibus meis in feodo et hereditate pro .ii. solidis per annum pro eius servitio. Et pro hac concessione et donatione dedit mihi predictus Wimerus dimidiam marcam argenti de gersuma, et de hoc tenemento est ipse meus affidatus. Hiis testibus: Baldewino de Toni, David de Bercholt, Waltero Lengleis, Roberto Quareme, Gerardo filio Wlfard, Iohanne fratre suo et pluribus aliis.

> Edward son of Wlfard of Bergholt was also know as Edward de Alneto (59), who is recorded in 1210–12 as holding twenty-shillings worth of land at East Bergholt retained by the king in his own hand, rendering account through the sheriff to the Exchequer (*Bk Fees*, 134). The last datable occurrence of Wimer is November 1196 (12), and the witnesses are consistent with a date around the first establishment of the canons at East Bergholt.
>
> For later charters relating to Flatford mill, see nos 55–57.

LANDS OF THE DODNASH FAMILY

For discussion of charters relating to the Dodnash family lands, see Introduction, pp. 7–10.

12. Final concord made in the *curia regis* before H[ubert], archbishop of Canterbury, and his fellow justices between Maurice of Dodnash, claimant, and Wimer the chaplain, defendant, concerning all the land in Dodnash with appurtenances which was held by Maurice's brother William son of Hervey, whereby Maurice demised and quitclaimed in perpetuity to Wimer and to the religious men there serving God and the Blessed Virgin, in free, pure and perpetual alms, all right and claim in William's land in Dodnash. For this concord and quitclaim Wimer gave Maurice forty marks of silver. Westminster, 14 November 1196

PRO, CP25/1/212/1/20; approx. 147 × 100 mm; chirograph, indented at top margin.

Pd., PRS os xx, no. 32.

Hec est finalis concordia facta in curia domini regis apud Westmonasterium in crastino sancti Bricii anno regni regis Ricardi .viii. coram H. Cantuariensi archiepiscopo, Radulfo de Hereford' archidiacono, Simone de Pateshull', magistro Toma de Husseburn', Ricardo de Heriard, Ogero filio Ogeri, tunc iusticiariis, et aliis fidelibus domini regis tunc ibidem presentibus inter Mauricium de Dodenesse petentem et Wimerum capellanum tenentem de tota terra que fuit Willelmi filii Hervei fratris eiusdem Mauricii cum pertinentiis suis in Dodenesse, unde placitum fuit inter eos in prefata curia, scilicet quod predictus Mauricius de Dodenesse dimisit et quietum clamavit predicto Wimero capellano et viris religiosis ibidem Deo et beate Marie servientibus in liberam et puram et perpetuam elemosinam totum ius et clamium suum quod habuit in predicta terra que fuit predicti Willelmi cum pertinentiis suis in predicta villa de Dodenesse de se et heredibus suis imperpetuum. Et pro hac fine et concordia et quieto clamio predictus Wimerus dedit predicto Mauricio quadraginta marcas argenti.

13. Grant in perpetuity by Maurice and Wimer, sons of Hervey of Dodnash, to the prior and canons, of part of their land at Dodnash, that is 'Osbernesfeld', 'Wacheslond', 'Sortecroft', 'Osberneslee', and their meadowland of 'Osberneslee' and 'Neubrege', and all the land once held by Wimund, with customs, services and appurtenances and with all the suit which is of the fee of Roger Bigod, earl of Norfolk, for an annual rent of a penny at Michaelmas, saving the service which they shall render as attorneys of the donors to the lord of the fee, that is 13½d a year. The prior and canons have given ten marks as entry-fine.

[Late twelfth – early thirteenth century]

Cartulary no. 23; approx. 195 × 77+ mm; endorsed: Mauricius et Wimarus fratres.

Sciant presentes et futuri quod ego Mauricius et ego Wimarus filii Hervei de
Dodenes dedimus et concessimus et hac presenti carta nostra confirmavimus Deo
et ecclesie beate Marie de Dodenes et priori et canonicis ibidem Deo servientibus
et servituris quandam partem terre nostre in Dodenes, scilicet Osbernesfeld,
Wacheslond, Sortecroft, Osberneslee, et pratum nostrum de Osberneslee et de
Neubrege, et totam terram quondam Wimundi, cum consuetudinibus et servitiis
et pertinentiis et cum omni sequela que est de feodo domini Rogeri le Bigot
comitis Norfolch(ie), habendam illis et tenendam de nobis et heredibus nostris
libere et quiete, plenarie et integre inperpetuum, reddendo inde nobis et heredibus
nostris singulis annis ad festum sancti Michaelis unum denarium pro omnibus
servitiis, consuetudinibus, exactionibus et demandis que ad nos pertinent, salvo
servitio quod predicti prior et canonici sicut aturnati nostri facient predicto domino feodi, videlicet tresdecim denarios et obulum per annum, scilicet ad festum
sancti Michaelis septem d. et ad Pascha sex d. et obulum. Pro hac autem donatione et concessione et huius carte nostre confirmatione sepedicti prior et canonici
dederunt nobis decem marcas argenti in gersumiam, et nos ad maiorem securitatem huic scripto sigilla nostra apposuimus. Hiis t(estibus): Helia de Amundevile,
Hugone Talemasch', Willelmo de Brumford et Huberto fratre eius, Willelmo de
Crepinge, Iohanne de Goudingham, Ermeiot de Wenham, Rogero filio Hugonis,
Roberto de Alneto, Mauricio de Dodenes et Thoma fratre eius, Ricardo filio
Roberti, Warino Testard et multis aliis.

For a later document relating to these lands, see no. 18.

14. Grant in perpetuity by Maurice son of Maurice of Dodnash to the prior and
canons of all the land which has come to him from his father by hereditary right,
that is, the land called 'Cardenei' of the fee of Roger, earl of Norfolk, the land
called 'Cumbwalle' of the fee of Ermeiot of Wenham, a tenement in Tattingstone
in the hamlet called 'Lourteburne', and 4d rent in Dodnash which Richard the
weaver rendered to him, to be held for the annual rent of a penny, saving the services due to the lords of the fees, that is, to Earl Roger 27d, to the lord Ermeiot of
Wenham 33d, and to the soke of Chelmondiston 10d *p.a.* The canons have given
him eight marks.   [Early thirteenth century, before August 1221]

Cartulary no. 66; approx. 183 × 97+ mm; endorsed: Dodenes, vi.

Sciant presentes et futuri quod ego Mauricius filius Mauricii de Dodenes concessi, dedi et hac presenti carta mea confirmavi priori et canonicis de Dodenes
presentibus et futuris totam terram quam hereditario iure ad me descendit de patre meo, scilicet totam terram que vocatur Cardenei de feudo domini Rogeri comitis Norffolchie, et totam terram que vocatur Cumbwalle de feudo domini
Ermeiotti de Wenham, et quoddam tenementum in Tatingeston in hameleto vo-
cato Lourteburne, et quatuor denarios in Dodenes quos Ricardus tixtor reddit
michi annuatim cum homagio et servitio suo, in mesuagiis, in pratis, in pasturis et
alnetis et omnibus aliis pertinentiis ad predictas terras pertinentibus, habenda et
tenenda eis in perpetuum de me et heredibus meis libere et quiete, reddendo inde
annuatim michi et heredibus meis unum denarium ad festum sancti Michaelis pro

omnibus servitiis, consuetudinibus et demandis, salvis servitiis dominis feo-
dorum, videlicet servitio domino comiti Rogero annuatim viginti septem denarios ad duos terminos, scilicet ad festum sancti Michaelis et ad Pascha, et domino
Ermeiotti de Wenham triginta tres denarios ad quatuor terminos censuales, et ad
socam de Chelmondiston' decem denarios ad quatuor terminos. Pro hac autem
concessione et carte mee confirmatione dederunt michi predicti prior et canonici
octo marcas argenti. Et ut hec mea donatio et carte mee confirmatio firma sit et
stabilis, presenti scripto sigillum meum apposui. Hiis testibus: Hugone Talmache,
domino Willelmo filio Roberti, domino Willelmo de Stratforde, Willelmo de
Holebrok, Ricardo de Boyton', Willelmo Argent', Radulfo de Braham, Mauricio
de Braham.

> Probably before the quitclaim of Maurice son of Maurice in 1224–25 (17), in
> which case the earl must be Roger I, who died before 2 Aug. 1221 (*HBC*, 473).
> Hugh Tollemache occurs in 1210–12 (*Bk Fees*, 134) and 1226 (35).

> In an earlier charter Maurice son of Hervey of Dodnash had quitclaimed to
> Thomas (possibly his son, but more likely a brother otherwise unrecorded) all
> the lands which he held after the death of his father, that is 'Lorteburne' of the
> king's socage, the land of Dodnash of the fee of Warin of Thunderley, and the
> land of 'Cumbwalle' of the fee of Ermeiot of Wenham (Ipswich, SRO, HD
> 1047/1/62); for 'Cumbwalle' see below, no. 20 and n. Another charter records
> the grant by Maurice (son of Maurice) of Dodnash to Richard the weaver, for an
> entry fine of 4s and 4d annual rent, of a piece of land in Dodnash between the
> water coming down from the mill of Thomas, Maurice's brother, and the water
> flowing down from his mill dams (Ipswich, SRO, HD 1047/1/68).

15. Notification by H[erbert] the prior, the precentor and the dean of Bury St
Edmunds that they have received a mandate of Pope Innocent III, dated at the
Lateran, 21 March 1215, recounting the complaint of the prior and chapter of
Holy Trinity, Ipswich, that the canons of Dodnash and certain other persons of
Norwich diocese have unjustly detained and refused to render certain tithes due
to them, and have caused them other injuries; they are to convoke the parties,
hear the evidence and reach a canonical judgement, with no appeal, enforcing
their verdict by ecclesiastical censure. Witnesses, should they withdraw through
favour, hatred or fear, are to be compelled to render truthful testimony. If all
judges cannot be present, two of them may proceed.

When the parties had convened before them, the representative of the prior and
convent of Ipswich alleged that all the tithes, lesser and other, from lands within
the parish of Bentley pertained by common law [of the Church] to the church of
Bentley, and that the prior and canons of Dodnash had occupied and detained
them unjustly, to their own grave prejudice, and therefore they sought judicial
sentence in their favour and that of the mother church. They also claimed the tithe
of hay, mills, assarts made or to be made and lands cultivated before this action
was brought, and of the hired servants of the canons of Dodnash dwelling in the
parish of Bentley. The prior of Dodnash sought, rather than litigation, the termi-
nation of this case by a form of peace, and at last the dispute was resolved as
follows: the prior and convent of Ipswich have retained for themselves and their

church of Bentley all tithes from the land which lies between the highway leading
to the church of Dodnash and the embankment of the old fishpond where of old
was the principal messuage of the lord of Dodnash, and also all tithes from the
great field lying between the great wood and 'Hulleney'; they have also retained
the parochial right which they claimed in relation to the servants of the canons of
Dodnash, so that their hired servants should attend the mother church of Bentley
at the three great festivals of the year, and when they die within the parish, they
should be buried there. All else that they had claimed they graciously remitted to
the prior and convent of Dodnash, undertaking to bring no action thereto pertaining in the future. This agreement was drawn up in the form of a chirograph with
the seals of the judges, and each party's copy was sealed by the other. Both
parties foreswore future litigation on these and related matters.

[Shortly after 21 March 1215]

Cartulary no. 27; first entry on long parchment, approx. 750 × 154 mm, compris-
ing two membranes, probably originally a roll, a thirteenth-century transcript.

Omnibus Cristi fidelibus ad quos presens scriptum pervenerit H(erbertus) prior et
precentor et decanus sancti Edmundi eternam in Domino salutem. Noverit universitas vestra nos mandatum domini pape in hec verba suscepisse: Innocentius
episcopus servus servorum Dei dilectis filiis priori, precentori et decano sancti
Edmundi Norwicensis diocesis salutem et apostolicam benedictionem. Ex parte
dilectorum filiorum prioris et capituli sancte Trinitatis de Gyppwico nobis est ob-
lata querela quod canonici de Dodenesch et quidam alii Norwicensis diocesis
quasdam decimas eorum ecclesie debitas contra iustitiam detinent et reddere con-
tradicunt, alias eis graves plurimum existentes. Quocirca discretioni vestre per
apostolica scripta mandamus quatinus, partibus convocatis et auditis hinc inde
propositis, quod canonicum fuerit appellatione postposita decernatis, facientes
quod decreveritis per censuram ecclesiasticam firmiter observari. Testes autem
qui fuerint nominati si se gratia, odio vel timore subtraxerint, per censuram
eandem appellatione remota cogatis veritati testimonium perhibere. Quod si non
omnes hiis exequendis potueritis interesse, duo vestrum ea nichilominus exe-
quantur. Dat' Lateran' .xii. kal' Aprilis pontificatus nostri anno octavodecimo.
Huius igitur auctoritate mandati, partibus coram nobis in iure constitutis, pars prioris et conventus sancte Trinitatis de Gypp(wic)o omnes decimas tam minutas
quam alias provenientes de terris suis infra parochiam suam de Benteley ad ecclesiam suam de Benteley de iure communi pertinere dicebat, asserens priorem et
canonicos de Dodenes eas in grave sui preiudicium minus licite occupasse et hac-
tenus iniuste detinuisse; unde petebat dictas decimas prenominatis canonicis
abiudicari et ecclesie matrici sententialiter adiudicari; idem etiam de decimis
feni, molendinorum, essartorum factorum et faciendorum et terrarum ante motam
questionem incultarum, et de famulis predictorum canonicorum de Dodenesch
conductitiis in parochia sua de Benteley commorantibus intendebat. Priore
siquidem de Dodenesch pro se et fratribus suis non ad litigandum sed potius ad
causam sub certa pacis forma terminandam in iure constituto, tandem inter partes
mota controversia in hunc modum conquievit. Dicti prior et conventus de
Gypp(wyco) retinuerunt sibi et ecclesie sue de Benteley omnes decimas proveni-

entes de tota terra que iacet inter viam magnam que ducit ad ecclesiam de Dodenesch et fossatum veteris vivari qui antiquitus fuit principale mesuagium domini
de Dodenesch, et omnes decimas similiter proveneniunt de campo magno iacente
inter magnum boscum de Hulleney; ius etiam parochiale quod sibi in famulis predictorum canonicorum de Dodenesch vendicaverunt sibi retinuerunt, ita videlicet
quod famuli eorum conductitii ecclesiam matricem de Benteley in tribus anni sol-
empnitatibus precipuis visitabunt divina ibidem percepturi, et cum in parochia
predicta decesserint, ecclesiastice in ea tradendi sepulture. Cetera vero omnia
superius expressa ob favorem religionis priori et canonicis de Dodenesch benigne
remiserunt prior et canonici de Gipp(wic)o, promittentes se de cetero eis super
hiis non moturos questionem. In cuius rei testimonium hoc scriptum in modum
cirographi confectum sigillorum nostrorum appositione communivimus, et ad
maiorem securitatem sepedicti priores et canonici sigilla sua utrimque apposuerunt, promittentes hinc inde specialiter quod super hac causa vel eius appenditiis
de cetero non movebunt questionem.

For discussion, see Introduction, pp. 11–12.

15A. Late medieval memorandum relating to tithes

Hit ys to be understand that thourgh the suggestion and compleynt of the pryor of
Yepswyche our holy fader [. . .] Pope Innocent, whether the furst or the seconde
hyt ys made no mencyon, sholde sende a certayn maundement to the pryor, pre-
sentor and dene of Seynt Edmundis to examyne whether the chanons of Dodenesche and other of the dyocyse of Northewych have wytholden certayn tythes of
the sayd pryor dywe. And hyt ys to be conceyved [that] in the sayd compleynt the
pryor of [Dodenesshe *deleted*] Seynt Maryes of the Altercar in Bergholt*ᵃ* ys name
ys not expressed but synguler [. . .] chanons of Dodenesche; wher as y suppose
ther be noon such, and in case hyt may be knowen or proved that eny suche
religyous sholde [. . .] in eny place veryly knowen and called by the sayd name of
Dodenesshe, then hyt were the mor lyke that the sayd pryor of Yepswyche sholde
reioyse and have suche tythes and dywtes as unto hym been awarded by the sayd
pryor, [presentor] and dene as theyr endentur of clayme maketh mynde.

But hyt ys veryly to be conceyved and feythefully to be understonde that the
sayd endentur whiche the sayd pryor gro[unds?] hym upon may in no wyse
charge ne bynde me ne my successors callyng us chanons of Dodenesshe, for hyt
ys opynly knowen and credybelly, as well by our holy faders bulles under lede as
by our furst founder and by other olde evydences that we ar founded and sette
withynne the precynct and parysshe [of Berg]holt and called the pryory of Seynt
Maryes of the Altcarre, and the Pope wryteth unto us in this forme – priori et
canonicis ecc[lesie] beate Marie de Alneto in Bergholt – thorugh vertu and effect
of whyche bulles and evydences we reioysen and posseden our lyvelode as well
temporell as spirituell.

Neverthelesse, hyt ys knowen in the contrey that we possedyn a lordeshyp
whiche is called Dodenesshe after a knyght whiche was called Sir Hywe of

Dodenesche, whiche olde maner stode sumtyme in the parysshe of Benteley, which maner and place, after hyt was appropred unto us, my predecessor lete take doun the mansyon and other houses of offyce such as hym semed, and sette theym at our dwellyng in the sayd alderca[rre in] such stedes as hym [seemed ?] most necessarye and profytabell.

Soo that by advyse my sayd predecessor seemed that the vacaunt place and grounde, wher as the sayd maner before stode, was most conveniyent for a vyneyerde, and after suche purpose at that tyme he dyde hyt to be occupyded and made suffycyent fense inclosyng and dykyng about the same vyneyerd, as hyt appereth well unto this day.

Notwithstondyng by processe and longe contenuance the sayd vyneyerd ne repeyred by other of my predecessors whiche succedyd hym, having no joye ne delyte to uphalden the sayd vynes and also sem[ed] the grounde not most apte ne convenabell to such entent, suffred the wode to [. . .] and thought the s[. . .] sholde be more profytabelly occupyed, wherthorugh hyt hathe syne tyme encresyd to a fayr wode.

And the sayd endentur [. . .] of Dodenesshe to yelde a certayn tythe of [dyverse londes *deleted*] a parcell of londe lying betwyxt the grete weye whiche ledethe to the churche of Dodenesshe and the [gret *deleted*] dyke of the [. . .] vyneyerd, whiche vyneyerd the sayd pryor of Yepswyche mysconstrueth and taketh hyt for a ryver, whiche by dyverse skylles may be proved the contrary as well by the maner of [wrytyng ?] as by the ground; the wrytyng ys vinarii with iij mynymes, wher as vivarii sholde after gode [gramere and ?] ortogrophie be so wryten; also hyt appereth evydently by the soyle and the old dykes [. . .] vyneyerd a[nd] no ryver neyther now ne in tyme past.

^a Bergholt *interlined*

Helmingham, T/Hel (S)/10/54; approx. 295 × 360 mm; on dorse, the canon of Pope Alexander III *Ex parte*, and a short rental, partially struck through.

For discussion, see Introduction, pp. 5–6.

16. Quitclaim by Thomas son of Maurice of Dodnash to the prior and canons, in pure and perpetual alms for the salvation of his soul and those of his wife, ancestors and successors, of all right which he might have to their possessions, that is, to all that they have acquired from their foundation to the eighth year of King Henry III, saving to him and his heirs the way which leads from Dodnash to 'Lemaneshei' and that which leads from Dodnash to 'Copedethorn' for chase and carriage, and saving all customary paths through the canons' lands; and saving to the canons all customary paths through his lands.

[28 October 1223 × 27 October 1224]

Cartulary no. 31; approx. 215 × 80+ mm; chirograph, indented at top margin; endorsed: Thome de Dodenes, xiii.

Sciant presentes et futuri quod ego Thomas filius Mauricii de Dodenes dimisi et concessi et hac carta mea quiete clamavi priori de Dodenes et canonicis ibidem

Deo servientibus et servituris totum ius et totum clamium quod habui vel habere potui in possessionibus eorum, scilicet in omnibus illis possessionibus quas predicti canonici adepti sunt ab initio fundationis ecclesie sue de Dodenes usque ad octavum annum regni regis Henrici filii regis Iohannis, tenendum et habendum illis libere et quiete pro me et heredibus meis inperpetuum, scilicet in terris, in boscis, in pratis, in alnetis, in pascuis, in bruariis et omnibus aliis rebus et libertatibus, in puram et perpetuam elemosinam pro anima mea et anima uxoris mee et animabus antecessorum et successorum meorum, salvis michi et heredibus meis via que extenditur a Dodenes versus Lemaneshei et via que extenditur a Dodenes versus Copedethorn ad caciandum et cariandum, et omnibus aliis viis debitis et consuetis per medium terrarum predictorum canonicorum sine detrimento eorum, et salvis omnibus viis debitis et consuetis per medium terrarum mearum predictis canonicis ad caciandum et cariandum sine detrimento meo. Hiis testibus: magistro Ricardo de Kodeh(am) decano, Thoma persona de Reindun', Ernaldo capellano, Ricardo capellano de Benetlee, Willelmo filio Roberti de Reindun', Roberto Petit, Willelmo Iuvenal, Roberto de Alneto, Rogero filio Hugonis, Roberto de Boitun', Thoma de Lodebroch, Willelmo Helewis, Thoma filio Hugonis, Roberto de Hulnei et multis aliis.

17. Quitclaim by Maurice son of Maurice of Dodnash to the prior and canons, made through the promptings of charity in pure and perpetual alms for the salvation of his soul and those of his wife, ancestors and successors, of all right he might have to their possessions acquired from their foundation to the ninth year of King Henry III, saving to himself and his heirs the way from Dodnash to Morell's land through 'Lemaneshei'. [28 October 1224 × 27 October 1225]

Cartulary no. 32; approx. 175 × 80+ mm; endorsed: Mauricii de Dodenes, viii.

Sciant presentes et futuri quod ego Mauricius filius Mauricii de Dodenes dimisi et concessi et hac carta mea quiete clamavi priori de Dodenes et canonicis ibidem Deo servientibus et servituris totum ius et totum clamium quod habui vel habere potui in possessionibus eorum, scilicet in omnibus illis possessionibus quas predicti canonici adepti sunt ab initio fundationis ecclesie sue de Dodenes usque ad nonum annum regni regis Henrici filii regis Iohannis, tenendum et habendum illis libere et quiete pro me et heredibus meis inperpetuum, scilicet in terris, in boscis, in pratis, in alnetis, in pascuis, in bruariis, in viis et omnibus aliis rebus et etiam libertatibus, intuitu caritatis in puram et perpetuam elemosinam pro salute anime mee et uxoris mee et omnium antecessorum et successorum meorum, salva michi et heredibus meis via a Dodenes usque ad terram Morelli per Lemaneshei. Et ut hec mea dimissio et concessio et quieta clamatio firma sit et stabilis, huic scripto sigillum meum apposui. Hiis t(estibus): Willelmo de Brumford, Willelmo de Wauding(efeld), Hugone de Holetun', Willelmo filio Willelmi de Kenebroch, Rogero filio Hugonis, Rogero Iuvencel, Isenbardo filio Hugonis, Willelmo Helte, Iohanne de la Mare et multis aliis.

Maurice had granted to his brother Thomas, for an entry fine of half a mark and 11d annual rent, all the land called 'Langeland' of the fee of Morell (Ipswich,

SRO, HD 1047/1/660; Hubert of Braiseworth had previously held this land (see below, no. 70n.).

18. Agreement made between J. prior of Dodnash on the one part and Maurice and Thomas of Dodnash on the other, whereby they have bound themselves by oath to combine to acquire together all the lands of Maurice and Wimer, sons of Hervey of Dodnash, as cheaply as possible, each of them contributing an equal sum of money towards the purchase. When by God's grace they have acquired this land, it shall be divided thus: the prior and church of Dodnash shall hold of the lords of the fee the land of Wimund with homages, customs and appurte-nances, 'Osbernesfeld', 'Sortecroft', 'Osberneslee' and its meadow, the holdings of the said sons of Hervey, and their meadow at 'Neubrege'; that part of the said meadow which Thomas of 'Osberneslee' has by inheritance from his father is to be granted to the church and prior in exchange for 'Wacheslond', which is granted to the said Thomas. Maurice, brother of Thomas, shall hold of the lords of the fee 'Holond', 'Holee' and the marsh and aldergroves of the fee of Hugh Tollemache, the wood of Selida Tatsalade and two acres in 'Cardenei' and 'Bernecroft'. Thomas, brother of Maurice, shall hold 'Millefeld', 'Quetecroft', 'Gulet', 'Sumerfalee' and the parts of the aldergrove adjacent to his house, and also 'Wacheslond' by exchange, as above. The three parties swore on oath to observe this agreement, and confirmed this by appending their seals.

[Early to mid thirteenth century]

Cartulary no. 79; approx. 152 × 90+ mm; no endorsement; slits for two seals.

Hec est conventio facta inter I. priorem de Dodenes ex una parte et Mauricium et Thomam de Dodenes ex altera, quod predicti prior et M. et T. obligaverunt se mutuo per fidem et corporale sacramentum prestitum quod per commune consi-lium et auxilium eorundem trium perquirent pro posse suo totam terram Mauricii et Wymari filiorum Hervei de Dodenes prout levius eam perquirere poterunt, ita tamen quod quilibet eorundem trium equalem portionem pecunie in dicte terre adquisitione apponet. Cum autem per Dei gratiam predictam terram adquisierint, adquisita ita dividetur inter predictos tres: priori et ecclesie de Dodenes he partes terre remanebunt tenende de dominis eiusdem feodi, scilicet terra Wimundi cum homagio et consuetudinibus et omnibus pertinentiis, et Osberneslee, Sortecroft, Osberneslee, pratum de Osberneslee predictorum filiorum dicti Hervei, et pratum eorundem apud Neubrege, et pars prati predicti Thome de Osberneslee quam habuit de hereditate patris sui cedet predicte ecclesie et priori in escambium pro Wacheslond que cedet eidem Thome. Predicto vero Mauricio fratri Thome he partes remanebunt tenende de dominis feodi, scilicet Holond, Holee et mariscus cum alnetis de feodo Hugonis Thalemasche, boscus Selide Tatsalade et due acre in Cardenei et Bernecroft. He autem partes remanebunt Thome fratri Mauricii, scilicet Millefeld, Quetecroft, Gulet, Sumerfalee et partes alneti iuxta domum suam, et Wacheslond que ei cedet in escambium pro Osberneslee sicut predictum est. Hanc autem conventionem fideliter et firmiter tenendam predictus prior in verbo veritatis et predicti M. et T. affidaverunt et iuraverunt et ad maiorem securitatem presentibus scriptis sigilla sua apposuerunt.

> Maurice son of Maurice occurs in 1224–25 (17) and was almost certainly dead by 1243, when his brother Geoffrey occurs (23); Thomas son of Maurice occurs in 1223–24 (16). The prior is almost certainly Jordan, who occurs in 1228 and 1234 (42, 66).

> For the lands to be held by the priory, see no. 13, which records the grant to the canons by Maurice and Wimer sons of Hervey, who also granted to Thomas of Dodnash, their uncle, their part of 'Millefeld' and 'Quetecroft', 'Gulet', 'Sumerfalee' and a flax-ground in 'Osbernesfeld' (Helmingham, T/Hel/49/6 (A2/7). The meadow of 'Neubregge' was subsequently granted back by the canons to Maurice (II, son of Maurice) of Dodnash, and was granted by his son Geoffrey to his uncle Thomas (Ipswich, SRO, HD1047/1/59).

> For Hugh Tollemache, see no. 24. For other Tollemache tenants in Bentley, see nos 31, 34–35, 41; and in Copdock, nos 101, 104.

19. Notification by the prior of Woodbridge and the deans of Lothingland and Claydon that they have received a mandate of Pope Gregory IX, dated at Perugia 21 May 1229, recounting the complaint of the prior and canons of Holy Trinity, Ipswich, that the prior and canons of the church of Dodnash, subject to their monastery, have refused to render the obedience and reverence due to their monastery, and that they and others of Norwich and Lincoln dioceses have caused them injury in things due to them and otherwise; they are to convoke the parties, hear the case and decide the matter in accordance with justice, with no appeal permitted, enforcing their judgement by ecclesiastical censure.

When the parties had convened before them, the prior of Holy Trinity, Ipswich, on behalf of the convent, demanded from the prior and canons of Dodnash the subjection and reverence which he asserted was due, and also the land which William son of Hervey had given them, on which the house of Dodnash was sited, also two acres of land which William the cripple, servant of the canons of Ipswich, held in Bentley, also an annual rent of twelve pence from the land called 'Ilmanescroft', also the tithe of grain from the great field of the new marl, also the wood which was the gift of Kebbel by the messuage which was held by Burdun in Bentley, also the tithes and obventions of the said Burdun, and also a third part of the tithe of hay and the lesser tithes of Maurice and Wimer sons of Hervey; all of which things they alleged that the prior and canons of Dodnash had unjustly detained and for which they brought a possessory action.

At last, after much altercation, the action between the parties was brought to a resolution, for the sake of peace, in the following manner. The prior and convent of Ipswich have withdrawn all complaint and action against the prior and canons of Dodnash relating to the above matters, in return for a rent of twenty pence. This agreement was made with the consent of Thomas, bishop of Norwich, and the document is sealed with the seals of the judges, the bishop and the parties.

16 May 1232

Cartulary no. 27; second entry of transcript described at no. 15.

Omnibus Cristi fidelibus ad quos presens scriptum pervenerit prior de Wodebrig' et de Lodeham et de Cleydon decani salutem in Domino. Mandatum domini pape suscepimus in hec verba: Gregorius episcopus servus servorum Dei dilectis filiis priori de Wodebrig' et de Lodeham et de Cleydon decanis salutem et apostolicam benedictionem. Dilecti filii prior et canonici sancte Trinitatis de Gypp(wic)o suam ad nos querimoniam destinarunt quod prior et canonici ecclesie de Doden(es) Norwycensis diocesis, monasterio ipsorum subiecti, obedientiam et reverentiam sibi debitam denegant exhibere; idem quoque et quidam alii eiusdem et Lincolniensis diocesum super debitis et rebus aliis iniuriantur eisdem. Ideoque discretioni vestre per apostolica scripta mandamus quatinus, partibus convocatis, audiatis causam et quod iustum fuerit appellatione remota statuatis, facientes quod statueritis per censuram ecclesiasticam firmiter observari. Testes etc. Quod si non omnes etc. Dat' Perusi xii kal. Iunii pontificatus nostri anno tertio.

Huius igitur auctoritate mandati partibus coram nobis vocatis et legittime comparentibus, dictus prior sancte Trinitatis pro se et conventu suo petiit a dicto priore de Dodenesch et conventu suo subscripta, videlicet subiectionem et reverentiam quas sibi et monasterio eorum de Gypp(wico) a dictis priore et canonicis de Dodenesch deberi asserebant, unacum terra quam Willemus filius Hervei eis contulit, in qua terra dicti canonici de Dodenesch siti sunt; item duas acras terre cum pertinentiis quas Willelmus contractus servus eorundem canonicorum de Gypp(wico) tenuit in Benteley, item annuum redditum duodecim denariorum de terra que vocatur Ilmanescroft; item decimas bladi de magno campo de novo marlato; item boscum de dono Kebbel iuxta mesuagium quod fuit Burdun in Benteley; item decimas et obventiones dicti Burdun; item decimas fenorum et minutas decimas de tertia parte Mauricii et Wymarc filiorum Hervey; que omnia dicunt dicti prior et conventus sancte Trinitatis dictos priorem et canonicos de Dodenesch iniuste detinuisse, et ad hec omnia intendant possessorium. Tandem vero post multas altercationes lis super omnibus predictis inter dictos priores pro se et conventibus eorum in hunc modum pro bono pacis conquievit, videlicet quod predicti prior et conventus de Gypp(wico) remiserunt predictis priori et canonicis de Dodenesch omnes questiones et actiones quas habebant ratione supradictorum contra dictos priorem et conventum de Dodenesch, ita quod dicti prior et canonici de Doden(esch) satisfecerunt dictis priori et conventui de Gypp(wico) in redditu viginti denariorum. In huius autem rei testimonium presenti scripto, interveniente etiam voluntate ac auctoritate venerabilis patris domini T(home) Norwycensis episcopi, sigilla nostra unacum sigillo dicti venerabilis patris domini T(home) et sigillis partium fecimus apponi. Acta apud Gyppwicum anno pontificatus eiusdem domini T(home) sexto, septimo decimo kal. Iunii.

For discussion, see Introduction, pp. 11–12.

20. Confirmation by William son of Ermeiot of Wenham to the prior and canons in perpetuity of all the land of his father's fee which is called 'Cumbwalle' with appurtenances, which Maurice brother of Geoffrey of Dodnash granted and sold to them. He has quitclaimed in perpetuity all homages pertaining to this land, together with reliefs, all manner of suit of court, aids for the knighting of sons and

the marriage of daughters, services, customs and all secular demands, saving to himself and his heirs an annual rent of 33d, with payment of 3½d to a scutage of 20s when it is levied, and *pro rata*. For this confirmation and quitclaim the canons have given him two marks in cash. [Mid thirteenth century]

Cartulary no. 88; approx. 150 × 140+ mm; endorsed: Carta Ermeiot (*sic*) de Wenham, xxiii; seal, round, approx. 28 mm, green wax, radiating device of eight petals, + SIGILL. WILLI DE WENHAM.

Sciant presentes et futuri quod ego Willelmus de Wenham filius Ermeioti de Wenham concessi et hac presenti carta mea confirmavi priori et canonicis sancte Marie de Dodenes et successoribus suis pro me et pro heredibus meis inperpetuum totam terram de Cumbwalle cum pertinentiis quam Mauricius de Doden(es) frater Galfridi de Doden(es) dictis priori et canonicis donavit et vendidit de feodo patris mei. Preterea remisi et omnino quietumclamavi pro me et pro heredibus meis dictis canonicis presentibus et futuris inperpetuum omnia homagia ad predictam terram pertinentia et spectantia cum releviis, omnimodis sectis curie, auxiliis tam ad filios milites faciendos quam ad filias maritandas, servitiis, consuetudinibus et omnibus secularibus demandis dictam terram contingentibus, salvo michi et heredibus meis annuo redditu triginta trium denariorum cum regali servitio, scilicet ad scutagium viginti solidorum quando currit tres denarios et obulum, et ad plus plus et ad minus minus. Pro hac autem concessione, remissione, quietaclamatione et huius carte mee confirmatione dederunt michi predicti prior et canonici duas marcas sterlingorum pre manibus. Et ut hec mea concessio, remissio, quietaclamatio et presentis carte mee confirmatio firma et stabilis permaneat inperpetuum, presenti scripto sigillum meum apposui. Testibus: domino Ricardo de Braham, domino Waltero fratre suo, domino Willelmo de Holebroc, Ricardo de Berchowte, domino Galfrido de Wenham persona, Iohanne fratre eius, Eadmundo de Capele, Roberto filio Ricardi de Boytun', Ricardo filio Willelmi de Boitun', Iurdano filio Henrici Bloman et aliis.

Four of the witnesses attest a document of 1250 (25). If the canons ever took possession of this land, they did not hold it for long, since Geoffrey son of Maurice granted the field called 'Cumbwalle' to his cousin Geoffrey son of Thomas of Dodnash for an annual rent of a clove (BL Add. ch. 9470).

21. Quitclaim by Geoffrey son of Maurice of Dodnash to Prior Robert and the canons of all right and claim in the lands, tenements, rents and homages, with all appurtenances, which Maurice his brother and Mary his mother have at any time held by hereditary right or in dower in Bentley, Tattingstone and Brantham, according to the charter of enfeoffment which they have from Maurice his brother, which enfeoffment he confirms. For this quitclaim and confirmation the canons have given him four marks for his advancement. [Mid thirteenth century]

Cartulary no. 81; approx. 185 × 25+ mm; endorsed: Dodenes, xx.

Notum sit omnibus tam presentibus quam futuris quod ego Galfridus filius Mauricii de Dodenes concessi, remisi, relaxavi et omnino quietum clamavi de me et heredibus meis domino Roberto priori sancte Marie de Dodenes et canonicis eiusdem loci et suis successoribus totum ius et clamium quod habui vel habere potui in terris, tenementis, redditibus, homagiis cum omnibus pertinentiis que Mauricius frater meus et Maria mater mea aliquo tempore tenuerunt et habuerunt iure hereditario seu nomine dotis in Benetleg', Tatingeston et Braham, cum omnibus que ad dicta tenementa et homagia aliquo modo contingere seu accidere possunt inperpetuum, sine ullo retenemento, habendas et tenendas omnes predictas terras et tenementa cum homagiis, redditibus et omnibus aliis pertinentiis suis predictis priori et canonicis de Dodenes et suis successoribus inperpetuum, sicut carta feoffamenti quam predicti prior et canonici de predicto Mauricio fratre meo inde habent plenarie testatur, ita quod nec ego nec heredes mei nec aliquis alius nomine meo vel heredum meorum in predictis terris, tenementis, homagiis, redditibus cum suis pertinentiis aliquid iuris vel clamei de cetero exigere vel vendicare possimus. Ratifico insuper et hoc presenti scripto meo pro me et heredibus meis confirmo feofamentum quod predicti prior et canonici habent de predictis terris et tenementis de predicto Mauricio fratre meo. Pro hac autem concessione, relaxatione, quietumclamatione, ratificatione et confirmatione dederunt michi predicti prior et canonici quatuor marcas argenti ad promotionem meam. In huius rei testimonium huic scripto sigillum meum apposui. Hiis testibus: domino Hugone Thalemache, domino Roberto de Reydon militibus, Galfrido filio Thome de Dodenes, Galfrido de Bosco de Spinersham, Willelmo de Wenham, Willelmo Cobum, Nicholao de Alneto, Rogero de Braham, Albrico de Braham, Willelmo Bartholomeu, Willelmo Ponting, Galfrido de la Mare, Willelmo Argent et aliis.

Geoffrey son of Maurice occurs in 1243 and 1250 (23, 25), Nicholas de Alneto in September 1256 (BL Add. ch. 9480), and Prior Robert 1252 × 57 (42).

22. Notification by Geoffrey son of Maurice of Dodnash (*Dodenes*) that he has granted to the canons, for an entry-fine of 40s, [*illeg.*] land lying between the canons' land and the stream of 'Tatsla. . . .' [*illeg.*], the other headland abutting on the canons' meadow called 'Os(berneslee)' beneath the aldergrove of 'Cumbwall', with pasture running down to the watercourse, to be held of him and his heirs for an annual rent of 4d in equal instalments at Michaelmas and Easter for all services, customs and demands. He has also quitclaimed to them all lands, pastures and possessions and all other things which they acquired from Hervey his brother of the land which was held by Maurice their father. Warranty is granted. Witnessed by [*illeg.*]   [Mid thirteenth century]

Ipswich, SRO, HD 1538/204/1; approx. 160 × 75+ mm; very badly stained by damp, in large part illegible; endorsed: Galfridus filius Mauricii de Dodenes.

23. Notification by Geoffrey son of Maurice of Dodnash that on 6 November 1243 at Ipswich, in the presence of William, bishop of Norwich, he received from the prior of Dodnash four marks of silver for the discharge of all debts owed to him, saving the daily corrody due to himself and his wife. To this document Mr

Roger, archdeacon of Suffolk, and William (? of Holbrook) appended their seals, as his own was not to hand.

Cartulary no. 82; approx. 175 × 45+ mm; no medieval endorsement.

Omnibus Cristi fidelibus presens scriptum visuris vel audituris Galfridus filius Mauricii de Dodenes salutem. Noveritis me die sancti Leonardi anno Domini M CC° XL tertio apud Gypewyc(um) coram venerabili patre Willelmo Dei gratia Norwycensi episcopo recepisse a priore de Dodenes quatuor marcas argenti, per quarum solutionem super omnibus debitis in quibus dictus prior michi obligatus fuerat fueram plenarie pacatus, exceptis cotidianis corrediis michi et uxori mee a domo supradicta assignatis. In cuius rei testimonium ad instantiam meam magister Rogerus archidiaconus Suff(olchie) apposuit signum suum huic scripto patenti, simul cum sigillo Willelmi (? de Hole)ᵃ-brok, quia sigillum meum proprium ad manum non habui.

ᵃ tear in ms.

24. Confirmation by Hugh Tollemache to the prior and canons in perpetuity, in return for six marks given to him and half a mark to his wife, of all the land which Geoffrey son of Maurice of Dodnash granted to them, to be held of Hugh and his heirs, to whom they shall render 4s *p.a.* for all services, etc., saving suit of court owed by Geoffrey and his ancestors and saving reliefs, that is, at the removal of any prior of Dodnash, by death or otherwise, the canons shall pay a relief according to the custom of other tenants of the same soke.

[Mid thirteenth century, before 1257]

Cartulary no. 84; approx. 176 × 92+ mm; endorsed: Carta Hugonis Thalmach; (modern): for Mr Hering, London, from Alexander Helmingham.

Sciant presentes et futuri quod ego Hugo Talemasch' concessi et hac presenti carta mea confirmavi priori et canonicis de Dodenes, pro sex marcis argenti quas michi dederunt et uxori mee dimidiam marcam, totam terram quam Galfridus filius Mauricii de Dodenes dedit Deo et ecclesie sancte Marie de Dodenes cum omnibus pertinentiis suis, habendam et tenendam dictis priori et canonicis et eorum eiusdem loci successoribus de me et heredibus meis libere et quiete, bene et in pace inperpetuum, reddendo inde annuatim michi et heredibus meis quatuor solidos ad quatuor terminos censuales, videlicet ad Pascha duodecim denarios et ad nativitatem sancti Iohannis Baptiste duodecim denarios et ad festum sancti Michaelis duodecim denarios et ad festum sancti Andree duodecim denarios, pro omnibus servitiis, consuetudinibus et exactionibus, salvis sectis ad curiam meam quas dictus Galfridus et antecessores sui michi soluti fuerunt facere, et salvis releviis, videlicet ad remotionem cuiuslibet prioris de Dodenes, sive vita privetur sive eo vivente removeatur, canonici eiusdem loci michi vel heredibus meis relevium facient secundum consuetudinem aliorum de eadem soka tenentium. Et ut hec mea concessio et carte mee confirmatio firma sit et stabilis, presenti scripto sigillum meum apposui. Hiis testibus: Ricardo de Braham, Albrico fratre suo, magistro Hugone de Waleys, magistro Rogero de Bikerwyker, Thoma de

Dodenes, Thoma de Meulinges, Alano de Braham, Stephano Helte, Hugone de Dodenes, Mauricio filio Mauricii de Dodenes, Iohanne filio Ricardi de Barun, Bald(ewino) de Coppedoc et multis aliis.

This Hugh Tollemache is to be distinguished from his ancestor of the same name who in 1212 held the manor of Bentley of the king in chief (*Bk Fees*, 134), as a William Tollemache (himself to be distinguished from that William who attests nos 2, 5 in 1188–89) intervenes, and William's widow Margaret in 1252–53 impleaded Hugh for a third part of the manors of Bentley, Acton and Copdock as her dower (Rye, *Fines*, 55 no. 196). This Hugh died shortly thereafter, before 1257, and in the document providing evidence for this, Prior Robert himself occurs (42). Hugh left as his heir his son Hugh, a minor, whose first datable occurrence is at Trinity 1269 (BL Add. ch. 9487). For subsequent generations of the family, see below, 147n, and Copinger, *Manors* vi, 9–11. Geoffrey son of Maurice of Dodnash occurs in 1243 and 1250 (23, 25), and although his widow was still alive in 1285 (27), no. 24A implies that he was dead by 1257. The Maurice son of Maurice of Dodnash who attests here is not the grantor of nos 14, 17–18, but is of a later generation. For the soke of Chelmondiston, see nos 14, 130.

24A. Recognition by Prior Robert and the canons that they and their successors are bound to pay to the lord Hugh Tollemache and his heirs 4s *p.a.* in four instalments for the land once held by Geoffrey son of Maurice of Dodnash. Hugh has relaxed and quitclaimed all suit of court which they used to render for this land. At the removal of any prior, either by death or deprivation, the next prior of the house shall pay a relief to Hugh and his heirs for the land once held by Geoffrey of Dodnash, according to the custom of other tenants of the soke [of Chelmondiston]. [Mid thirteenth century, before 1257]

Helmingham, T/Hel/44/1 (Tollemache cartulary) no. 6 (damaged).

Omnibus Cristi fidelibus ad quos presens scriptum pervenerit Robertus Dei gratia prior de Dodenes et eiusdem loci canonici salutem. Noveritis nos et successores nostri deb[ere annua]tim reddere domino Hugoni Talemasch et heredibus suis quatuor solidos sterlingorum ad quatuor terminos anni, videlicet ad festum sancti Michaelis .xii.d et ad festum sancti Andree .xii.d et ad Pascha .xii.d et ad nativitatem sancti Iohannis Baptiste .xii.d pro terra quondam Galfridi filii Mauricii de Dodenes. Et sciendum quod prefatus dominus Hugo Talemasch relaxavit et quietum clamavit nobis et successoribus nostris pro se et pro heredibus suis omnimodas curie sue sectas quas soliti fuimus facere pro predicta terra. Sciendum est iterum quod ad remotionem cuiuslibet prioris nostre domus de Dodenes, sive vita privetur sive vivens remotionem dignitatis prioratus patiatur, prior subsequens nostre domus de Dodenes faciet relevium prefato domino Hugoni vel heredibus suis secundum consuetudinem aliorum de eadem soka tenentium pro prefata terra quondam prefati Galfridi de Dodenes. Et ut [di]stat cavilatio, presens scriptum sigillo capituli nostri roboravimus. Hiis testibus: domino Ricardo de Braham, domino Waltero fratre suo, Albrico de Braham, Ricardo de

Holebroc, Galfrido de Dode(nes), Stephano Helte, Iohanne de Barun, Roberto de Coppedok, Willelmo filio Agnetis, Sew [*illeg.*]cher, Roberto de Prithes, Roberto filio Samsonis et aliis.

See no. 24.

25. Quitclaim by Geoffrey son of Maurice of Dodnash and Isabella his wife of all prebends and corrodies, in food and drink, in corn and money and in all else, which they used to receive daily, weekly, monthly or yearly from the prior and canons, which they were obliged to provide in accordance with their charters, which Geoffrey and Isabella have in the presence of discreet men returned to them. Quitclaim also of all right in and claim to the land called 'Sortecroft' with its appurtenances, so that neither they nor their heirs may henceforth in perpetuity make any claim thereto. They have pledged on oath that, should they contravene this quitclaim, they shall pay the canons 40s as a penalty, on pain of excommunication by the bishop of Norwich, and shall pay to the crown a fine of 40s, on pain of distraint by the sheriff of Suffolk, and they renounce all legal appeal in this matter. For this quitclaim the canons have paid £19 6s 8d in cash.

May 1250

Cartulary no. 87; approx. 165 × 97 + 13 mm; no medieval endorsement; slits for two seals.

Notum sit omnibus hominibus presentibus et futuris quod ego Galfridus de Dodenes filius Mauricii de Dodenes et Ysabella uxor mea remisimus et quietumclamavimus pro nobis inperpetuum omnes prebendas et omnia correda, tam in cibis et potibus quam in bladis et denariis et in omnibus aliis debitis que nos solebamus recipere de priore et canonicis de Dodenes singulis diebus, septimanis, mensibus et annis, sicut predicti prior et canonici fuerunt nobis per cartas suas obligati, quas scilicet cartas dictis priori et canonicis coram discretis viris manifeste et solute reddidimus et inperpetuum quiete deliberavimus. Remisimus etiam et quietumclamavimus similiter omne ius et clamium quod habuimus vel habere potuimus in quadam terra que vocatur Sortecroft cum pertinentiis dictis canonicis et successoribus suis pro nobis inperpetuum, ita quod nec nos nec aliquis nomine nostro aliquid iuris de cetero in predicta terra cum pertinentiis nobis vendicare possimus. Ego autem dictus Galfridus et Ysabella uxor mea tactis sacrosanctis iuravimus et fide media nos et omnia nostra bona mobilia et inmobilia obligavimus tam episcopo Norwycensi quam vicecomiti Suffolchie qui pro tempore fuerit ut ipse episcopus per sententiam excommunicationis in personas nostras latam ad solutionem .xl. solidorum nomine pene dictis canonicis faciendam sine cause cognitione possit nos compellere, et dictus vicecomes qui pro tempore fuerit possit nos distringere per captionem averiorum nostrorum ubicumque fuerint inventa ad solutionem .xl. solidorum nomine pene domino regi faciendam, si contra hanc remissionem et quietumclamationem in aliquo, quod absit, contraire ceperimus, renuntiantes omni cavillationi et exceptioni iuris et facti et omni appellationi et omni iuris remedio in hac parte. Pro hac remissione et quietaclamatione dederunt michi et Ysabelle uxori mee predicti prior et canonici viginti

novem marcas et .x. solidos sterlingorum pre manibus. Et ad maiorem securita-
tem optinendam ego dictus G. et Ysabella uxor mea presenti scripto sigilla nostra
apposuimus. Hiis testibus: domino Ricardo de Braham, domino W(illelmo) de
Holebroc militibus, magistro Hugone rectore ecclesie de Braham, Willelmo
Godesw(ein), Roberto Davi burgensi de Gypp(ewico), Michaele de Frest(un),
Willelmo Roger de Bercholte, Willelmo dispensatore, Ranulfo filio suo, Herveo
Glanvile, Iordano filio Henrici, Bartholomeo clerico, Eadmundo de Capele et
aliis. Actum anno regni regis Henrici filii regis Iohannis XXXIIII^{to} mense Maii.

26. Quitclaim by William son of Geoffrey son of Maurice of Dodnash to Prior
Ralph and the canons of all right and claim in the lands and tenements once held
by Geoffrey his father in the vill of Bentley (*Benethl'*), together with the annual
rent of a penny which they used to pay him for the tenement which they held of
him and his ancestors there, so that neither he nor any of his heirs may henceforth
make any claim therein. For this concession, confirmation and quitclaim they
have given him a sum of money.
Hiis testibus: domino Hugone Talemache, domino Fulcone de Vallibus, Roberto
de Reydone, Willelmo de Braham, Iohanne de Belstede, Willelmo de Creppinge,
Waltero Baldewyne, Waltero de Berholt, Andrea^a Helte, Roberto de Spina,
Willelmo de Bruera, Radulfo clerico et aliis.   [c.1279 × 1304]

^{a} MS: Andree

Cartulary no. 94; approx. 210 × 128+ mm; endorsed: Willelmus de le Waldoune,
xxiiii; de clamio Willelmi de Dodenes de toto tenemento patris sui et uno d. redditus; seal, round, approx. 30 mm, natural wax, radiating device of five petals,
. . .LI FIL. GALFRIDI . . .

Geoffrey son of Maurice was dead by 1285 at latest (27). For a further quitclaim
by William, see no. 28; by 1316 he had taken the name 'de Waldoune' (BL Add.
ch. 9579). Prior Ralph occurs 1285–1301; his predecessor occurs 21 Sept. 1279,
and he was no longer prior in April 1304.

27. On Monday 12 March 1285 the following agreement was made (*ita convenit*) between Prior Ralph and the convent on the one part and Isabelle widow of
Geoffrey son of Maurice of Dodnash (*Dodenes*), whereby the prior and convent
are by their unanimous consent bound to render to Isabelle each year for the
duration of her life two quarters of rye, one quarter of barley, six bushels of peas
and two bushels of beans, beginning next Easter with two quarters of rye, one
quarter of barley, six bushels of peas and two bushels of beans, and thereafter
each Michaelmas and Easter half of the foresaid quantities, for the whole term of
her life. If the prior and convent should default in whole or in part in these payments, the prior wills and concedes for himself and his successors that the sheriff
of Suffolk for the time being or his bailiffs may distrain upon all their goods,
movable and immovable, wherever they may be found, until full satisfaction is
made to Isabelle, and the sheriff shall receive from them 2s each time distraint is
made because of non-payment and restoration is made to Isabelle by view of the

sheriff.[a] In return for this grant Isabelle has utterly quitclaimed to the prior and convent and their successors all right etc. in all lands and tenements held in the name of her dower which were once held by Geoffrey her husband in Bentley (*Benetl'*), Tattingstone (*Tatingstun*) and Brantham (*Braham*). This agreement is drawn up in the form of a chirograph sealed alternately by the parties.

Hiis testibus: Hugone Talemach milite,[b] Galfrido de Dodenes, Thoma de Frestone, Hamone de Wlferstun, Radulfo clerico, Iohanne de la Mare, Ricardo le Blund, Petro Overbrok et aliis.

[a] MS damaged at this point   [b] milite *underlined*

Cartulary no. 110; approx. 182 × 134 + 12 mm; chirograph, indented at top margin; no endorsement; seal, oval, approx. 40 × 26 mm, eagle displayed, + S. IZA-BELE. . . TO. . .AN, not extant, illustrated as brown

28. Notification by William son of Geoffrey of Dodnash (*Dodeneys*) that he has relaxed and quitclaimed, for himself and his successors, to Prior John of Dodnash and the canons and their successors all right or claim which he had or in any way might have in all lands and tenements which the prior and canons hold in Dodnash in the vill of Bentley (*Bentlegh*), which they shall have and hold in perpetuity, so that neither William, his heirs nor anyone in their name may henceforth make any claim therein. For this relaxation and quitclaim the prior and canons have given him £4 in cash. Sealed in testimony.

Testibus: Iohanne de la Dale, Hugone Horold, Thoma Stace, Rogero de Godelysford, Rogero de Wyvermerysch, Alexandro de Freston, Roberto Daniel, Iacobo de Godelysford et aliis.   Ipswich, Saturday 8 April 1307

Cartulary no. 116; approx. 187 × 95+ mm; endorsed: xxiiii; seal, round, approx. 40 mm, greenish-black wax, radiating device of four serrated petals, + S. WILL. FIL. GALFRID.

OTHER PROPERTIES IN BENTLEY AND DODNASH

29. Grant by M[artin], abbot of St Martin's, Aumale, to the canons in perpetuity of all the woodland which he holds in 'Hulney' with the pasture thereto pertaining, for an annual rent of 4s. For this grant they have paid 3 marks entry-fine
[Late twelfth – early thirteenth century]

A1 = Cartulary no. 6; approx. 168 × 98 + 20 mm; endorsed: Aubemarle, xviii; seal, vessica, approx. 60 × 40 mm, St Martin vested as bishop, right hand raised in benediction, crozier in left hand, . . .INI . . .IS; not extant, illustrated as brown.

A2 = Cartulary no. 5; approx. 170 × 62+ mm; endorsed: xviii, Martinus abbas; seal, vessica, approx. 52 × 36 mm, natural wax varnished brown, abbot fully vested for mass, crozier in right hand, book in left, + SIG. MARTINI ABBATIS STI MARTINI ALBEMARLIS.

Universis sancte matris ecclesie filiis ad quos presens scriptum pervenerit M(artinus) Dei gratia abbas ecclesie sancti Martini Albermar' salutem in Domino. Noverit universitas vestra nos dedisse et concessisse et hac presenti carta nostra confirmasse priori sancte Marie de Dodenes et canonicis ibidem Deo servientibus totum nemus quod habemus in Hulenheia cum pascua ad nemus illud pertinente, illis et successoribus eorum tenendum in perpetuum de ecclesia beati Martini de Albermar' et de nobis et successoribus nostris libere, solute et quiete, solvendo inde nobis annuatim quatuor solidos sterlingorum ad duos terminos anni, scilicet ad Pentecosten duos solidos et ad festum sancti Martini in hieme duos solidos pro omni servitio et exactione. Pro hac itaque donatione, concessione et confirmatione predictus prior et canonici beate Marie de Dodenes dederunt nobis in gersumam tres marcas argenti. Hiis testibus: Huberto de Bromford,[a] Ricardo fratre eius,[b] Galfrido de Bromford clerico nostro, Weremundo servienti nostro, Hugone de Belested,[c] Roberto fratre suo, Weremundo[d] et Benedicto servientibus nostris, 'Eustachio de Braham et Rogero filio eius, Milone[f] Lenveise, Willelmo de Maneston',[e] David de Bercholt, [g]Warino de Bercholt, Warino de Frames(den), Roberto de Glanvill' de Framesd(en), Mauricio,[g] Walkelino clerico et multis aliis.

[a] Bramford A2   [b] suo A2   [c] Belsted A2   [d] Wueremundo A2; this witness is named twice in both recensions   [e...e] omitted A2   [f] Miles A1   [g...g] omitted A2, which substitutes Roberto de Framesden'.

Martin abbot of Aumale occurs in 1205 (*Fines* ii, no. 441); Eustace of Brantham last occurs in 1202 (*CRR* ii, 136). The abbey of Aumale held the manor of Washbrook (Great Belstead) in Samford hundred (*VN*, 462), of which this woodland is almost certainly an appurtenance.

30. Quitclaim by Robert of 'Hulney' to the canons, in pure and perpetual alms, for the salvation of himself and his ancestors, of all right and claim in the pasture below 'Hulney', as surrounded by its embankments, from the land of Robert Hareis to that of Geoffrey Burdoun, and also in the heath beyond the road which leads from 'Hulney' towards Ipswich.   [Early to mid thirteenth century]

Cartulary no. 57; approx. 288 × 69+ mm; no endorsement.

Omnibus sancte matris ecclesie filiis ad quos presens scriptum pervenerit Robertus de Hulney salutem in Domino. Sciatis me concessisse et remississe et quietumclamasse pro me et heredibus meis in puram et perpetuam elemosinam, pro salute anime mee et animarum antecessorum meorum, Deo et ecclesie beate Marie de Dodenasch et canonicis ibidem Deo servituris totum ius et clameum quod habui vel habere potui in pastura subtus Hulney sicut precingitur fossato a terra Roberti Hareis usque ad terram Galfridi Burdoun, et preterea totum ius quod habui vel habere potui in bruario ultra viam que extenditur de Hulney versus Gippewicum. Ego autem ad maiorem securitatem huic scripto in testimonium sigillum meum apposui. H(iis) t(estibus): magistro Ricardo decano de Codeham, Thoma persona de Reinden', Ricardo capellano de Bentley, Willelmo de Waudigfeld, Mauricio de Dodenassch, Roberto de Boitone etc.

Robert of 'Hulney' occurs in 1236–37 (Ipswich, SRO, HD 1047/2/55). Thomas, parson of Raydon, and Richard, chaplain of Bentley, occur in 1223–24 (16), and William of Waldingfield and Maurice of Dodnash in 1224–25 (17).

31. Grant by Edith, Matilda and Avice [daughters of Richard] to the canons in free and perpetual alms of half of their heathland, which lies next to the canons' heath, which is of the fee of Hugh Tollemache, to the east, for an annual rent of a penny. The canons have paid 2s as entry-fine.   [Early thirteenth century]

Cartulary no. 63; approx. 200 × 64 + 15 mm; endorsed: de bruario, xxii; de bruario de Benetle qui nunc est Marlar; three slits for seals; right: missing; central: round, approx. 35 mm, natural wax, fleur-de-lys, + SIGILLUM MAHAUT FIL. RIC.; left: round, approx. 32 mm, natural wax, stylised flower, a sexfoil within an octofoil, + SIGILL EDIETH F. . . RICARDI .

Sciant presentes et futuri quod ego Hediht et Matildis et Avicia dedimus et concessimus et hac presenti carta nostra confirmavimus ecclesie beate Marie de Dodenes et canonicis ibidem Deo servientibus et servituris medietatem partis bruarii nostri quod iacet inter bruarium canonicorum quod est de feodo Hugonis Talemasche versus orientem, tenendam de nobis et heredibus nostris in pura et perpetua elemosina, reddendo inde annuatim unum denarium, scilicet ad festum sancti Michaelis, pro omnibus servitiis, consuetudinibus et auxiliis. Pro hac autem donatione et concessione predicti canonici nobis dederunt duos solidos in gersumiam. Et ut hec nostra donatio et concessio perpetuis temporibus rata et inconcussa permaneat, presentia scripta*a* sigillorum nostrorum appositione corroboravimus. Hiis testibus: Eustachio de Braham, Rogero de Coppedoc, Radulfo de Gerevile, Martino de Guleford, Hugone de Braham, Willelmo de Boitun', Willelmo Helt', Ysembardo filio Hugonis, Roberto de Rameis et multis aliis.

a MS: presentibus scriptis

Eustace of Brantham was active from 1165 to 1202 (*Sibton Cartularies* iii, no. 741 n.). William of Boyton occurs 1227–28 (Rye, *Fines*, 25 no. 39). William Helte occurs 1224–26 (17, 35). Text, endorsement and seals suggest that the father of these ladies was Richard de Bruario.

32. Grant by Walter Tibi and Avice his wife to the canons in perpetuity of all that part of their heath in Dodnash lying next to 'Ailmerescroft', to be held for an annual rent of ½d, and for which the canons have given 2s as entry-fine.
[Early to mid thirteenth century]

Cartulary no. 29; approx. 145 × 80 mm; endorsed: Prior et canonici de Dodenes, Walterus Tibi et Avicia, xxvi; V iii; slits for two seals, on right, seal, round, approx. 32 mm, natural wax varnished brown, tendrils, + SIGILUM AVICIE FIL. RIC.

Sciant presentes et futuri quod ego Walterus Tibi et Avicia uxor mea concessimus et dedimus et hac carta nostra confirmavimus Deo et ecclesie beate Marie de Dodenes et canonicis ibidem Deo servientibus et servituris totam partem bruarii nostri in Dodenes iacentem iuxta Ailmerescroft, habendam et tenendam prenominatis canonicis de nobis et heredibus nostris inperpetuum libere et quiete, reddendo inde nobis et heredibus nostris quolibet anno ad festum sancti Michaelis unum obulum pro omni servitio, consuetudine et demanda. Pro hac autem concessione et donatione et huius carte nostre confirmatione dederunt nobis prefati canonici duos solidos in gersumiam. Hiis testibus: Willelmo de Waudingefeld, Mauricio de Dodenes, Willelmo Helte, Ysebardo filio Hugonis, Rogero Iuvencel, Warino Testard, Iohanne de Mara, Roberto de Boitun', Roberto de Bucheli, Willelmo Wisman, Hugone et aliis.

Avice is certainly one of the three sisters of no. 31, as revealed by her seal. Most of the witnesses occur 1223–26 (16–17, 35).

33. Confirmation by Avice, widow of Walter Tibi, to the canons in perpetuity of that part of their heath which Walter and she granted to them, for annual rent of ½d at Michaelmas and ¼d at Easter. The canons have paid her 2s as entry-fine.

[Early to mid thirteenth century]

Cartulary no. 64; approx. 140 × 72+ mm; endorsed: Avicia Tibi, xxvi.

Sciant presentes et futuri quod ego Avicia quondam uxor Walteri Tibi concessi et hac presenti carta mea confirmavi in viduitate mea Deo et ecclesie beate Marie de Dodenes et canonicis ibidem Deo servientibus et servituris totam illam partem bruarii quam Walterus sponsus meus et ego predictis canonicis carta nostra dedimus et confirmavimus, habendam et tenendam prenominatis canonicis de me et heredibus meis, reddendo quolibet anno tres quadrantes ad duos terminos anni, scilicet ad festum sancti Michaelis unum obulum et ad Pascha .i. quadrantem, pro omni servitio, consuetudine et demanda. Pro hac autem concessione et huius carte mee confirmatione dederunt michi predicti canonici duos solidos in gersumiam. His t(estibus): domino Ranulfo de Braham, Willelmo de Waudrigfeld, Mauricio de Dodenes, Willelmo Helte, Ysebardo filio Hugonis, Rogero Iuvencel, Warino Testard, Thoma filio Hugonis de Benethleya, Iohanne de Mara, Roberto de Boitun', Roberto de Bucheli, Willelmo Wisman, Ricardo filio Hugonis et aliis.

Ranulf of Brantham occurs 1227–30 (Rye, *Fines*, 39 no. 118, 30 no. 4); William of Waldingfield occurs 1224–25 (17), and Roger Iuvencel 1224–26 (17, 35); Robert of Boyton occurs from 1223–24 (16) to 1243–44 (Rye, *Fines*, 47 no. 16).

34. Quitclaim by Avice of 'Lemaneshei' of the parish of Bentley to the prior and canons, for her salvation and that of her ancestors, of an annual rent of ½d which they used to pay her at Michaelmas for a parcel of land lying between their own land, held of the fee of Hugh Tollemache (*Thalemach*), to be held by them in pure and perpetual alms. She and her heirs will grant warranty against all men and women in perpetuity.

Hiis testibus: domino Hugone Thalemach', Galfrido de Dodenes, Simone de Hulnhey, Ricardo de Bruera, Radulfo clerico, Roberto de Falceham, Iordano Scileman et multis aliis.

[Mid to late thirteenth century]

Cartulary no. 98; approx. 168 × 75+ mm; endorsed: Benetlegh, xxviii; seal, oval, approx. 33 × 19 mm, natural wax varnished green, eagle displayed, + SIG. . . SECRETUM . . .

Avice of 'Lemaneshei' may be the same person as, or perhaps more likely the daughter of, the Avice of nos 31–3. Geoffrey of Dodnash occurs from 1252 × 57 to 1285 (27, 42); Jordan Skileman in 1257 (63); Ralph the clerk from 1276 (48) to 1308 (BL Add. ch. 9566); and Richard de Bruera in 1284 (206).

35. Lease by Ranulf the smith and Edith his wife to the prior and convent for a term of ten years from Michaelmas 1226 of all the land which they hold of the prior of Holy Trinity, Ipswich, for an annual rent of 6d payable in four instalments. They have also leased to them the land in Bentley which they hold of Hugh Tolle-mache for three sowings, and for the same term half the proceeds of their wood of 'Scarbotewalle'. For this lease the canons have given them 5s.   Late 1226

Cartulary no. 33; approx. 160 × 75+ mm; endorsed: carta Ranulfi fabri.

Sciant presentes et futuri quod ego Ranulfus faber et Edith uxor mea dimissimus et concessimus et presenti carta nostra confirmavimus priori de Dodenes et canonicis ibi Deo servientibus et servituris totam terram nostram quam tenemus de priore sancte Trinitatis de Gipewico in villa de Benethleia, habendam et tenen-dam de nobis et heredibus nostris a festo sancti Michaelis post mortem Pandulfi episcopi Norwicensis usque in decem annos proximo sequentes per servitium sex denariorum ad quatuor terminos anni percipiendorum, scilicet ad festum sancti Michaelis .iii. ob. et ad festum sancti Andree apostoli .iii. ob. et ad Pascha .iii. ob. et ad festum sancti Iohannis Baptiste .iii. ob. pro omnibus servitiis. Et preterea concessimus eisdem totam terram nostram quam tenemus de feodo Hugonis Thalemach in prenominata villa de Benethleya ad tertiam garbam seminandam, et medietatem commoditatis bosci nostri cum pastura de Scarbotewalle usque ad predictum terminum. Nos autem prenominata tenementa contra dominos feodo-rum defendemus et plenarie acquietabimus de omnibus servitiis, consuetudinibus et demandis. Pro hac dimissione et concessione predicti prior et canonici ad pro-motionem nostram quinque solidos argenti nobis dederunt. Hanc concessionem et conventionem fideliter observandam iuravimus et bona fide promisimus, et huic scripto in testimonium sigillum nostrum apposuimus. Hiis t(estibus): Hugone Thalemach, Willelmo de Waldingfeld, Mauricio de Do(de)nes et Thoma fratre eius, Roberto de Alneto, Oseberto de Braham, Willelmo Helt, Rogero Iuvencle, Roberto de Boitun, Iohanne de la Mare et multis aliis.

Pandulph, bishop of Norwich, died at Rome on 16 September 1226.

Edith is almost certainly one of the three daughters of Richard de Bruario of no. 31. In a grant to them by William of Holbrook of land in Bentley, Ranulf and Edith are described as 'of Coddenham' (BL Add. ch. 9471).

36. Grant in perpetuity by Ranulf the smith and Edith his wife to the canons of all their part of 'Fendlond' adjoining 'Scarbotewelle', and two other parcels of

land in 'Fenlond' which they have received from Walter Tibi and Avice his wife in exchange for two other parcels in 'Tunstedel'. For this grant the canons have given 4s entry-fine. [Early to mid thirteenth century, *c.* 1226]

Cartulary no. 34; approx. 139 × 62+ mm; endorsed: x.

Sciant presentes et futuri quod ego Ranulfus faber et Edith uxor mea concessimus et dedimus et hac carta nostra confirmavimus Deo et ecclesie beate Marie de Do-denes et canonicis ibidem Deo servientibus et servituris totam partem nostram in Fendlond iuxta Scarebotewelle et duas alias partes terre iacentes in predicto Fen-lond, quas accepimus in escambium a Waltero Tibi et uxore eius Avicia pro duabus aliis partibus terre iacentibus in Tunstedel, habendas et tenendas prenomi-natis canonicis de nobis et heredibus nostris inperpetuum libere et quiete, red-dendo inde nobis quolibet anno in festo sancti Michaelis unum denarium pro omnibus servitiis, consuetudinibus et demandis. Pro ista autem concessione et donatione et huius carte nostre confirmatione dederunt nobis predicti canonici quatuor solidos in gersumiam. Hiis t(estibus): Willelmo de Waudingf(eld), Mauricio de Dodenes et Galfrido filio eius, Willelmo Helte, Ysenbardo filio Hugonis, Rogero Iuvencel, Warino Testard, Iohanne de Mara, Roberto de Boitun', Roberto de Bucheli, Willelmo Wisman, Ricardo filio Hugonis et aliis.

Six of the witnesses also attest no. 35.

37. Grant in perpetuity by Ranulf the smith and Edith his wife to the canons of all their part of the heath in Dodnash adjoining 'Ailmerescroft', for an annual rent of ½d at Michaelmas. The canons have given 2s entry-fine.
[Early to mid thirteenth century, *c.* 1226]

Cartulary no. 35; approx. 128 × 75+ mm; endorsed: xxv.

Sciant presentes et futuri quod ego Ranulfus faber et Edith uxor mea concessimus et dedimus et hac carta nostra confirmavimus Deo et ecclesie beate Marie de Do-denes et canonicis ibidem Deo servientibus et servituris totam partem bruarii nostri in Dodenes iacentem iuxta Ailmerescroft, habendam et tenendam prenominatis canonicis de nobis et heredibus nostris inperpetuum libere et quiete, reddendo inde nobis et heredibus nostris quolibet anno ad festum sancti Michaelis unum obulum pro omni servitio, consuetudine et demanda. Pro hac autem concessione et donatione et huius carte nostre confirmatione dederunt nobis predicti canonici duos solidos in gersumiam. Hiis t(estibus): Willelmo de Waudingef(eld), Mauricio de Dodenes, Willelmo Helte, Ysebardo filio Hugonis, Iohanne de Mara, Roberto de Boitun', Roberto de Bucheli, Willelmo Wisman, Rogero Iuvencel, Warino Testard, Ricardo filio Hugonis et aliis.

Five of the witnesses also attest no. 35.

38. Final concord made in the king's court before Thomas of Moulton and his fellow justices between Ranulf the smith and Edith his wife and Hamo Ened[a] and

Avice his wife, claimants, and Prior Jordan, defendant, concerning five acres of land with appurtenances in Bentley. An assize of *mort d'ancestor* was summoned, and the claimants quitclaimed in perpetuity, for themselves and the wives' heirs, to Prior Jordan and the convent all right and claim in the land, and for this the prior gave them 15s.   Ipswich, 20 November 1234.

PRO, CP25/1/213/10/78; approx. 150 × 80 mm, chirograph indented at top margin.

Hec est finalis concordia facta in curia domini regis apud Gipewic' die lune proxima post octabas sancti Martini anno regni regis Henrici filii regis Iohannis nonodecimo coram Thoma de Multon, Roberto de Lexinton, Oliveru de Vallibus, Ada filio Willelmi et Roberto de Bellocampo, iusticiariis itinerantibus, et aliis domini regis fidelibus tunc ibidem presentibus inter Rannulfum Fabrum et Edytham uxorem eius [et] Hamonem Ened*a* et Aviciam uxorem eius, petentes, et Iordanum priorem de Dodenash, tenentem, de quinque acris terre cum pertinentiis in Benetleg', unde assisa mortis antecessoris summonita fuit inter eos in eadem curia, scilicet quod predicti Rannulfus et Edyth, Hamo et Avicia remiserunt et quietum clamaverunt de se et heredibus ipsarum Edyth et Avicie predicto priori et successoribus suis et ecclesie sue de Dodenash totum ius et clamium quod habuerunt in tota predicta terra cum pertinentiis suis inperpetuum. Et pro hac remissione, quieta clamantia, fine et concordia idem prior dedit predictis Rannulpho et Edyth, Hamoni et Avicie quindecim solidos sterlingorum.

a Reading uncertain.

39. Grant in pure and perpetual alms by Adam son of William Flanke to the canons of all land with appurtenances which may in any way have come to him by hereditary right after the death of Matilda his mother in the field once called 'Bruere', which lies in the parish of Bentley between the canons' land on both sides and abuts on the way leading from the house of Jordan son of Henry to the wood of 'Lemaneshey', for an annual rent of ½d. Warranty is granted.

[Mid thirteenth century]

Cartulary no. 74; approx. 180 × 116+ mm; endorsed: De Ada Flanke de Bruer in Benetle quod nunc est Marlar, xxviii; seal, round, approx. 35 mm, natural wax varnished greenish brown, radiating device of sixteen petals within double circle, + S. ADE FLAUNK.

Sciant presentes et futuri quod ego Adam filius Willelmi Flanke de Benetleye concessi, dedi et hac presenti carta mea confirmavi Deo et ecclesie sancte Marie de Dodenes et canonicis ibidem Deo servientibus et inperpetuum servituris in liberam et perpetuam elemosinam totam terram cum pertinentiis que michi descendit aut accidere potuit vel alieno modo poterit iure hereditario post mortem Matildis matris mee in campo qui quondam vocabatur Bruere, iacente in parochia de Benetleye inter terras predictorum canonicorum ex utraque parte in longitudine, et abuttat super viam que ducit de domo Iurdani filii Henrici versus boscum de Lemeneshey, tenendam et habendam de me et de heredibus meis illis et successoribus suis vel quibuscunque suis assignatis inperpetuum, libere, quiete et hereditarie, bene et in pace, reddendo inde michi et heredibus meis annuatim unum obulum, scilicet ad festum sancti Michaelis, pro omnibus servitiis, consuetudinibus, curiarum sectis, releviis, auxiliis et demandis. Et ego predictus Adam et heredes mei warantizabimus, acquietabimus et defendemus predictam terram cum pertinentiis predictis canonicis presentibus et futuris et eorum assignatis per predictum servitium contra omnes tam Iudeos quam Cristianos inperpetuum. Testibus: Galfrido filio Thome de Dodenes, Willelmo de Wenham, Roberto de Boytun', Ricardo de Boyt(un), Iurdano filio Henrici, Willelmo Henry, Galfrido de la Mare, Willelmo Mikeleboy, Ricardo Andreu, Iurdano Overbroc, Roberto clerico, Willelmo Mahew et aliis.

> Matilda is almost certainly the third of the three sisters, daughters of Richard de Bruario, of no. 31. Geoffrey son of Thomas of Dodnash and Geoffrey de la Mare occur in the mid thirteenth century (21); Robert of Boyton occurs from 1223–24 (16) to 1243–44 (Rye, *Fines*, 47 no. 16); Jordan son of Henry occurs in 1250 (25).

40. Quitclaim by Adam son of William Flanke to the canons and their assigns of all right and claim by inheritance from his mother Matilda in all the land called 'Bruere' adjacent to 'Ailmerescroft' in Bentley, and of all right in 'Ailmerescroft' itself, by whatever means he might claim such, for an annual rent of ½d to be paid to him and his heirs, who will acquit and defend the land against the capital lords for suit of court and all services.   [Mid thirteenth century]

> Cartulary no. 71; approx. 137 × 105+ mm; endorsed: xxvii; seal as no. 39, dark green wax.

Sciant presentes et futuri quod ego Adam filius Willelmi Flanke concessi, remisi et quietumclamavi pro me et heredibus meis inperpetuum Deo et ecclesie sancte Marie de Dodenes et canonicis ibidem Deo servientibus et inperpetuum servituris et eorum assignatis totum ius et clamium quod habui vel habere potui et quod michi descendere potuit de hereditate Matildis matris mee in tota terra que vocatur Bruere iuxta Ailmerescroft in villa de Benetleye, et totum ius meum in Ailmerescroft quod michi quocumque modo descendere poterit, tenendum et habendum predictis canonicis et successoribus suis inperpetuum, libere, quiete et hereditarie, reddendo inde michi et heredibus meis annuatim unum obulum ad festum sancti Michaelis pro omnibus servitiis, consuetudinibus, curiarum sectis et demandis. Et ego predictus Adam et heredes mei tam de curiarum sectis quam de omnibus aliis servitiis dictam terram (cum) contingentibus contra capitales dominos acquietabimus illos et defendemus inperpetuum. Testibus: Galfrido de Doden(es), Willelmo de Wenham, Radulfo de Alneto, Rogero de sancta Osyda, Roberto de Boit(un), Ricardo de Boit(un), Iurdano filio Henrici, Willelmo Henr', Galfrido de la Mare, Willelmo Mikeleboy, Iurdano Overbroc et aliis.

> Nine of these witnesses attest no. 39, and Ralph de Alneto occurs in 1256 (BL Add. ch. 9480).

41. Quitclaim in pure and perpetual alms by Adam Flanke of the parish of Bentley (*Benetleg'*) to the prior and canons, for the salvation of himself and his ancestors, of the annual rent of ½d which they used to pay for a parcel of land lying between their land and his, which he holds of the fee of Hugh Tollemache (*Thalemach*). Warranty is granted against all men in perpetuity.

Hiis testibus: domino Hugone Thalemache, Galfrido de Dodeneys, Symone Chattherol, Ricardo de Bruera, Radulfo clerico, Roberto de Falcenh(am), Iordano Schileman et multis aliis. [Mid to late thirteenth century]

> Cartulary no. 73; approx. 175 × 70+ mm; endorsed: xxvii; seal, oval, approx. 34 × 19 mm, natural wax varnished brown, perching bird facing to right, + SIG WIL. . . MAR.[1]
>
> [1] It is stange that, since he had his own seal (39–40), Adam Flanke was here using the seal of another man (? William de Mara, Marlar).
>
> Geoffrey of Dodnash occurs from 1252 × 57 to 1285 (27, 42), Jordan Skileman in 1257 (63), and Ralph the clerk of Bentley from 1276 to 1308 (48; BL Add. ch. 9566).

42. Notification by Artald de Saint-Romain (*de sancto Romano*) that he has conceded, remitted and utterly quitclaimed to the lord prior Robert and the canons of Dodnash and their successors all suit of court and customs thereto pertaining (*omnes curiarum sectas et sectarum consuetudines*) of the court of Bentley (*Benetleye*) relating to all the tenements which the prior and canons hold of the fee of the late Hugh Thalemasche, whose lands and heirs Artald holds in custody by the gift of the lord Edward, son and heir of King Henry. He wills and concedes that the prior and canons should be free, quit and absolved of such suit of court and related customs until the heirs of the said Hugh Thalemasche shall attain the age of majority. For this remission etc. the prior and canons have given him half a mark of silver. Sealed in testimony.

Testibus: Galfrido de Dodenes, Galfrido de la Mare, Willelmo de Wenham, Willelmo Mikeleboy, Ricardo Andrew, Iurdano filio Henrici, Willelmo fratre eius, Roberto clerico et aliis. [28 October 1252 × Michaelmas 1257]

> Cartulary no. 105; approx. 245 × 54+ mm; endorsed: Benthileye.
>
> For Artald de Saint-Roman, see Tout, *Chapters* i, 278–80. He was attached to the king's service from about 1240; in January 1255 he was appointed keeper of the Wardrobe; he died around Michaelmas 1257. The Hugh Tollemache here described as deceased was still alive in 37 Henry III, 1252–53 (Rye, *Fines*, 55 no. 196), and the first datable occurrence of his heir, also Hugh, is in 1269 (BL Add. ch. 9487).

43. Grant by Robert son of Hugh to William son of William of Kembroke, in fee and heredity, for his homage and service and for 3s entry-fine and an annual rent of 4d, of all his part of 'Smeriesmedwe' and 4d annual rent, with homage and service and all other appurtenances, from Richard the weaver.

[Early thirteenth century]

Helmingham, T/Hel/98/4 (A23/15); approx. 132 × 77 + 15 mm; endorsed: Prior de Dodenasch; parchment tag, fragment of seal in linen bag.

Sciant presentes et futuri quod ego Robertus filius Hugonis concessi et dedi et hac presenti carta confirmavi Willelmo filio Willelmi de Kenebroke, pro homagio et servitio suo et tribus solidis quod michi dedit in gersumam, totam partem meam de Smeriesmedwe et quatuor denarios annui redditus*a* cum homagio et servitio et omnibus aliis pertinentiis de Ricardo textore, habend(am) et tenend(am) dicto Willelmo et heredibus suis vel assignatis de me et heredibus meis libere et quiete, bene et pacifice, in feodo et hereditate, reddendo inde annuatim michi et heredibus meis quatuor denarios ad tres terminos, scilicet duos denarios ad festum sancti Michaelis et unum denarium ad festum sancti Andree et unum denarium ad Pascha, pro omnibus servitiis et consuetudinibus, exactionibus et demandis. Hiis testibus: Ada*b* Bullok, Thoma filio Hugonis, Semanno de Pomerio, Andrea de Sampford, Ricardo filio suo, Willelmo de Finesford, Huberto Muckeleboy, Ada*b* Muckeleboy et aliis.

a annui redditus *repeated* *b* MS: Adam

Robert son of Hugh attests an early to mid thirteenth century charter (79). For William of Kembroke see no. 44n. For (probably another) rent of 4d paid by Richard the weaver, see no. 14.

44. Grant by William son of William of Kembroke to the canons, in pure and perpetual alms for the salvation of his soul and those of his ancestors, of the homage and service of Richard the weaver for an acre of land lying between that of Baldwin Brawod and that of Robert le Bur, that is, 4d.

[Early to mid thirteenth century]

Cartulary no. 75; approx. 183 × 74 mm; no endorsement.

Sciant presentes et futuri quod ego Willelmus filius Willelmi de Kenebroch concessi et dedi et hac carta mea confirmavi Deo et beate Marie de Dodenes et priori et canonicis ibidem Deo servientibus et servituris homagium Ricardi telarii et totum servitium quod michi fecit vel debuit facere de una acra terre iacente inter terram Baldewini Brewod et terram Roberti le Bur, scilicet quatuor denarios per annum, ad Pascha unum denarium, ad nativitatem sancti Iohannis Baptiste unum denarium, ad festum sancti Michaelis unum denarium et ad festum sancti Andree unum denarium, pro salute anime mee et antecessorum meorum in puram et perpetuam elemosinam. Ut autem hec mea concessio et donatio et carte mee confirmatio firma sit et stabilis, huic scripto sigillum meum apposui. His t(estibus): Willelmo de Waudingefeld, Ranulfo de Braham, Roberto de Alneto, Alano filio Rogeri de Braham, Ysebardo filio Hugonis, Osberto clerico de Stutitun et Alexandro filio eius, Rogero Warre, Rogero filio Edwini, Gerardo de Andredest' et multis aliis.

'Kenebroch' is Kembroke Hall in Bucklesham. William son of William of Kembroke occurs in 1224–25 (17); in the early thirteenth century he received a messuage in Bentley from Prior William and the canons of Leighs, in exchange for tenements in Sweffling and North Glemham (BL Add. ch. 9489); he also held land in Bentley of Geoffrey son of Maurice of Dodnash granted to him by Robert of 'Fletesmuthe' and Edith his wife, and land granted by Matilda daughter of John Kebbel (BL Add. ch. 9497, 9501). Maurice of Dodnash had granted to William, for an entry fine of 30s and annual rent of 4d, a piece of land in Bentley called 'Frelond' (Ipswich, SRO, HD1047/1/69).

45. Quitclaim by John Skileman of Bentley (*Benetleya*) to the prior and canons, for his salvation and that of his ancestors, of an acre of land lying lengthwise along the embankment stretching from Dodnash to Ipswich, of which one head-land abuts on the land once held by William of Holbrook to the east, and the other on John's messuage to the west. The canons have given him two marks in cash. Warranty is granted in perpetuity.
Hiis testibus: domino Ricardo de Holebroc, domino Iohanne de Wenham, Galfrido de Dodenes, Ranulfo clerico de Benetleye, Ricardo de Bruario, Willelmo de Bruario, Roberto de Spina de Capel'.				[Probably 1272–73]

Cartulary no. 93; approx. 235 × 55+ mm; endorsed: xxx, Iohannes Scileman.

In 1272–73 John Skileman brought a case against the prior and others concerning a tenement in Dodnash (PRO, C66 (Patent Rolls)/92, m. 6d). Several of the witnesses occur from 1276–85 (27, 48, 206). Ranulf the clerk is probably in error for Ralph (Radulfo).

46. Quitclaim by John Skileman of Bentley (*Benethleya*) to the prior and canons of all his lands and tenements which he had of their fee, together with a messuage and buildings and all other appurtenances in the vill of Bentley, so that neither he nor any of his heirs or assigns may henceforth make any claim therein. Sealed in testimony.
Hiis testibus: domino Ricardo de Holebrok, domino Iohanne de Wenham militibus, Galfrido de Dodenes, Rogero de Braham, Radulfo de Braham, Andrea Helte, Galfrido de la Mare, Roberto de Waldingefeld, Roberto de Spina, Ricardo de Glaunvile, Ricardo de Bruar', Willelmo de Bruar', Radulfo de Benethl(eia) clerico et multis aliis.				[Shortly after 1272–73]

Cartulary no. 92; approx. 200 × 98+ mm; endorsed: xxxi.; dating as no. 45.

47. Quitclaim in perpetuity by Roger Russel of Bentley (*Benetleye*) to the prior and canons of all right in a messuage and in all the land in Bentley which his father once held of the prior, and also in a parcel of land called 'Schortecroft' in Bentley which he himself purchased from the prior, so that neither he, his heirs nor anyone in his name may henceforth make any claim therein. For this quitclaim the prior has given him 40s in cash.
Testibus: domino Hugone Talemache, domino Gerardo de Wachesham militibus, Edwardo Charles, Waltero Baldewyn, Willelmo de Braham, Radulfo clerico,

Iohanne de Coppedok, Roberto le Clerk de Falcenham, Willelmo le Neuman, Iohanne Oliver et aliis.   [Late thirteenth – early fourteenth century]

> Helmingham, T/Hel/98/1 (A2/9); approx. 202 × 110 + 24 mm; endorsed: xxxii, de Rogero Russel; parchment tag, seal missing.

> Ralph the clerk occurs from 1276 (48) to 1308 (BL Add. ch. 9566); Walter Baldwin and William of Brantham attest no. 26, 1279 × 1304. This is the only occurrence in this collection of the donor and five of the witnesses.

48. Notification by Alice Kasenel of Bentley (*Benetlee*) that, on behalf of herself and her heirs or assigns, she has quitclaimed to the prior and canons all right and claim which she had or in any way might have had in a parcel of land with all its appurtenances which lies in the field called 'le Marledlonde' in the vill of Bentley, between the lands of the prior and canons and the road which leads from Dodnash (*Dodenes*) towards 'le Kantissestrate', of which one headland abuts to the south on the land of the prior and canons and the other to the north on the land of Ralph the clerk, to have and to hold to the prior and canons and their successors of Alice and her heirs or assigns freely, well, wholly, in peace, in fee and heredity and in perpetuity so that neither she nor her heirs nor anyone in their name may henceforth make therein any claim. For this concession etc. the prior and canons shall give her annually for the duration of her life a bushel of rye for all actions and demands. Sealed in corroboration.
Hiis testibus: domino Roberto de Schelton, domino Hugone Thalemache militibus, Galfrido de Dodenes, Rogero de Braham, Radulfo de Braham, Iohanne de Belsted, Willelmo de Houton, Roberto Anneys, Radulfo clerico et aliis.

Dodnash, Thursday 14 May 1276.

> Cartulary no. 106; approx. 204 × 99 mm; endorsed: Alicia Kasnel; Kentisstrete quod Alicia Casnel ven(didit) in Benetlee, xxviii.

49. Notification[1] that a dispute had arisen between the prior and convent of Holy Trinity, Ipswich, appellants, and the prior and convent of Dodnash, defendants, concerning the unjust spoliation of the great tithe of two acres of land or more of the tenement of a certain Kasenel in the parish of Bentley (*Benteley*), which is appropriated to the prior and convent of Ipswich, and concerning also the unjust detention of the lesser tithes of a certain curtilage and a dovecote in the same parish, recently perpetrated, which tithes, great and lesser, the prior and convent of Holy Trinity, Ipswich, assert pertain to them by the common law [of the Church] by right of their church of Bentley, the prior and canons of Dodnash asserting to the contrary, according to the common law indulted to the whole Order of canons regular and according to a specific indult granted to them by the apostolic see. After a lengthy judicial dispute between the parties, at last and through the intervention of mutual friends, the dispute was resolved to restore peace between the parties in the following manner. The Prior and convent of Holy Trinity, Ipswich, and their successors shall in future and in perpetuity receive, in the name of their

church of Bentley, all the tithes proceeding in any manner whatsoever from the said two acres, with all increments and emoluments, without contradiction or hindrance by the prior and canons of Dodnash and their successors or any of their servants; the prior and convent of Ipswich and their successors shall surrender to the prior and convent of Dodnash and their successors in peace and tranquillity the tithes of the said curtilage and dovecote, making no claim against them nor doing them any harm therein, in such wise that if the curtilage and dovecote are alienated in any way, or occupied by some other person, or are given at farm or are worked by any other person, then the tithes of the curtilage and dovecote shall for the duration be rendered to the church of Bentley, legitimately and with no contradiction by their possessors. This settlement was approved by the prior and convent of both houses, who appended their capitular seals to each other's copy, together with the seal of the Officiality of Norwich.

Ipswich, 1 August 1282

Cartulary no. 27 (described at 15), dorse.

[1] The salutation is not copied; the sealing clause indicates that this is a notification by the Official of Norwich diocese.

For earlier litigation before papal judges-delegate relating to tithes in Bentley, see nos 15, 19. For the papal indult to Dodnash, which is of dubious authenticity, and a general ruling concerning tithe-paying by Augustinian houses, see no. 111 and n.

50. Agreement made between the prior and canons and Ralph of Brantham, layman. They each hold parcels of meadow and aldergrove at Dodnash, to the east of the monastery by the bank of the stream which flows from Dodnash to 'Neubrege'; the rise in water level and flooding has in some places broken the bank at the bend of the river and has obscured the boundaries of these parcels. Controversy might easily arise between the parties because of this, and wishing to avoid such, they have agreed that by the judgement and view of Robert de Bruario of Capel [St Mary] and Robert le Pas of Brantham, the stream shall run directly through the middle of the respective parcels, so that the canons shall have all the land formerly pertaining to Ralph which has been removed from the south of the stream, and similarly Ralph shall have all the land formerly the canons' which has been removed from the north. This agreement, in the form of a chirograph, has been sealed alternately by the two parties.

[Late thirteenth century, probably 1287]

Cartulary no. 72; approx. 208 × 110 + 10 mm; chirograph, indented at top margin; endorsed: Carta Radulfi de Braham de escambio; carta inter priorem de Dod' et Radulfum de Braham laicum de escambio, xiiii.

Universis Cristi fidelibus presens scriptum visuris vel audituris prior et canonici de Dodenes et Radulfus de Braham laycus salutem in Domino. Ad universitatis vestre notitiam volumus pervenire tenore presentium quod cum nos particulariter portiones prati et alneti habeamus apud Dodenes iacentes ex parte orientali monasterii de Dodenes iuxta ripam que fluit de Dodenes apud Neubrege, et dicta ripa per subreptionem fluminis et aque alluvionem dictas portiones nostras in quibusdam locis ita detraxerit in amfracto et transverso in quibusdam locis ita ussurpaverit quod fines dictarum portionum prefate ripe confudit inundatio, et ita ratione dicte confusionis de facili posset inter nos suscitari materia litis et contentionis, nos unanimiter et concorditer cuiuslibet a nobis contentionis amputare volentes causam, desiderantes etiam multiplicare pacis et amoris tranquillitatem atque fovere, ita providimus quod iuxta arbitrium Willelmi de Bruario de Capeles et Roberti le Pas de Braham pariter et observationem antedicta ripa per medias dictas portiones nostras linialiter et directe suum fluxum habebit et cursitationem, ita videlicet quod illas terras omnes, sive plus sive minus fuerint in eisdem, spectantes ad dictum Radulfum detractas vel ussurpatas per illam ripam ex parte australi eiusdem ripe habeant et optineant [prior et canonici] sine qualibet calumnia vel contradictione, vice versa portionem et particulam spectantem ad priorem et canonicos detractam vel ussurpatam per dictam ripam ex parte boreali habeat et possideat*a* dictus Radulfus. Et ut hec robur et firmitatem habeant inter partes ratione permutationis et escambii, et ad huius rei evidentiam pleniorem, factum est instrumentum in modum cirograffi confectum, cuius unam partem pars prioris et canonicorum habet penes se sigillo Radulfi de Braham consignatam, alteram autem partem habet Radulfus de Braham sigillo dictorum prioris et canonicorum roboratam.*b* Hiis testibus: domino Hugone Thalemache, Willelmo de Braham, Galfrido de Dodenes, Andrea Helte, Willelmo de Houtune, Radulfo clerico de Benethlee, Willelmo de Bruario de Capeles, Roberto le Pas de Braham, Willelmo de Michelefeld, Radulfo de Braham et multis aliis.

a MS: habead et possidead
b MS: habent dicti prior et canonici sigillo Radulfi de Braham roboratam.

Ralph of Brantham occurs in 1276 (48), the 1270s/80s (46, 85–6) and soon after 1279 (130); William de Bruera occurs as bailiff in 1297 (73); and Ralph the chaplain from 1276 (27) to 1308 (BL Add. ch. 9566). Geoffrey de la Mare was still alive in 1283 (BL Add ch. 9519).

It is very likely that this agreement was made in the aftermath of the great rise in the water level and flooding of 1287 (J.M. Lambert *et al.*, *The Making of the Broads*, Royal Geographical Society Research Papers 3, London 1961, 100–1). See also M. Bailey, '*Per impetum maris*: Natural Disaster and Economic Decline in Eastern England, 1275–1350', in B.M.S. Campbell, ed., *Before the Black Death: Studies in the Crisis of the Early Fourteenth Century*, Manchester 1991.

51. Grant in fee and heredity by Nicholas of 'Bertham' to Ralph the clerk, for his service and for 7s in silver which he gave in cash as an entry-fine, of a parcel of land in Bentley (*Benethl'*) with appurtenances, lying between the land of Selova Casenel on one side and that of Nicholas son of Ralph the clerk on the other, abutting at one headland to the south on the wood of the prior of Holy Trinity, Ipswich, which is called 'Lemaneshey', and at the other to the north on Ralph's land, to be held by him, his heirs, assigns or whosoever to whom he may wish to give, sell, bequeath or in any way assign it in perpetuity, rendering annually to Nicholas and his heirs 1¼d, that is, ½d at Easter and ¼d at each of the other

usual terms, for all services etc., saving only to the prior and convent of Holy Trinity, Ipswich, one day's work in the autumn at 'Cherchehus' in Bentley, with food provided. Warranty is granted against all persons in perpetuity. Sealed in testimony.

Hiis testibus: Galfrido de Dodenesse, Galfrido de la Mare, Iohanne filio suo, Petro Overbroc, Iohanne Bonchevaler, Roberto le Sireve, Hamone de Chatesham, Ricardo le Blunt, Roberto clerico, Petro filio Thome, Rogero Underwode et multis aliis.   [Late thirteenth century]

> Cartulary no. 104; approx. 177 × 105+ mm; endorsed: Bentleigh; seal, vessica, approx. 50 × 30 mm, brown wax, radiating device of four major alternating with four minor petals, + S. NICHOLAI DE BERTHAM.

> 'Bertham' is probably Barham, up the Gipping valley from Ipswich, in Claydon hundred. Ralph the clerk occurs from 1276 (48) to 1308 (BL Add. ch. 9566). He was married to Isabelle (BL Add. ch. 9494), and had sons Nicholas (BL Add. ch. 9508) and William, who himself had a son John, who occurs in 1334 (BL Add. ch. 9598). In April 1295 Selova Casenel granted land in Bentley to Nicholas, himself a clerk (BL Add. ch. 9534). Geoffrey of Dodnash was still alive in 1285 (27). It is not clear why this charter is included in the priory's 'cartulary', although it is possible that this land did subsequently pass to the canons.

52. Grant by King Edward III to the prior and canons of free warren in all their demesne lands in Bentley, Falkenham and [East] Bergholt. Nottingham, 22 October 1327.

> Cal., *C Ch R 1327–41*, 58.

EAST BERGHOLT

53. Grant by Ada de Tosny to the canons, in pure and perpetual alms, of that parcel of land below 'Sigrimeslegh' which was held by Robert Godibure, and that below 'Estlegh' held by Alan son of Seward, in exchange for a similar amount of meadow which the canons have granted to her. For this exchange they have given her two marks of silver.   [Late twelfth – early thirteenth century]

> Cartulary no. 4; approx. 196 × 80+ mm; endorsed: Ada de Toeni, iii.

Ada de Toni omnibus suis hominibus et omnibus amicis suis, Francis et Anglicis, presentibus et futuris, salutem. Sciatis me dedisse et concessisse et hac presenti carta mea confirmasse in puram et perpetuam elemosinam priori et canonicis ecclesie beate Marie de Dodenes illam particulam prati quam Robertus Godibure tenuit sub Sigrimeslega et illam particulam prati quam fuit Alani filii Sewardi sub est lega, pro escambiis tanti prati quod predictus prior et predicti canonici dederunt predicte Ade, tenendas^a libere, quiete et solute, bene et in pace et honorifice in perpetuum per predictam escambiam. Pro hac donatione et concessione huius escambii predictus prior et prefati canonici dederunt predicte Ade duas marcas argenti. Hiis testibus: Eustacio de Braham, Rogero de Braham filio suo, Waltero et Ricardo fratribus suis, Roberto Quaram, Willelmo de Manent, Edwardo de Alneto, Gerardo fratre suo, Rogero filio Hugonis, Herberto filio Ricardi, David de Bercolte, Rogero filio Godwini, Eadwardo filio Willelmi, Ricardo de Cat(iwade) et multis aliis.

a MS: tenendum

After no. 4, because referring to the canons of Dodnash rather than 'de Alneto de Bergholt'. Ada was still alive after Michaelmas 1201 (*PR 4 John*, 115).

54. Grant by Roger Bigod, earl of Norfolk, made through the promptings of charity, to the canons of the homage and service of Adam Buris with all his tenement in the vill of [East] Bergholt, and all the land held by Alan son of Seward with his *sequela*, and all the land held in demesne by William of Bramford, which lies between the house of Gerard Luvegos and Bergholt heath, and all the aldergrove of the same fee between the messuage of Adam Buris and 'Sigrimesley', for the annual render of a pair of gilded spurs for all service etc. All this is confirmed as granted to him by the charter of William of Bramford.

[Late twelfth – early thirteenth century]

Cartulary no. 9; approx. 154 × 105+ mm; endorsed: Comes Rogerus, non demonstretur.

Rogerus Bigot comes Norf(olchie) omnibus hominibus et amicis suis Francis et Anglis tam presentibus quam futuris salutem. Sciatis me caritatis intuitu concessisse, dedisse et presenti carta confirmasse Deo et ecclesie beate Marie de Dodeneys et canonicis ibidem Deo servientibus homagium et servitium Ade Buris in villa de Berkholt cum toto tenemento suo et cum tota sequela sua, et totam terram quam Alanus filius Sewardi tenet in eadem villa, et totam terram quam Willelmus de Bromford habuit in dominico de feodo illo, que iacet inter domum Gerardi Luvegos et brueram de Berkholt, et totum alnetum quod est de feodo illo et quod est inter mesuagium Ade Buris et Sigrimesleg, illis autem habenda et tenenda libere et quiete de me et heredibus meis inperpetuum, reddendo inde annuatim ad Pascha unum par calcariorum deauratorum de pretio sex denariorum pro omni servitio, consuetudine et exactione. Hec autem omnia predicta predictis canonicis de Dodeneys concessi et dedi, sicut Willelmus de Bromford ipsa michi concessit et dedit et carta sua confirmavit. Hiis testibus: Rogero de Braham, Gaufrido de Grimill', Willelmo de Verdun, Roberto filio Oseberti, Reginaldo de Pyrhou, Rogero de Ribof, Huberto de Bromford, Ricardo fratre ipsius, Ada Malvoisyn, Willelmo de Braham, Ricardo fratre ipsius, Mauricio et Thoma de Dodeneys, Ricardo de Kattiwad, Edwardo filio Iosce, Willelmo de Reimes, Willelmo de Bosco, Gaufrido filio Henrici de Grimill' et multis aliis.

Roger Bigod was created earl of Norfolk on 25 Nov. 1189 and died in 1221, before 2 Aug. (*HBC*, 473); William of Bramford made a grant to the canons at Bergholt (9); he occurs in 1202 and 1211 (*Fines* ii, nos. 345, 543), and was probably still alive in 1228 (*CRR* xiii, no. 1201).

55. Grant in pure and perpetual alms by Edward son of Wlfard of the Aldergrove to the canons, for his salvation and that of his ancestors, of all his mill of Flatford in the vill of [East] Bergholt with all appurtenances, free from all secular service.
[Late twelfth – early thirteenth century]

Cartulary no. 11; approx. 170 × 85+ mm; endorsed: Edwardus de Alneto, xix; seal (not illustrated), round, approx. 34 mm, natural wax varnished brown, wolf facing right, looking back over shoulder, + SIGILL. . .ALNET.

Sciant presentes et futuri quod ego Edwardus de Alneto filius Wulphardi de Alneto pro me et pro heredibus meis concessi et in puram et perpetuam elemosinam dedi, pro salute anime mee et omnium antecessorum meorum, Deo et ecclesie sancte Marie de Dodeneys et canonicis ibidem Deo servientibus totum molendinum meum de Flotford in villa de Berkholt cum omnibus ad illud pertinentibus, ita scilicet quod predicti canonici predictum molendinum cum pertinentiis habeant et teneant in perpetuum bene et in pace et ab omni seculari exactione et servitio quietum et solutum. Hiis testibus: Henrico de Grimill', Rogero de Braham, Milone Lenveis, Waltero de Raveningham, Willelmo Lenveis, Gaufrido de Grimill, Reginaldo de Pyrhou, Rogero de Ribof, Roberto filio Oseberti, Thoma de Braham, Bartholomeo de Beylham, Willelmo et Huberto de Bromford, Rogero filio Godwini, Waltero filio Thedrici, Mauricio de Dodeneys et Thoma fratre eius et multis aliis.

For an earlier grant by this donor to Wimer the chaplain, see no. 11. Miles Lenveise was active in 1198, was the earl's attorney in the *curia regis* in 1200, and was dead by 1224; for him, and Roger of Brantham, see *Sibton Cartularies* iii, no. 741n. William Lenveise was Bigod's constable in 1216, and Reginald de Pirho was in the Framlingham garrison that year (R.A. Brown, 'Framlingham Castle and Bigod, 1154–1216', in *Castles, Conquests and Charters*, Woodbridge 1989, 207). Bartholomew of Bayling granted land to Hickling priory in 5 John (Bodl. MS Tanner 425, fo. 28r).

56. Confirmation in pure and perpetual alms by Roger Bigod, earl of Norfolk, to the canons of his mill of Flatford in the vill of [East] Bergholt with all appurtenances, just as Edward son of Wlfard of the Aldergrove granted it to him and confirmed it by charter. [Late twelfth – early thirteenth century]

Cartulary no. 12; approx. 146 × 82+ mm; endorsed: Comes Rogerus.

Rogerus Bigot comes Norf(olchie) omnibus hominibus suis Frangcis et Angilis tam presentibus quam futuris salutem. Sciatis me caritatis intuitu concessisse, dedisse et presenti carta confirmasse Deo et ecclesie beate Marie de Dodeneys et canonicis ibidem Deo servientibus totum molendinum meum de Flotford in villa de Bercholt cum omnibus ad illud pertinentibus, habendum et tenendum in puram et perpetuam elemosinam; et hoc vero predictum molendinum predictis canonicis de Dodeneys concessi et dedi sicut Edwardus de Alneto filius Wlvardi de Alneto illud mihi concessit et dedit et carta sua confirmavit. Hiis testibus: Rogero de Braham, Willelmo de Verdun, Gaufrido de Grimill', Roberto filio Oseberti, Reginaldo de Pyrhou, Rogero de Ribof, Huberto de Bromford et Ricardo fratre eius, Ada Malvoisyn, Willelmo de Braham et Ricardo fratre ipsius, Mauricio et Thoma de Dodeneys, Ricardo de Kattiwad, Edwardo filio Iosce, Willelmo de Reimes, Willelmo de Bosco, Gaufrido filio Henrici de Grimill' et multis aliis.

> Roger Bigod was created earl on 25 Nov. 1189 and died in 1221, before 2 Aug. (*HBC*, 473).

57. Acknowledgement by Nicholas of the Aldergrove that he and his heirs are bound to the payment to the prior and canons of an annual rent of 11s 7d, which his ancestors used to pay for the mill of Flatford. Right of distraint is granted in the event of non-payment. He has confirmed for the canons his ancestor's charters of enfeoffment and confirmation.   [Mid thirteenth century]

> Ipswich, SRO, q s 271 (Fitch's *Monasticon*), vol. ii, at p. 186; approx. 180 × 70 + 14 mm; very fragile and now backed, so endorsement invisible; tag and seal missing.

Notum sit omnibus presentibus et futuris quod ego Nicholaus de Alneto et heredes mei tenemur priori et canonicis de Dodenes presentibus et futuris in annuo redditu .xi. solidorum et .vii. denariorum singulis annis pro molendino de Floteford, solvendo in perpetuum sicut predecessores nostri quondam fecerunt ad quatuor anni terminos, scilicet ad festum sancti Andree .xxxiiii. d., ad Pascha .xxxiiii. d., ad nativitatem sancti Iohannis Baptiste triginta et quatuor denarios et ad festum sancti Michaelis tres solidos et unum denarium. Et si ita contingat quod ego vel heredes mei ad aliquem prefixum terminum dicte solutionis negligenter vel contemptu defecerimus, liceat priori et canonicis et successoribus suis tam infra molendinum predictum quam extra sicut iustum fuerit distringere quoad pro predicto annuale redditu plenarie fuerit solutio. Ego autem nec heredes mei vel mei assignati aliquod impedimentum vel obstaculum faciemus quo minus predicti prior et canonici et successores eorum predictum annuum redditum ad terminos prescriptos pacifice possint habere et absque alicuius contradictione gaudere. Preterea tam cartas feffamenti quam confirmationes quas predicti prior et canonici de antecessoribus meis libere possident ratas et gratas pro me et pro heredibus meis predictis canonicis et successoribus eorum inperpetuum confirmavi possidendas. Et ad maiorem securitatem super hiis perpetuo optinendam, presenti confirmationi mee sigillum meum apposui. Testibus: domino Ricardo de Braham, domino Waltero fratre suo, Roberto de Waudingfeld, Ricardo de Cnichtewde, Ricardo de Boyt(un), Roberto de Boytun', Wymer Page, Gerardo de Lodebroc, Radulfo filio clerici, Rogero de sancta Osytha, Roberto clerico.

> Nicholas de Alneto, or de Launey, attests charters of the mid thirteenth century (21, 40, with Roger of St Osyth), and specifically in September 1256 (BL Add. ch. 9480). He died on 23 April 1274. He held a tenement in East Bergholt of the king in chief worth 60s *p.a.*, of which 20s was to be paid at the king's Exchequer, and 9s to other lords; and also a tenement in Stratford St Mary of mr Roger of Holbrook, by the service of half a knight's fee, worth 41s 11d *p.a.* (*CIPM* ii, no.

197). Robert of Boyton occurs from 1223–24 (16) to 1243–44 (Rye, *Fines*, 47 no. 16); Sir Richard of Brantham attests in 1250 (25).

58. Grant in perpetuity by Alexander son of Christiana to the canons of all the land which Pentecost held in the vill of [East] Bergholt, between the way which leads from 'le Quelne' towards the house of Godwin Luvegos and the stream which divides Dodnash from Bergholt, with the field called 'Gokesfeld', to be held for an annual rent of 3s to the lords of the fee for all services *etc.*, saving scutage. The canons have paid a mark as entry-fine.

[Late twelfth – early thirteenth century]

Cartulary no. 25; approx. 206 × 75+ mm; endorsed: Bergholt.

Sciant presentes et futuri quod ego Alexander filius Christiane concessi et dedi et hac carta mea Deo et ecclesie beate Marie de Dodenes et canonicis ibidem Deo servientibus et servituris totam illam terram quam Pentecuste tenuit in villa de Berchoute inter viam que vadit del Quelne versus domum Godwine Luvegos et rivulum qui dividit Dodenes de Berchoute, cum campo qui vocatur Gokesfeld, tenendam et habendam prenominatis canonicis et eorum successoribus inperpetuum libere et quiete et honorifice, reddendo inde per annum dominis feodi tres solidos, scilicet ad festum sancti Michaelis .ix. d., ad festum sancti Andree .ix. d., ad Pascha .ix. d., ad nativitatem sancti Iohannis Baptiste .ix. d. pro omnibus servitiis et consuetudinibus, salvo servitio domini regis. Pro hac autem concessione et donatione et huius carte mee confirmatione et huic scripto sigilli mei appositione dederunt michi predicti canonici unam marcam argenti in gersumiam. His t(estibus): Eustachio de Braham et Rogero filio eius, Clerenbaldo de Alno, Roberto filio Roberti, Hamone Petit, Edwardo de Alneto et Gerardo fratre eius, Roberto Quareme et Willelmo Quareme, Hamone de Ho et aliis.

Eustace of Brantham occurs from 1165–1202, and Roger his son from 1195–1223 (*Sibton Cartularies* iii, no. 741n). Edward of the Aldergrove, Robert Quareme and Gerard Lovegos all attest in the late twelfth century (2, 6–10).

59. Grant in pure and perpetual alms by John son of Alexander, for his salvation and that of his father, his mother Clarice and his ancestors and successors, to the canons of an annual rent of 3d to be received from John son of Amyas and his heirs for a parcel of land lying by the messuage once held by Roger le Lung and beyond the road leading southwards, which is of the fee of Simon son of Simon. Right of distraint is conceded in the event of non-payment.

[Mid thirteenth century]

Cartulary no. 26; approx. 125 × 95+ mm; endorsed: hospitale de Gyp' de .iii.d.; carta de .iii. d. de ospitali Gipp'.

Omnibus sancte matris ecclesie filiis ad quos presens scriptum pervenerit Iohannes filius Alexandri salutem. Sciatis me concessisse, dedisse et hac carta mea confirmasse priori et canonicis de Dodenes presentibus et futuris tres denarios

76

annui redditus percipiendos de Iohanne filio Amisii et heredibus suis de quadam
pecia terre iacente contra mesuagium quondam Rogeri le Lung ultra viam versus
suth, que est de feodo Simonis filii Symonis, scilicet ad festum sancti Michaelis
tres obulos et ad Pascha tres obulos, habendos illis inperpetuum in puram et perpetuam elemosinam pro salute anime mee et patris mei Alexandri et matris mee
Claricie et omnium antecessorum et successorum meorum. Et si forte, quod absit,
prenominatus Iohannes vel heredes sui predictis priori et canonicis ad predictos
terminos prefixum redditum non solverint, liceat priori et canonicis predictis distringere prenominatum Iohannem et heredes suos in predicta terra. Ut autem hec
mea concessio, donatio et confirmatio perpetuam habeat stabilitatem, huic scripto
sigillum meum apposui in testimonium. Hiis testibus: Iohanne Costin, Helia filio
Iohannis, Iohanne de Beaumes, Silvestro filio Waukelin, Hugone et Rogero de
Langestun fratribus, Galfrido de Beaumes, Petro filio Everardi, Co(n)stentin
Fader et multis aliis.

There are none of the usual witnesses to charters in this collection. Hugh of
'Langestun' occurs from 1239–40 to 1256–57 (Rye, *Fines*, 42 no. 72; 59 no. 31);
Geoffrey de Beaumes occurs 1261–62 (ibid., 63 no. 116B). This land was presumably subsequently held of Dodnash by one of the four hospitals established
in Ipswich (*MRH*, 366).

60. Grant in perpetuity by Roger de Akeni to the prior and canons of all the land
with appurtenances which Brictwald on the day of his death held of his fee in
[East] Bergholt, and the field called 'Gokesfeld' with appurtenances, and four
crofts with appurtenances which Richard Hauec once held there, which lie between Bergholt heath and the land of Gerard Lovegos called 'Wrongeland', and
the aldergrove called 'Hauekesfen', and the meadow in 'Sturemede' called
'Hauekesmede', and a parcel of land called 'Walpictel', with appurtenances, saving
the tenement of 'Walpictel', and the curtilage of Robert Scad, which is of the
foresaid land held by Hauek, and the common pasture pertaining to these lands,
for an annual rent of 6s 8½d, saving to his men the exchanges of meadow which
the prior and canons gave to them for the overflow from their pond. Warranty is
granted.

[Early to mid thirteenth century, probably soon after Michaelmas 1228]

Cartulary no. 54; approx. 190 × 115+ mm; endorsed: Carta Rogeri de Akeney de
campo de Bergh', xi.

Sciant presentes et futuri quod ego Rogerus de Akeni concessi et dedi et hac carta
mea confirmavi priori et canonicis de Dodenes presentibus et futuris totam terram cum pertinentiis quam Brictwaldus tenuit de feodo meo in Berchoute die qua
obiit, et campum qui vocatur Gokesfeld cum pertinentiis, et quatuor cruftas de
terra quam Ricardus Hauec tenuit quondam in Berchoute, scilicet que iacent inter
bruarium de Berchoute et terram Gerardi Luvegos que vocatur Wrongelond, cum
pertinentiis eisdem cruftis pertinentibus, et alnetum quod vocatur Hauekesfen, et
pratum in Sturemede quod vocatur Hauekesmed', et unam peciam terre que vocatur Walpictel cum pertinentiis eidem pecie terre pertinentibus, salvo tenemento

tenentium Walpictel, et curtilagium Roberti Scad quod est de predicta terra quam Hauek tenuit, et communam pasture predictis terris pertinentem, tenenda et habenda predictis priori et canonicis inperpetuum, libere et quiete et honorifice, bene et in pace, de me et heredibus meis, solvendo inde annuatim michi et heredibus meis sex solidos et octo denarios et obolum, scilicet ad Pascha .xx.d. ob. et ad nativitatem sancti Iohannis Baptiste .xx. d. et ad festum sancti Michaelis .xx. d. et ad festum sancti Andree .xx. d. pro omnibus servitiis et consuetudinibus et demandis, salvis hominibus meis escambiis prati que predicti prior et canonici eisdem dederunt pro refullo stagni sui. Et ego et heredes mei warantizabimus omnia predicta tenementa predictis priori et canonicis contra omnes homines. Pro hac autem donatione et concessione et huius carte mee confirmatione dederunt michi predicti prior et canonici decem marcas argenti in gersumiam. His testibus: Willelmo de Ambli, Willelmo filio Roberti de Reindun', Hugone Talemasch, Ricardo de Brumford, Willelmo de Cheverevile, Roberto de Alneto, Roberto de Manetun', Edwardo Davi, Alano filio Rogeri de Braham, Warino Testard, Augustino de Blakeham, Ricardo de Hintlisham, Alexandro de Stutton et multis aliis.

The Akeni family originated from Acquigny (Eure, arr. and cant. Louviers), and were tenants of Tosny in Cambridgeshire and Oxfordshire (Loyd, *Anglo-Norman Families*, 2). They held the manor in East Bergholt which became known as 'Spencer's' (Coppinger, *Manors* vi, 19). Roger de Akeni occurs in 1228–29 (Rye, *Fines*, 29 nos 130, 133), as does Robert of Manton (ibid., 29 no. 130). At Michaelmas 1228 Roger brought actions in the *curia regis* against Prior Jordan for twenty-eight acres of land and an acre of woodland at Bergholt, against William of Bramford for fifteen acres of land there and two acres of meadow in Stratford, against Robert of the Aldergrove for twenty-eight acres in Bergholt, and against Ralph son of Gerald for thirty acres, to which the prior and the others had no right of entry except through Ada, widow of Roger de Tosny, who had held all this land in dower (*CRR* xiii, no. 1201). This charter probably represents the resolution of that conflict with regard to the priory.

61. Grant in pure and perpetual alms by Roger de Akeni, for his salvation and that of his ancestors, to the canons of all his land in [East] Bergholt which is contained between 'Sigrimeslee' and the aldergrove of Gerard Luvegos, as it is embanked right up to the water which divides Bergholt from Dodnash.

[Early to mid thirteenth century]

Cartulary no. 55; approx. 226 × 70+ mm; endorsed: Carta Rogeri de Akenei de campo de Bercholt, x; seal, round, approx. 34 mm, natural wax varnished brown, shield of arms, a maunche; S. . .LL. ROGER DE AKEN.

Sciant presentes et futuri quod ego Rogerus de Akeni concessi et dedi et hac carta mea confirmavi priori et canonicis de Dodenes presentibus et futuris, pro salute anime mee et animarum antecessorum meorum et successorum, totam terram illam in Bercholte que continetur inter Sigrimeslee et alnetum Gerardi Luvegos sicut fossatum cingit iam dictam terram maxime usque aquam que dividit Bercholt de Dodenes, in liberam et puram et perpetuam elemosinam. Ut autem hec mea concessio et donatio et confirmatio firma sit et stabilis, huic scripto sigillum meum apposui. His testibus: domino Widone de Ambli, Hugone Thalemasch, Ranulfo de Braham, Willelmo filio Roberti de Reindun', Thoma Locun persona de Reindun', Patricio persona de Laleford, Radulfo de Berchout capellano, Roberto de Alneto, Roberto de Manetun, Edwardo Davi, Warino Testard, Alexandro de Stutton et multis aliis.

See no. 60.

62. Final concord made in the king's court at Ipswich on 13 October 1228 before the named justices between Robert de Pavilly and Alice his wife, complainants, and Prior Jordan of Dodnash, defendant, concerning thirty acres of land with appurtenances in [East] Bergholt; and also between the said Robert and Alice, complainants, and Thomas Lochon, defendant, concerning two acres of land with appurtenances in Stratford [St Mary]. An assize of *mort d'ancestor* was summoned, but Robert and Alice remitted and quitclaimed in perpetuity, for themselves and for Alice's heirs, to the prior and his successors and the church of Dodnash, and to Thomas Lochon, all right and claim which they had in the foresaid land and meadow with appurtenances. For this remittance etc. the prior and Thomas have given them two marks of silver.

A1 = Cartulary no. 111, top left-hand portion of tripartite chirograph; approx. 190 × 98 mm; endorsed: xii.

A2 = PRO, CP25/1/213/7/14; chirograph indented at top margin; approx. 175 × 110 mm; endorsed: Et sciendum quod Rogerus de Akeni apponit clamium.

Hec est finalis concordia facta in curia domini regis apud Gipiswic' a die sancti Michaelis in quindecim dies anno regni regis Henrici filiii regis Iohannis duodecim coram Martino de Patershill decano sancti Pauli London', Stephano de Segrave, Thoma de Heyden, Willelmo de Insula, Willelmo de London' iusticiariis et aliis domini regis fidelibus tunc ibi presentibus, inter Robertum de Pavily et Aliciam uxorem eius petentes et Iordanum priorem de Dodenes tenentem de triginta acris terre cum pertinentiis in Burcholt, et inter eosdem Robertum et Aliciam petentes et Thomam Lochon tenentem de duabus acris prati cum pertinentiis in Straford, unde recognitio assise mortis antecessorum summonita fuit inter eosdem in eadem curia, scilicet quod predicti Robertus et Alicia remiserunt et quietum clamaverunt de se et de heredibus ipsius Alicie predicto priori et successoribus suis et ecclesie de Dodenes' et predicto Thome et heredibus suis totum ius et clameum quod habuerunt in tota predicta terra et prato cum pertinentiis in perpetuum. Et pro hac remissione, quieta clamantia, fine et concordia predicti prior et Thomas dederunt predictis Roberto et Alicie duas marcas argenti.

For the Pavilly family, see Loyd, *Anglo-Norman Families*, 77. In 1204–5 Tiffany, widow of Roger de Pavilly, was plaintiff for her dower in Hillington, Norf., her son Thomas, who had adhered to the king of France, being vouched to warranty (*CRR* iii, 183, 259). The family held the manor of Stutton Hall, in Stutton, and in 1275 a Roger de Pavilly claimed free warren there. In 1311 the manor passed by fine to the Visdelou family (Copinger, *Manors* vi, 98; Rye, *Fines*, 64, nos 126, 135; 126, no. 41). For the grant by William of Bramford to the priory of the homage and service of Thomas Lochon, see no. 121.

63. Notification by Hubert le Sponere of [East] Bergholt that he had conceded, granted and by this charter confirmed to God and St Mary of Dodnash and the canons there serving God, for the salvation of his soul and those of his parents, an annual rent of 2d to be received in equal instalments at Easter and Michaelmas from a parcel of arable land called 'Barunnislond' lying in the fields of Bergholt between the land of Warin of 'Ayescryb' to the west and that of Alan of 'Ayescryb' to the east, abutting on the common road from Bergholt to Brantham and at the other headland on the land of Hamo le Reve, to have and to hold to the canons and to all their successors. Warranty is granted against all persons in perpetuity. Sealed in testimony.

Hiis testibus: Nicholao de Launey, Roberto de Launey, Ricardo de Bercholt, Ada de Lodebrock, Stephano Hylte, Iordano Skyleman, Theobaldo de Redislond, Hugone Schad et aliis.   11 June 1257.

Cartulary no. 103; approx. 172 × 104+ mm; endorsed: Hubertus le Sponer', xvii.

64. Final concord made in the *curia regis* at Ipswich on 1 December 1286 before Matthew of Rochester, Walter of Hopton, Richard of Boyland, Robert Fulks, Mr Thomas of Siddington and Walter Stirchley, justices itinerant, between Prior Ralph, plaintiff, and John de la Mare, defendant, represented by William Gubyoun, relating to the plea that the prior holds thirty-nine acres with appurtenances in [East] Bergholt by the service of 6s 8½d *per annum* for all services, customs and demands, but that John has distrained the prior to render suit at his court of [East] Bergholt every three weeks, against the tenor of the prior's charters. John has remitted and quitclaimed to the prior and his successors and the church of Dodnash all right and claim to demand suit of court every three weeks for this tenement, and the prior has received John and his heirs into all [spiritual] benefits and prayers of the house forever.

PRO, CP 25/1/215/38/29; approx. 262 × 148 mm, indented at upper margin.

This is the rent agreed with Roger de Akeni, c. 1228 (60). In 1279 the manor later known as 'Spencer's' was held by John de Akeni (*HR* ii, 189), but by 1286 it was held by John de la Mare (Copinger, *Manors* vi, 19).

65. At the court of the Prior of the Hospital of St John of Jerusalem in England the prior conceded, *extra seisinam suam*, to the prior and convent of Dodnash (*Dodenessh*) and their successors three acres of land with appurtenances in East Bergholt (*Estbergholt*) which Alan le Buk, while he lived, held of him by homage, fealty, suit of court and an annual rent of 5¾d, and which after Alan's death reverted to the Prior of the Hospital by escheat, to be held by them and their successors for a term of one hundred years, rendering annually to the Prior of the

Hospital the foresaid service, that is, suit of court and the said rent. Thursday 7 January 1350.

Helmingham, T/Hel/98/22 (A2/144); copy of court roll; approx. 265 × 120 mm

Henry I had given four librates of the land which he retained in his own hand after his grant to Roger de Tosny (see above, p. 7) to Peter de Liscamp, and Peter granted this land to the Templars (*Bk Fees*, 134), from whom it passed to the Hospitallers; it became known as the manor of 'Commandry's' or 'St John's' (Copinger, *Manors* vi, 20–21).

66. Grant by Henry de Brokes of East Bergholt (*Estbergholte*) to the venerable prior Henry and the canons now and in the future serving God in the church of St Mary of Dodnash of an annual rent of 20d to be received in equal instalments at Michaelmas and Easter from all the lands and tenements in East Bergholt which he has recently purchased from John le Buk' and Alexander Vivien. If at any term the rent shall be in arrears, they may distrain upon these lands and tenements, or any part thereof, into whosesoever hands they may have come, and may remove and retain those things restrained until full satisfaction is made for arrears, and to this he pledges himself, his lands and tenements, his heirs and executors and all his goods.
Testibus: Iohanne le Spenser, Iohanne Tofts, Willelmo Atheʒe, Willelmo Marigon, Ricardo Ade et aliis.   East Bergholt, Sunday 24 July 1351.

Cartulary no. 136; approx. 270 × 95 mm; descriptive endorsement.

67. Grant in perpetuity by Richard Ade of East Bergholt (*Eastbergholt*) to the venerable lord Prior Henry and the canons of an annual rent of 28d, to be received in equal instalments at the usual terms, that is, Michaelmas, the feast of St Andrew, Easter and the Nativity of St John the Baptist, from all his lands and tenements in East Bergholt, which William le Buk purchased from John le Catour and which lie between the grantor's house and his land in the same vill. If at any term the rent is in arrears, they and their successors may distrain upon the said lands and tenements or any part of them, into whosesoever hands they may have come, and may remove and retain those things distrained until full satisfaction is made, and to this he pledges himself, his heirs and executors and all his goods. Sealed in testimony.
Testibus: Iohanne le Spenser, Iohanne Tofts, Willelmo at Hege, Willelmo Marigon, Henrico del Brok et aliis.   East Bergholt, Sunday 31 July 1351

Helmingham, T/Hel/98/21 (A2/144); approx. 257 × 110 + 15 mm; endorsed: Ric' Ade, xxiiii; parchment tag, fragment of vessica shaped seal, natural wax varnished brown, device indecipherable.

68. Quitclaim by John, son and heir of John le Buk, of [East] Bergholt to the canons, for the salvation of himself and his father and mother, of all right and

claim which he had, or in any way might have, in the land called 'Adislond', which William le Bouk purchased from John le Catour, which lies lengthwise next to the land of Richard Adi of Bergholt, so that neither he, his heirs nor anyone in their name may henceforth claim any right therein. Warranty is granted against all persons in perpetuity.

Hiis testibus: Iohanne le Spenser, Simone David, Iohanne Lodebrok, Willelmo Marigon, Ricarda Ad' et aliis.   [East] Bergholt, 23 May 1352

> Ipswich, SRO, HD 1538/204/5; approx. 290 × 78 mm; tongue for sealing torn away.

69. Grant by William Marigon of [East] Bergholt (*Bergholte*) to Prior Roger and the canons of a messuage and seven acres of land and pasture, be there more or less, which he holds of the said prior and canons in the vill of Bergholt, to have and to hold with all appurtenances of the capital lords of the fee by the due and legally accustomed services. Warranty is granted against all persons in perpetuity. Sealed in testimony.

Hiis testibus: Rogero de Wlferston, Waltero Cosyn, Willelmo Haucoun, Willelmo fabro, Ricardo Wynne et aliis.   [East] Bergholt, Thursday 30 September 1372

> Cartulary no. 147; approx. 260 × 84+ mm; descriptive endorsement; seal (not illustrated), round, approx. 22 mm, greenish-black wax, device very faint, probably star.

> William Marigon was among those licensed on 12 July 1366 to alienate lands to the priory (155). On 25 April 1373 the canons leased to him at farm the land which they recently had by his gift (182), and on 30 April 1375 granted a further lease to him of meadow in Capel St Mary (190).

BRAISEWORTH

70. Grant in pure and perpetual alms by Hubert of Braiseworth to the canons, made out of devotion and for the salvation of himself, Clarice his wife, his father and all his ancestors, of an annual rent of 6d from the land held of his fee by William the priest, which was formerly the messuage of Josce son of Hubert, priest, to be received from William, his assigns or from whoever holds the land, in two instalments each year. If payment is not made at any term, the canons may distrain upon the land until payment is rendered in full.

[Early to mid thirteenth century]

> Ipswich, SRO, q s 271 (Fitch's *Monasticon*), vol. ii, at p. 167; approx. 131 × 92 mm, no turn-up; endorsed: Briseworf, xiiii; tag and seal missing.

Omnibus Cristi fidelibus presentibus et futuris hoc scriptum visuris Hubertus de Brisewrthe salutem. Noverit universitas vestra me pie devotionis intuitu et pro salute anime mee et Claricie uxoris mee et pro salute anime patris mei et omnium antecessorum meorum concessisse, dedisse et hac carta mea confirmasse Deo et ecclesie beate Marie de Dodenes et priori et canonicis ibidem Deo servientibus et servituris sex denarios de redditu annuos de terra illa quam Willelmus sacerdos tenet de me de feodo meo in villa de Brisewrthe, que iam fuit mesagium Goscii filii Huberti sacerdotis, habendos et percipiendos de predicto Willelmo et eius assignatis vel de illis qui predictam [terram] tenebunt, ad duos terminos, ad festum sancti Michaelis .iii. denarios et ad Pascha .iii. denarios, in puram et perpetuam elemosinam.[a] Et si forte contingat, quod absit, quod qui predictam terram tenent non solverint predictum redditum ad terminos prenominatos, concedo pro me et heredibus meis quod sepedicti canonici sine alicuius contradictione distringant prenominatam terram ad plenariam solutionem. Et ut hec mea concessio et donatio et huius carte mee confirmatio inconcusse et stabiles permaneant, huic scripto sigillum meum apposui in testimonium. His testibus: Huberto Gernegan, Galfrido de Badel', Huberto de Randestun, Ada de Brom capellano, Matheo de Gerardvill, Michaele de Brisewrth, Willelmo de Cranlee, Roberto de Cranle, Willelmo de Bosvill', Willelmo de la More, Philippo de Bunege et aliis.

[a] MS: elemosinam perpetuam

For the Braiseworth family, see *Eye Cartulary* ii, 62–3. The family held the manors of Cotton and Braiseworth as mesne tenants of the Sackville family, who themselves held one knight's fee of the honour of Eye, including manors at Bures and Bergholt. The witness of nos 5–6 is Hubert I, who first occurs 1168 × 1179, and died probably in 1194–95. The charter above is of Hubert II, who occurs from 1209 to *c.* 1240. Most of the witnesses are tenants of the honour of Eye; Adam of Brome occurs *c.* 1230, Geoffrey of Badley c. 1230–40 (*Eye Cartulary* i, nos 180, 182). The gift of this isolated property is probably explained by the fact that Hubert of Braiseworth held land of Morell's fee of Maurice of Dodnash in the vill of Bentley, which he subsequently granted to Maurice's brother Thomas (Bodl. Suffolk ch. 195 (c)).

BRANTHAM

71. Grant in pure and perpetual alms by Eustace of Brantham to the canons, for the souls of his father and mother and his ancestors, of a salt-house in Brantham held by William son of Thedrich, his man.

[Late twelfth – early thirteenth century]

Cartulary no. 16; approx. 210 × 63+ mm; endorsed: Eustacius de Braham, de salina et de commune marisci, ii.

Eustachius de Brahamia omnibus hominibus suis et amicis, Francis et Anglicis, presentibus et futuris, salutem. Noveritis me dedisse et concessisse et hac presenti carta mea confirmasse Deo et ecclesie beate Marie de Dodenes et canonicis ibidem Deo servientibus unam salinam in Braham quam Willelmus filius Thedric3 homo meus tenuit, in puram et perpetuam elemosinam pro anima patris mei et matris mee et antecessorum meorum. His testibus: domino Rogero comite Norfolch, Hugone filio eius, Godefrido de Bellomonte, Thoma de Braham, Hugone filio Alani, Hugone filio Osberti, Isebardo filio eius, Hugone de Braham, Luca et

Ricardo fratribus eius, Willelmo clerico de Tating(eston), Waltero fratre eius, Eadwardo de Alneto, David de Bircholt, Girardo de Lothebroc, Mauricio de Doden(es), Thoma fratre eius et multis aliis.

Eustace of Brantham occurs from 1165 (*PR 14 Henry II*, 28) to 1202 (*CRR* ii, 136; *PBKJ* ii, no. 939); he was a prominent Bigod tenant, and his son Roger served as the earl's steward in the early thirteenth century (see *Sibton Cartularies* iii, no. 741n). Geoffrey archdn of Suffolk became archdn shortly after Nov. 1188, last occurs in 1206 and had been succeeded by 1214 (*Fasti* ii, 67–68).

For the location of the saltings at Brantham, see S. Podd, *Earthwork Reconnaissance in Suffolk: Rapid Identification Survey*, Archaeological Section, Suffolk County Council, 1995, map 5A.

72. Grant in pure and perpetual alms by Eustace of Brantham to the canons, out of the promptings of devotion for his salvation and that of his father, mother and ancestors, of a salt-house in Brantham held by William son of Thedrich, his man, with common rights in the marsh.   [Late twelfth – early thirteenth century]

Cartulary no. 15; approx. 202 × 75+ mm; endorsed: Heustachius de Braham.

Eustachius de Brahamia omnibus hominibus et amicis suis Francis et Anglicis, presentibus et futuris, salutem. Noveritis me bone devotionis intuitu dedisse et franchiasse et hac presenti carta mea confirmasse Deo et ecclesie beate Marie de Dodenes et canonicis ibidem Deo servientibus unam salinam in Braham quam Willelmus filius Tedriʒ homo meus tenuit, cum communione communis marascii, in puram et perpetuam elemosinam pro salute anime mee et pro animabus patris et matris mee et antecessorum meorum. Hiis testibus: domino Rogero comite Norfolch, Hugone filio eius, Galfrido archidiacono, Alano decano de Braham, Roberto capellano de Frameling(ham), Godfrido de Bellomonte, Thoma de Braham, Hugone filio Alani, Hugone filio Osberti, Hugone filio Eustachii de Braham, Luca et Ricardo fratribus eius, Waltero clerico de Tatingest(on), David de Birholt, Girardo de Lodebroc, Mauricio de Framesd(en) et multis aliis.

See no. 71.

73. Quitclaim by Roger Pycston of Brantham (*Braham*) to Prior Ralph and the canons of all right and claim which he had or in any way might have in a salt-house (*salina*) with commons (*communitate*) of a marsh and all other appurtenances in Brantham, and in a parcel of arable land in the same vill, lying lengthwise between the land of John le Sezere and that of Peter Monjoye, and abutting at one headland on the stream running from 'Cotebrig' to the north and at the other on 'Sinothemere' to the south, which salt-house and land his father had once held of the prior and canons, so that neither he, his heirs nor anyone in his name may henceforth make any demand or claim therein for any reason. Sealed in testimony.
Testibus: Willelmo Baldewyne, Willelmo de Braham, Ricardo Hilte, Willelmo de Bruar' tunc ballivo, Roberto Warin, Ricardo de Boyton et aliis.

Dodnash, 1 May 1297

Cartulary no. 113; approx. 190 × 78 mm; endorsed: xvii.

74. Grant in pure and perpetual alms by Hugh son of Alan of Brantham to the canons, for the salvation of his soul and those of his parents and ancestors, of all his land of 'Chimecroft' which lies between the land of Thedrich Lutehare and that of Hugh son of Alan of Stutton, with appurtenances in water, pastures and alder-groves, also of all his meadow in 'Clakesmedwe' and all his meadow which lies by the land of Clarembald de Alneo at 'Garmingeho'. Warranty is granted against all men.   [Late twelfth – early thirteenth century]

> A1 = Cartulary no. 13; approx. 236 × 76 + 16 mm; endorsed: Hugo filius Alani de Braham, xii; carta Hugonis de Braham.
>
> A2 = Helmingham, T/Hel/98/7 (A2/18); approx. 256 × 65 + 17 mm; endorsed: Hugo filius Alani; parchment tag, seal missing.

Hugo filius Alani de Braham omnibus hominibus et amicis suis tam presentibus quam futuris salutem. Sciatis me dedisse et hac presenti carta mea confirmasse Deo et beate Marie de Dodenes et priori et canonicis ibidem Deo servientibus totam terram meam de Chimecroft que iacet inter terram Thedrici Lutehare de Braham et inter terram Hugonis filii Alani de Stuttune cum pertinentiis, in aquis, in pascuis et in alnetis et in*ᵃ* omnibus, et totum pratum meum quod iacet in Clakesmedwe, et totum pratum meum quod iacet iuxta pratum domini Clerembaldi de Alneo apud Garmingeho, in puram et perpetuam elemosinam pro salute anime mee et animarum patris et matris mee et antecessorum meorum. Et ego predictus Hugo et heredes mei warantizabimus predictam terram predictis canonicis contra omnes homines. Hiis testibus: domino Rogero comite Nor(folchie),*ᵇ* Hugone filio eius, Godefrido de Belmunt, Eustachio de Braham, Thoma filio eius et Ricardo et Eustachio et Hugone filiis eius, Hamone Petit, Roberto filio eius,*ᶜ* Eadwardo de Alneto,*ᵈ* Willelmo clerico de Tatinkestun', Waltero fratre eius, Gerardo de Lode-broch, Mauricio de Framesd(en) et multis aliis.

> *ᵃ* et in *omitted* A2   *ᵇ* Bigoth A2   *ᶜ*et Hamone Petit et Roberto filio eius A2
> *ᵈ* A1 *ends here with* et multis aliis.
>
> For Eustace of Brantham, see no. 71; his attestation suggests a date before, or not long after, 1200.

75. Confirmation by Hubert de Montchesney to the canons in pure and perpetual alms, for his salvation and that of his father and mother and his ancestors, of the grant made by Hugh son of Alan of Brantham of all his land in 'Chimecroft', all his meadow in 'Clakesmedwe' and all his meadow next to that of Clarembald of the Aldergrove at 'Garmingeho', which is of his fee, as detailed in Hugh's charter [no. 74] which they have.   [Late twelfth – early thirteenth century]

> Cartulary no. 14; approx. 175 × 75+ mm; endorsed: Hub' de Monachanesi xii.

Universis Cristi fidelibus presentibus et futuris Hubertus de Montchensia salutem. Noveritis me concessisse et ratum habuisse et hac presenti carta confirmasse Deo et ecclesie beate Marie de Dodenes et canonicis ibidem Deo servientibus donationem quam Hugo filius Alani de Braham fecit eisdem canonicis de tota terra sua in Chimecroft et de toto prato quod iacet in Clakesmedwe et de toto prato quod iacet iuxta pratum*ᵃ* Clerenbaldi de Alneo apud Garmingeho quod est de feodo meo, cum onmibus pertinentiis, sicut in carta ipsius Hugonis predicti quam ab eo possident continetur, in puram et perpetuam elemosinam pro salute anime mee et animarum patris et matris mee et antecessorum meorum. Hiis testibus: domino Rogero Bigot comite de Norf(olchia), Hugone filio eius, Galfrido archidiacono Suffol(chie), Alano decano, Eustachio de Braham, Mil(on)e Lenveise, Godefrido de Bellomonte, Willelmo Testepin de Hintlesham, Girardo de Ve, Ada*ᵇ* Gernun, Willelmo Spontemalveis, Iohanne filio Reginaldi, Roberto de Monchensia, Mauricio de Framesd(en), Simone de Beri.

ᵃ MS: pratum iuxta   *ᵇ* MS: Ade

For Hubert, son and heir of Stephen de Montchesney, see *GEC* ix, 415. He was a knight before Easter 1205 (*CRR* iii, 284). He was active in opposition to King John, but his lands in Norfolk, Suffolk and Essex were restored to him in October 1217 (*Rot. Litt. Claus.* i, 332, 375). He occurs as a litigant to 1220, and was certainly dead by 1229, when he had been succeeded by William I de Montchesney. The attestation of Geoffrey archdn of Suffolk and Eustace of Brantham, and of Alan the dean, who had been present at the dedication (4), suggests a date not later than the earliest years of the thirteenth century.

76. Quitclaim by Richard son of Hugh son of Alan to the prior and canons of all right and claim in the land of 'Chimecroft' with two parcels of meadow lying in the meadows of 'Stamford' and 'Clakesmede', with the homage and service of William son of William of Kembroke, Seman of the Apple-orchard, Roger Vescunte the son of Seman and the heirs of Roger Hoeles, and with other appurtenances. For this quitclaim the canons have paid 30s.

[Early to mid thirteenth century]

Cartulary no. 78; approx. 165 × 76 + 8 mm; endorsed: Ricardi filii Hugoni de Brah', xii.

Sciant presentes et futuri quod ego Richardus filius Hugonis filii Alani remisi et quietum clamavi inperpetuum pro me et heredibus meis priori de Dodenes et canonicis presentibus et futuris totum ius et clamium quod habui vel habere potui in terra de Chimecroft cum duabus peciis prati iacentibus in prato de Stamford et Clakesmede et cum homagiis et servitiis Willelmi filii Willelmi de Kenebroch et Semanni de Pomario et Rogeri Vescunte filii Semanni et heredum Rogeri Hoeles et aliis pertinentiis. Ut autem ista remissio et quieta clamatio perpetuam optineat firmitatem, huic scripto sigillum meum apposui. Pro hac autem remissione et quieta clamatione dederunt michi predicti prior et canonici triginta solidos sterlingorum. Hiis t(estibus): Willelmo filio Roberti de Reindun', Mauricio de Dodenes et Hugone filio eius, Thoma de Dodenes et Hugone filio eius, Ricardo filio Roberti, Thoma filio Hugonis de Benetlee, Gerardo de Andredest', Willelmo filio Willelmi de Kenebroch, Semanno de Pomario, Rogero filio Semanni Viscunte, Simone Cole et aliis.

William son of William of Kembroke occurs in 1224–25 (17), and Maurice and
Thomas of Dodnash from 1224–26 (16–17, 35).

77. Grant in pure and perpetual alms by William son of Helte to the canons, for
the salvation of his soul and those of his father, mother and ancestors, of that part
of his land at Brantham above 'Aldefeld', which abuts on the castle of Hamo
Petit. [Early thirteenth century]

> Cartulary no. 30; approx. 218 × 72 mm; endorsed: Willelm' Helte, xvi; seal,
> round, approx. 40 mm, natural wax varnished brown, five-stemmed plant with
> trefoil terminals, + SIGILL WILLELMI HELTE DE BRAHAM.

Omnibus hominibus et amicis suis tam presentibus quam futuris Willelmus filius
Helte de Braham salutem. Noveritis me bone devotionis intuitu dedisse et franchiasse et hac carta mea confirmasse Deo et beate Marie de Dodenes et canonicis
ibidem Deo servientibus, pro salute anime mee et pro anima patris mei et matris
mee et antecessorum meorum, illam partem terre mee in Braham super Aldefeld
que abutat castello Hamonis Petit in puram et perpetuam elemosinam. Et ut hec
donatio mea et confirmatio firma et stabilis permaneat, sigilli mei appositione
corroboravi. T(estibus): Alano decano de Braham, Willelmo capellano suo,
Eustachio de Braham, Rogero filio eius, Luca et Hugone fratribus suis, Hugone
filio Alani, Ricardo filio eius, Willelmo de Bromford, Ysebardo filio Hugonis de
Braham, Mauricio de Doden(es), Thoma fratre eius et multis aliis.

> William Helte occurs 1224–26 (17, 35); Alan dean of Brantham occurs in 1188
> (4) and Eustace of Brantham last in 1202 (71n.). William of Bramford occurs
> before 1196 and probably until 1224–25 (9 and n.). A later Hamo le Petit
> claimed franchises in a curacate of land at Brantham which constituted half a
> knight's fee (*HR* ii, 177).

78. Grant in pure and perpetual alms by Hugh Maupetit to the canons, for his
salvation and that of his wife and ancestors, of the homage and service of John de
la Mare, that is, 3d *p.a.*, for the land lying between the lands of William son of
Thomas and abutting on the path leading from 'Redeslond', and the homage and
service of William Barun, that is, 2d *p.a.*, for the land lying between that of John
of 'Avesrib' and that of Constantine of 'Avesrib', with payment of scutage of ¼d
whenever scutage is levied. [Early to mid thirteenth century]

> Cartulary no. 43; approx. 135 × 102+ mm; endorsed: xi, de Hugone Maupetit de
> homagio et servitio.

Sciant presentes et futuri quod ego Hugo Maupetit concessi et dedi et hac presenti carta mea confirmavi Deo et ecclesie beate Marie de Dodenes et canonicis
ibidem Deo servientibus et servituris homagium et servitium Iohannis de la Mare
de tribus deneratis de servitio quos solebat michi reddere, scilicet ad festum
sancti Andree tres obolos et in festo sancti Iohannis Baptiste tres obolos, de terra
iacente inter terras Willelmi filii Thome et abutante super viam venientem de

Redeslond, et homagium et servitium Willelmi Barun de duobus denaratis de servitio quos solebat michi reddere, scilicet in festo sancti Andree unum denarium et in festo sancti Iohannis unum denarium, de terra iacente inter terram Iohannis de Avesrib et terram Constantini de Avesrib, cum scutagio unius oboli ad quodlibet scutagium, habenda et tenenda in puram et perpetuam elemosinam pro salute anime mee et uxoris mee et antecessorum meorum. Et ut hec mea concessio et donatio firma sit et stabilis, eam sigilli mei appositione corroboravi. His t(estibus): magistro Ricardo decano de Samford, Thoma persona de Reindun, Bartholomeo persona de Holebroch, Roberto persona de Capele, Willelmo de Tatingest'. Willelmo de Brumford milite, Willelmo de Creping', Mauricio de Dodenes et Mauricio nepote eius et aliis.

> Thomas, parson of Raydon, occurs in 1223–24 (16), and Maurice of Dodnash 1224–26 (17, 35). This is almost certainly an earlier John de la Mare than the litigant of no. 64, who was himself dead by 1 December 1298 and was succeeded by yet another John (Helmingham, T/Hel/49/20).

79. Grant in pure and perpetual alms by John de Mara to the canons, made by the promptings of charity and for the salvation of himself, Alice his wife, Sinoth and Aldith and all his ancestors, of all his messuage in the croft of 'Ismere' with the flax-ground and three selions outside the messuage, and also half an acre of 'Withiaker' and half an acre above 'Lunedune', and all his part of the assart at 'Lunedune', and the headland at 'Ismere' at the head of the land of Hugh Pas, and all his part of 'Linch', and all the marsh pertaining to the messuage of 'Ismere'. The canons have granted to them that at their deaths they shall have all due to brethren of the house.   [Early to mid thirteenth century]

> Cartulary no. 42; approx. 165 × 95+ mm; endorsed: iii, Braham Ysmer; carta Iohannis de Mara de Braham, quod dominus I. le Pas tenet.

Omnibus sancte matris ecclesie filiis ad quos presens scriptum pervenerit Iohannes de Mara salutem in Domino. Sciatis me concessisse, dedisse et hac carta mea confirmasse mesagium meum in crufta de Ismere cum linario et cum tribus seilinis extra mesagium, et dimidiam acram de Withiaker et dimidiam acram super Lunedune et totam partem meam assarti de Lunedune et forarium apud Ismere ad capud terre Hugonis Pas et totam partem meam de Linch et totum mariscum pertinens ad predictum mesagium de Ismere cum pertinentiis, Deo et ecclesie beate Marie de Dodenes et canonicis ibidem Deo servientibus et servituris intuitu pietatis et pro salute anime mee et Alicie uxoris mee et Sinoth et Aldith et omnium antecessorum meorum in puram et perpetuam elemosinam. Predictus autem prior et canonici concesserunt nobis in die obitus nostri fratribus suis debita. Ego autem Iohannes et heredes mei warantizabimus prenominatis canonicis et eorum successoribus inperpetuum prenominatas terras cum pertinentiis contra omnes homines et acquietabimus et defendemus. Ego autem Iohannes in huius rei testimonium huic scripto sigillum meum apposui. His testibus: domino Ranulfo de Braham, Thoma persona de Reindune, Luca persona de Wlferestun, Willelmo persona de Holetune, Roberto de Alneto, Mauricio de Dodenes et Thoma fratre eius et Galfrido et Hugone filiis eorum, Alano filio Rogeri et Mauricio fratre eius, Rogero Iuvencel, Roberto filio Ricardi de Boitun', Ysenbardo filio Hugonis, Roberto filio Hugonis, Roberto filio Willelmi, Osberto de Wogate, Edwardo Davi, Warino Testard et aliis.

John de Mara occurs 1224–26 (17, 35); Ranulf of Brantham occurs 1227–30 (Rye, *Fines*, 29 no. 118; 30 n. 4). Five witnesses occur in 1226 (35). For the tenure of John le Passh, chaplain, see no. 185.

80. Grant in pure and perpetual alms by John de Mara to the canons, for his salvation and that of his ancestors and successors, of all the homage and service which John Godsuein used to render him for an acre of land in Brantham lying between the land of Alan son of Roger and that of John Henry, that is 5d *p.a.* Warranty is granted. [Early to mid thirteenth century]

Cartulary no. 51; approx. 165 × 55+ mm; endorsed: iii; seal, round, approx. 42 mm, natural wax varnished brown, seeded fleur-de-lys, + SIGILL IOHANNIS DE. . .

Sciant presentes et futuri quod ego Iohannes de Mara concessi et dedi et hac carta mea confirmavi priori et canonicis de Dodenes presentibus et futuris homagium et totum servitium quod Iohannes Godswein solebat vel debebat michi facere de una acra terre in villa de Braham iacente de longo in longum inter terram Alani filii Rogeri et terram Iohannis Henrici, scilicet quinque denarios de redditu annuos, ad festum sancti Michaelis duos d. et obolum et ad Pascha duos d. et obolum, percipiendos de predicto Iohanne et heredibus eius inperpetuum et habendos illis in puram et perpetuam elemosinam et ab omni seculari servitio quietam, pro salute anime mee et animarum antecessorum meorum et successorum. Ego autem Iohannes et heredes mei wararantizabimus prenominatis canonicis predictum redditum contra omnes homines. Ego autem Iohannes in testimonium huic scripto sigillum meum apposui. His t(estibus): Alano filio Rogeri et Mauricio fratre eius, Ysenbardo filio Hugonis, Hugone Maupetit, Osberto de Wogate, Hugone Plumer, Ricardo le King, Ricardo Martini, Martino Sant et aliis.

For John de Mara, see no. 79. Isembard son of Hugh occurs 1224–25 (17).

81. Quitclaim by Alice, widow of John Godswein, to the prior and canons and their successors and to Nicholas del Broc of Brantham and his heirs of all right and claim to an annual rent of 2s which Nicholas used to pay to her late husband, and which he gave in pure and perpetual alms to the canons, as his charter which they have bears witness. [Early to mid thirteenth century]

Cartulary no. 48; approx. 165 × 58+ mm; endorsed: xviii.

Sciant presentes et futuri quod ego Alicia quondam uxor Iohannis Godswein in viduitate mea concessi, remisi et omnino inperpetuum quiete clamavi priori et canonicis de Dodenes et successoribus eorum et Nicholao del Broc de Braham et heredibus suis totum ius et clamium quod habui et habere potui in duorum solidorum redditu quos dictus Nicholaus solebat reddere viro meo Iohanni God-swein, quod scilicet redditum dictus Iohannes Godswein quondam vir meus dictis canonicis in puram et perpetuam elemosinam dedit et sua carta confirmavit, sicut carta dicti Iohannis quam ipsi canonici habent de eo testatur. Ut autem hec mea concessio, remissio et quiete clamatio firma et stabilis inperpetuum permaneat tam dictis priori et canonicis atque successoribus eorum quam dicto Nicholao et heredibus suis, huic scripto sigillum meum apposui. Hiis testibus: domino Ricardo de Braham, domino Ermegout de Wenham, Thoma de Dodenes, Thoma God(s)wein, Alano de Braham, Iohanne Cobelot, Roberto de Boit(un), Ricardo filio eius, Willelmo de Achowt, Ricardo Giffard tunc ballivo de Sanford', Galfrido de Dodenes, Mauricio de Dodenes et multis aliis.

> Robert of Boyton occurs from 1223–24 (16) to 1243–44 (Rye, *Fines*, 47 no. 16); Richard of Brantham in 1219–20 (ibid., 21 no. 97); Thomas and Maurice of Dodnash in 1224–26 (16–17, 35), and Ermeiot of Wenham in 1246 (BL Add. ch. 9485).

82. Grant in pure and perpetual alms by Ranulf of Brantham to the canons, for his salvation and that of his ancestors, of the liberty, insofar as it is his right, of crossing his water between 'Stuttetflet' and Cattawade, that is, of lading and un-lading their own boats and others employed for their use, without payment of any toll or due. [Early to mid thirteenth century]

> Cartulary no. 52; approx. 128 × 61+ mm; endorsed: Carta Ranulfi de Braham de pas' et car'.

Omnibus sancte matris ecclesie filiis ad quos presens scriptum pervenerit Ranulfus de Braham salutem. Sciatis me concessisse et dedisse et hac presenti carta mea confirmasse, pro salute anime mee et antecessorum meorum, Deo et ecclesie beate Marie de Dodenes et canonicis ibidem [Deo] servientibus et servituris libertatam per totam aquam meam que est inter Stuttetflet and Katewade quantum mei iuris est transeundi, videlicet et honerandi et exhonerandi in propriis navibus suis et etiam alienis navibus in eorum propriis usibus laborantibus, sine omni passagio, pacagio et theloneo, in puram et perpetuam elemosinam. Et ut hec mea concessio et donatio et huius carte mee confirmatio perpetuam optineant firmitatem, eas presenti scripto et sigilli mei appositione munivi. His t(estibus): Hamone Lenveise, Iohanne Lenveise, Michaele de Blaveni, Iacobo Lenveise, Mauricio de Dodenes, Rogero filio Hugonis, Rogero Iuvencel, Galfrido de Capele clerico, Iohanne de Mara et multis aliis.

> Ranulf of Brantham (or Braham) occurs 1227–30 (Rye, *Fines*, 29 no. 118, 30 no. 4). Hamo Lenveise first occurs in 1210 and was dead by Easter 1232 (*Sibton Cartularies* ii, no. 390n.; *CRR* xiv, nos. 1212, 2447). The manor of Braham Hall is adjacent to Cattawade.

83. Grant in perpetuity by Aubrey of Brantham, rector of Wacton, to the canons, made by the promptings of charity, of an annual rent of 18d in Brantham which

Martin Lenfant and Emma his wife sold to him, to be received from the heir of
John de Viggeber', with the homage and relief of John's heirs, and whatever
Aubrey had or might have there.   [Mid thirteenth century]

> Cartulary no. 85; approx. 170 × 61 + 7 mm; endorsed: Albricus de Braham rec-
> tor omnium sanctorum.

Omnibus sancte matris ecclesie filiis hoc presens scriptum visuris vel audituris
Albricus de Braham rector ecclesie omnium sanctorum de Waketun salutem in
Domino. Noverit universitas vestra me caritatis intuitu concessisse et dedisse et
hac presenti carta mea confirmasse Deo et ecclesie beate Marie de Dodenes et
canonicis ibidem presentibus et futuris decem et octo denarios annui redditus
quos Martinus Lenfant et Emma uxor sua michi vendiderunt in villa de Braham,
percipiendos de herede Iohannis de Viggeber' cum homagio et relevio heredum
predicti Iohannis, et quicquid ibidem habui vel habere potui sine aliquo retenemento inperpetuum. Et ut hec mea donatio et concessio rata sit et perpetua, huic
scripto sigillum meum apposui. Hiis testibus: domino Ricardo de Braham, Teho-
baldo de Lestun', Iuliano de Braham, Petro de Hand', Willelmo dispensatore,
Iohanne Gotsuueyn, Willemo filio Bartholomei de Holebroc et aliis.

> Sir Richard of Brantham occurs from 1219–20 (Rye, *Fines*, 21 no. 97) to 1250
> (25), when William *dispensator* also occurs. John Godswein may be the son of
> the deceased man of the same name of no. 81.

84. Grant in free and perpetual alms by Osbert son of John Henry to the canons
of the homage and service of Hugh Pichot, his brother, with all the tenement he
holds in Brantham, that is, an annual rent of 4d with appurtenances, free from all
secular service. For this grant the canons have paid 4s. Warranty is granted.
                                                       [Probably mid thirteenth century]

> Cartulary no. 97; approx. 186 × 112 mm; endorsed: Braham, vi; carta Osberti
> filii Iohannis Henri de tenemento Hugonis Pichot; Willelmus Mage tenet iunior
> et Matildis Marin; fragment of seal, round, approx. 28 mm, green wax, fleur-de-
> lys, S. OSBERT. . .

Sciant presentes et futuri quod ego Osbertus filius Iohannis Henry concessi, dedi
et hac presenti carta mea confirmavi in liberam et perpetuam elemosinam Deo et
ecclesie sancte Marie de Dodenes et canonicis ibidem Deo servientibus et inperpetuum servituris homagium et servitium Hugonis Pichot fratris mei cum toto
tenemento suo quod de me tenuit in villa de Braham, scilicet annuum redditum
quatuor denariorum cum pertinentiis ad quatuor anni terminos, scilicet ad nativitatem sancti Iohannis Baptiste unum denarium, ad festum sancti Michaelis unum
denarium, ad festum sancti Andree unum denarium et ad Pascha unum denarium,
tenendum et habendum dictis canonicis et successoribus suis vel quibuscumque
eorum assignatis inperpetuum, libere, quiete et hereditarie absque omni seculari
servitio michi vel heredibus meis vel alicui inde faciendo. Pro hac autem concessione, donatione et presentis carte mee confirmatione dederunt michi predicti
prior et canonici de Doden' quatuor solidos. Et ego predictus Osbertus et heredes

mei warantizabimus, acquietabimus et defendemus homagium et servitium predicti Hugonis et heredum suorum cum toto tenemento suo et cum predictis quatuor denariis annui redditus cum pertinentiis predictis priori et canonicis et
successoribus suis contra omnes tam Iudeos quam Cristianos inperpetuum. Hiis
testibus: Galfrido filio Thome de Doden', Iohanne Cobelot, Ricardo Ysenbawd,
Willelmo Aderm, Mauricio filio Rogeri, Willelmo de Howtun, Willelmo Maupetit,
Rogero Pas, Iurdano filio Henri(*sic*), Ricardo de Boitun, Galfrido de la Mare,
Ricardo de Bruar' et aliis.

> Richard of Boyton occurs 1233–34 (Rye, *Fines*, 32 no. 47); Jordan son of Henry
> occurs 1250 and 1252 × 57 (25, 42) and Geoffrey de la Mare 1252 × 57 (25).

85. Grant in pure and perpetual alms by John Attebroc of Brantham (*Braham*) to
the canons of a parcel of land in Brantham, lying lengthwise between the land of
Robert le Knettere and that of Richard the clerk, abutting to the east on the way
leading from the house of Peter Lays to Brantham church and to the west on the
land of Roger Munjoye and that of Robert of Stratford (? *Stratforde*, reading uncertain), to be held in fee and heredity. Warranty is granted against all persons in
perpetuity.
Hiis testibus: domino Hugone de Talemache, domino Iohanne de Wenham,
Willelmo de Creppinge, Andrea Helte, Radulfo de Braham, Radulfo clerico,
Willelmo de Bruar', Roberto le Pas, Willelmo de Houtone*ᵃ* et aliis.
[Late thirteenth century, probably 1270s–1280s]

> *ᵃ* Last witness repeated.

> Cartulary no. 100; approx. 215 × 78+ mm; endorsed: iiii, carta Ade Attbrok de
> Braham; Bartholomeus Moptyt tenet pro xvi d.

> Ralph of Brantham and William of Holton occur in 1276 (48), Ralph the clerk
> from 1276–84 (27, 48, 206) and William de Bruario in 1284 (206); the other wit-
> nesses attest late thirteenth-century charters.

86. Grant in pure and perpetual alms by Adam son of John Attebroke of Brantham (*Braham*) to the prior and canons of a parcel of land in Brantham, lying between the land of John le Sethere and that of Peter Munjoye, of which one
headland to the north abuts on the stream running from 'Cotesbregge' towards the
marsh, and the other to the south on 'Sinothemere', to be held in fee. Warranty is
granted in perpetuity.
Hiis testibus: domino Hugone Talemach', domino Iohanne de Wenham, Willelmo de Crepingge, Andrea Hylte, Radulfo de Braham, Radulfo de Benetleye,
Willelmo de la Bruere, Roberto le Pas, Willelmo le Maupetit, Willelmo de Houton
et aliis.
[Late thirteenth century, probably 1270s–1280s]

> Cartulary no. 102; approx. 225 × 102+ mm; endorsed: Carta Ade filii Iohannis
> Attbrok de Braham; W. Maggs senior et W. Brente; seal, vessica, approx. 45 × 31
> mm, natural wax, radiating device of eight petals, S. ADEME. . . BROC.

CAPEL ST MARY

87. Grant by Robert son of Richard of Boyton to the canons, in pure and perpetual alms, out of piety and devotion and for the souls of himself, his father and mother and all his ancestors, of all the pasture of his fee which lies below 'Hulneia', with the aldergrove and with the embankment with which it is ringed. Warranty is granted. [Early thirteenth century]

> Cartulary no. 38; approx. 225 × 60 mm; endorsed: Roberti de Boitune, i; seal, round, approx. 39 mm, brown wax, cockerel walking to right, + SIGILL. ROBERTI FILII RICARDI.

Universis sancte matris ecclesie filiis ad quos presens scriptum pervenerit Robertus filius Ricardi de Boitune salutem. Noverit universitas vestra me pie et bone devotionis intuitu dedisse et concessisse et hac presenti carta mea confirmasse Deo et ecclesie beate Marie de Dodenes et canonicis ibidem Deo famulantibus totam pasturam que est de feudo meo infra Hulneiam cum alneto et cum fossato sicut fossatum eam cingit, in puram et perpetuam elemosinam pro salute anime mee et animabus patris et matris mee et omnium antecessorum meorum. Ego vero et heredes mei warantizabimus predictam elemosinam predictis canonicis contra omnes homines qui possint mori. Hiis t(estibus): Roberto decano de Gip(ewico), Alano decano de Braham, Thoma persona de Reindun', Radulfo capellano de Bircholt, Stephano capellano de Benet(elee), Willelmo clerico de Thatingest', Roberto capellano de Boitun', Ermegoth de Wenham, Willelmo de Boitun', Warino Testard, Mauricio de Dodenes, Thoma fratre eius, Rogero filio Hugonis de Braham, Ricardo fratre eius, Ricardo filio Eustachii de Braham.

> The first dated reference to Robert of Boyton is 1223–24 (16); but Robert dean of Ipswich and Alan the dean attest in 1188 (4); Thomas of Dodnash and Thomas, parson of Raydon, occur in 1223–24 (16).

88. Grant by Robert son of Richard of Boyton to the canons of four acres of land of the fee of William of Boyton in 'Michelefeld', adjoining lengthwise the land of 'Longecroft' and abutting on 'Brunblilond', for an annual rent of 12d and payment of ½d towards scutage of 20s, and *pro rata*. Warranty is granted. The canons have paid 25s as entry fine.

[Early to mid thirteenth century, before Easter 1232]

> Cartulary no. 58; approx. 178 × 71+ mm; endorsed: Robertus de Boitune; prior et canonici de Dodenes.

Sciant presentes et futuri quod ego Robertus filius Ricardi de Boitune concessi et dedi et hac presenti carta mea confirmavi Deo et ecclesie sancte Marie de Dodenes et canonicis ibidem Deo servientibus et servituris quatuor acras terre mee de feodo Willelmi de Boitun' in Michelefeld, iacentes in longum iuxta terram de Longecroft, et abuttant super Brunblilond, habendas illis et tenendas de me et heredibus meis inperpetuum, libere et quiete et honorifice, reddendo michi et heredibus meis de servitio duodecim denarios per annum ad quatuor terminos pro omni servitio, consuetudine, exactione et demanda, scilicet ad festum sancti Michaelis .iii. d., ad festum sancti Andree .iii. d., ad Pascha .iii. d. et ad festum sancti Iohannis Baptiste .iii. d., salvo servitio domini regis ad scutagium viginti solidorum obulum, et ad plus plus et ad minus minus. Et ego et heredes mei warantizabimus prenominatis canonicis prenominatam terram contra omnes homines. Et pro ista concessione et donatione dederunt michi prenominati canonici viginti quinque solidos in gersumam. Et ego Robertus huic scripto sigillum meum apposui. His t(estibus): Hamone Lenveise, Willelmo de Brumford et Huberto fratre eius, Ermeiot de Wenham, Mauricio de Dodenes et Thoma fratre eius, Roberto le Petit, Rogero filio Hugonis et Ricardo fratre eius, Rogero Iuvencel, Ricardo Godefrei, Willelmo Helte et multis aliis.

> Robert of Boyton occurs from 1223–24 (16) to 1243–44 (Rye, *Fines*, 47 no. 16); but Hamo Lenveise, who first occurs in 1210, died between Easter 1231 and Easter 1232 (*Sibton Cartularies* ii, no. 390n.).

89. Grant by Richard son of Robert of Boyton to the prior and canons in heredity of an annual rent of 2s which they used to pay for the land which they held of himself and his father in Boyton, for which they shall henceforth render each year at Easter a pair of gloves worth ½d for all services. The canons have paid him 15s in cash. Warranty is granted.   [Mid thirteenth century, before 1253]

> Cartulary no. 86; approx. 270 × 72+ mm; endorsed: Ricardus filius Roberti de Boitune de .ii. s. redditus quieti, iiii; ii.

Sciant presentes et futuri quod ego Ricardus filius Roberti de Boytun concessi et dedi et hac presenti carta mea confirmavi priori et canonicis de Dodenes ibidem Deo et beate Marie servientibus duos solidatos annui redditus quos predictus prior et canonici predicti michi debuerunt annuatim pro terra illa quam tenuerunt quondam de predicto Roberto patre meo et de me in Boytune, habendos et tenendos de me et de heredibus meis predictis priori et canonicis et eorum successoribus libere, quiete, bene et in pace, hereditarie, reddendo inde annuatim michi et heredibus meis unum par cirotecarum pretii unius oboli in Pasca pro omnibus servitiis, consuetudinibus, exactionibus, sectis et secularibus demandis. Pro hac autem concessione, donatione et carte huius confirmatione dederunt michi predictus prior et canonici predicti quindecim solidos esterlingorum pre manibus. Et ego prenominatus Ricardus et heredes mei warantizabimus et acquietabimus ac defendemus illos supradictos duos solidatos annui redditus et predictam terram cum suis pertinentiis predictis priori et canonicis et eorum successoribus vel suis assignatis ut predictum est per servitium predictum contra omnes homines et feminas tam Iudeos quam Christianos inperpetuum. Et ut hec autem concessio, donatio et carte huius confirmatio perpetuam optineat stabilitatem, hoc scriptum presens sigilli mei appositione roboravi. Hiis testibus: domino Ricardo de Braham, domino Hugone Talemasche, domino Willelmo Talemasche militibus, Willelmo de Holebroc, Willelmo filio Bartholomei de Braham, Hugone de Dodenes, Mauricio Argent', Roberto de Capeles, Edmundo filio Galfridi de Capeles,

Willelmo filio Rogeri de Bercholt, Michaele de Frestun', Mattheo Testar et aliis multis.

Robert of Boyton last occurs 1243–44 (Rye, *Fines*, 47 no. 16). William of Holbrook, Edmund of Capel and Michael of Freston occur 1250 (25). William Tollemache was dead by 1253 (Rye, *Fines*, 55 no. 196).

90. Grant by William of Boyton to the canons in pure and perpetual alms, for his soul and those of Juliana his wife, their parents and all their ancestors, of all his part of 'Smethewdedune', that is, half of all the broom and bracken there.

[Early to mid thirteenth century]

Cartulary no. 70; approx. 134 × 55+ mm; endorsed: Willelm' de Boitune.

Omnibus sancte matris ecclesie filiis ad quos presens scriptum pervenerit Willelmus de Boitune salutem. Sciatis me concessisse et donasse et hac presenti carta mea confirmasse Deo et ecclesie sancte Marie de Dodenes et canonicis ibidem Deo servientibus et servituris totam partem meam de Smethewdedune, scilicet medietatem totius genest(eie) et totius fugere prenominate terre, tenendam et habendam in perpetuum in puram et perpetuam elemosinam pro salute anime mee et Iuliane uxoris mee et parentum nostrorum et omnium antecessorum. Et ego et heredes mei warantizabimus prenominatis canonicis prenominatam concessionem et donationem contra omnes homines. Hiis testibus: Willelmo de Brumford et Huberto fratre eius, Adam Mauveisin, Ermeiot de Wenham, Mauricio de Dodenes et Thomas fratre eius et Mauricio et Wimaro nepotibus eorum, Ricardo filio Roberti, Rogero Iuvencel, Willelmo Helte, Iohanne de la Mare et multis aliis.

William of Boyton occurs 1227–28 (Rye, *Fines*, 25 no. 39); Maurice and Thomas of Dodnash 1224–26 (16–17, 35); Roger Iuvencel, William Helte and John de la Mare also in 1224–25 and 1226 (17, 35)

91. Quitclaim by John son of Roger Bruning to the prior and canons of all right and claim in the land called 'Furlong' once held by his father, for which they shall render to Alan his brother 6d *p.a.* For this quitclaim Alan has granted to John and his heirs in perpetuity two acres of the fee of Ermeiot of Wenham.

[Early to mid thirteenth century]

Cartulary no. 41; approx. 150 × 70+ mm; endorsed: x; (later) ii.

Omnibus presens scriptum visuris et audituris Iohannes filius Rogeri Bruning salutem. Sciatis me concessisse et remisisse et quietum clamasse pro me et heredibus meis inperpetuum priori et canonicis de Dodenes omne ius et clamium quod habui vel habere potui in tota terra illa que vocatur Furlong que fuit quondam Rogeri patris mei cum omnibus pertinentiis, habendum et tenendum predictis priori et canonicis libere et quiete, reddendo inde per annum Alano fratri meo et heredibus suis sex denarios pro omnibus servitiis, consuetudinibus et demandis. Pro hac autem concessione et remissione et quieta clamatione predictus Alanus frater meus concessit michi et heredibus meis inperpetuum duas acras terre de feodo Ermeiot de Wenham. His t(estibus): Willelmo de Brumford, Ermeiot de Wenham, Willelmo de Waudingefeld, Rogero de Horshae, Mauricio et Thoma de Dodenes fratribus et Galfrido et Hugone filiis eorum, Roberto de Alneto, Rogero Iuvencel, Warino Testard, Galfrido de Capele clerico, Alano de Capele, Gileberto de Spina et Rogero fratre eius et aliis.

William of Bramford occurs from 1202 (*Fines* ii, no. 345) to 1228 (*CRR* xiii, no. 1201). William of Waldingfield was dead by 22 Aug. 1230 (*CRR* xiv, no. 990). Other witnesses occur in the 1220s (16–17, 35).

The location of this land cannot be known with certainty, but the abutment of the land of Alan of Capel in no. 92 and the attestation of William Waldingfield (cf. 97–99) suggest that Capel St Mary is the most likely vill.

92. Grant in pure and perpetual alms by Alan Bruning to the canons, for his salvation and that of his ancestors, of three acres of land in 'Furlong' with appurtenances, which were held by Roger his father and which lie between the land of Roger Iuvencel and that of Alan of Capel. Warranty is granted.

[Early to mid thirteenth century]

Cartulary no. 40; approx. 137 × 88+ mm; endorsed: Alanus Bruning in puram elemosinam, x; relaxatio redditus alterius carte.

Sciant presentes et futuri quod ego Alanus Bruning concessi et dedi et hac presenti carta mea confirmavi Deo et ecclesie beate Marie de Dodenes et priori et canonicis ibidem Deo servientibus et servituris tres acras terre in furlong cum pertinentiis que fuerunt Rogeri patris mei, iacentes inter terram Rogeri Iuvencel et terram Alani de Capele, habendas et tenendas illis inperpetuum in puram et perpetuam elemosinam pro salute anime mee et antecessorum meorum. Ego autem Alanus et heredes mei warantizabimus et defendemus predictam terram cum pertinentiis sepedictis canonicis contra omnes homines. Et ut hec mea concessio et donatio firma sit et stabilis, huic scripto sigillum meum in testimonium apposui. His testibus: domino Ricardo de Codeham decano, Thoma persona de Reindun, Willelmo de Brumford, Willelmo de Waldinggefeld, Mauricio et Thoma de Dodenes et Galfrido et Hugone filiis eorum, Roberto de Alneto, Rogero Iuvencel, Henrico Bonchevaler, Roberto de Boitun', Galfrido de Capele clerico, Iohanne de Mara et multis aliis.

See no. 91.

93. Grant in perpetuity by Richard son of Warin of Raydon to the prior and canons of a parcel of land called 'Wdelee' with appurtenances, which lies below the wood of Ralph de Capervilla, to be held for an annual rent of 6d to Richard and his heirs. The canons have given three marks as entry-fine.

[Early to mid thirteenth century]

Cartulary no. 36; approx. 138 × 80+ mm; endorsed: De Ricardo filio Warini, Reydon', xii; seal, round, approx. 38 mm, brown wax, fleur-de-lys, + SIGILE RICARDI FILII WARIN.

Sciant presentes et futuri quod ego Ricardus filius Warini de Reindune concessi et dedi et presenti carta mea confirmavi priori et canonicis de Dodenes Deo servientibus et servituris unam partem terre que vocatur Wdelee cum pertinentiis iacentem sub bosco Radulfi de Kevreville, habendam et tenendam illis de me et heredibus meis inperpetuum libere et quiete, reddendo inde nobis per annum sex denarios ad duos terminos, scilicet ad festum sancti Michaelis tres d. et ad Pascha tres d. pro omnibus servitiis, consuetudinibus, exactionibus et demandis. Pro hac autem concessione et donatione et huius carte mee confirmatione et warantizatione dederunt michi predicti prior et canonici tres marcas argenti in gersumiam. Hiis t(estibus): Willelmo de Brumford, Radulfo de Keureville, Willelmo de Waudingef(eld), Rogero de Horshae, Ermeiot de Wenham, Willelmo Angot, Rogero Iuvencel, Rogero filio Hugonis de Braham, Willelmo Helte, Galfrido de Capele clerico, Rogero medico, Iohanne de la Mare et multis aliis.

> William of Bramford occurs in 1202, 1211, and 1228 (9 n.); William of Walding-field, William Helte and Roger Juvencal all occur 1224–25 (17) and John de la Mare 1226 (35). Ralph de Capervilla was a juror in a plea concerning land in Raydon in 1200 (*CRR* i, 314), and was still alive in the 1230s (*Sibton Cartularies* ii, nos 409–10).

94. Grant in pure and perpetual alms by Richard son of Warin of Raydon to the canons, for his salvation and that of his ancestors and successors, of a parcel of land called 'Wdelee' with appurtenances, which lies below the wood of Ralph de Capervilla. Warranty is granted.   [Early to mid thirteenth century]

> Cartulary no. 56; approx. 187 × 62+ mm; endorsed: Testard de Reindun; Ricardus filius Warini de Reindune in puram elemosinam, xii; seal, round, approx. 38 mm, natural wax varnished brown, a radiating device of eight major alternating with eight minor petals, + SIGILL RICARDI FIL WARINI.

Omnibus sancte matris ecclesie filiis ad quos presens scriptum pervenerit Ricardus filius Warini de Reindun' salutem in Domino. Sciatis me concessisse et dedisse et hac carta mea confirmasse Deo et ecclesie beate Marie de Dodenes et canonicis ibidem Deo servientibus et servituris unam partem terre que vocatur Wdelee cum pertinentiis iacente sub bosco Radulfi de Chevreville, habendam et tenendam illis in puram et perpetuam elemosinam pro salute anime mee et antecessorum et successorum meorum. Ego autem Ricardus et heredes mei warantizabimus prenominatam terram cum pertinentiis prenominatis canonicis contra omnes homines et contra omnes feminas. His t(estibus): magistro Ricardo de Kodeham decano, Thoma persona de Reindun', Willelmo de Brumford, Radulfo de Chevrevile, Willelmo de Waudingef(eld), Rogero de Horshae, Ermeiot de Wenham, Rogero Iuvencel, Mauricio de Dodenes, Willelmo de Kenebroch, Rogero medico, Iohanne de Mara et multis aliis.

> Most of the witnesses of this charter occur 1223–26 (16–17, 35).

The endorsement of this charter indicates that the grantor's father was that Warin Testard who is a frequent witness. It is notable that Richard son of Warin changed his seal for one with a completely different device (cf. 93).

95. Grant in perpetuity by Matilda daughter of Gilbert to the prior and canons of all the part of her land of the fee of William son of Robert of Raydon in the parish of Capel [St Mary], lying alongside the way leading from 'Copedethorn' to Dodnash, for an annual rent of 3d for all service, except for payment of ½d to a scutage of 20s, and *pro rata*. The canons have given 3s as entry-fine.

[Early to mid thirteenth century]

Cartulary no. 53; approx. 130 × 58+ mm; endorsed: iii; ix; seal, round, approx. 38 mm, natural wax varnished brown, seeded fleur-de-lys, . . .MATILDIS. . .

Sciant presentes et futuri quod ego Matildis filia Gyleberti concessi et dedi et hac presenti carta mea confirmavi Deo et ecclesie beate Marie de Dodenes et priori et canonicis ibidem Deo servientibus et servituris totam partem terre mee de feodo Willelmi filii Roberti de Reindune in parochia de Capele, iacentem iuxta viam descendentem de Copedethorn versus Dodenes, habendam et tenendam illis inperpetuum de me et heredibus meis libere, quiete et honorifice, solvendo inde michi et heredibus meis tres denarios per annum ad tres terminos, scilicet ad festum sancti Michaelis unum d. et ad Pascha unum d. et ad nativitatem sancti Iohannis Baptiste unum d., pro omni servitio, consuetudine, exactione et demanda michi et heredibus meis pertinente, salvo servitio domini regis, scilicet ad scutagium viginti solidorum obolum, et ad plus plus et ad minus minus. Pro hac autem donatione et huius carte confirmatione et warantizatione et huic scripto sigilli mei appositione dederunt michi predicti prior et canonici tres solidos in gersumiam. His t(estibus): Hugone Talemasche, Willelmo de Brumford, Willelmo de Crepyng, Ermeiot de Wenham, Willelmo de Boitun', Roberto de Alneto, Mauricio et Thoma de Dodenes fratribus, Ricardo Godefridi, Warino Testard et aliis.

William of Bramford occurs in 1202 and 1211 (*Fines* ii, nos 345, 543), and it is probably the same man still alive in 1228 (*CRR* xiii, no. 1201). William of Boyton occurs in 1227–28 (Rye, *Fines*, 25 no. 39); Maurice and Thomas of Dodnash occur 1224–26 (16–17, 35).

96. Grant by Geoffrey of Capel [St Mary], clerk, to the prior and canons of an acre and a half of his land of the fee of William son of Robert of Raydon in the parish of Capel [St Mary], lying by the road from 'Copedethorn' to Dodnash, for an annual rent of 6d and payment of ½d towards scutage. The canons have given one mark as entry-fine. [Early to mid thirteenth century]

Cartulary no. 62; approx. 142 × 54+ mm; endorsed: Galfridus clericus de Capele, ix.

Sciant presentes et futuri quod ego Galfridus de Capele clericus concessi et dedi et hac presenti carta mea confirmavi Deo et ecclesie beate Marie de Dodenes et priori et canonicis ibidem Deo servientibus et servituris unam acram et dimidiam terre mee de feodo Willelmi filii Roberti de Reindun' in parochia de Capele, iacentem iuxta viam descendentem de Copedethorn versus Dodenes, tenendam illis inperpetuum de me et heredibus meis libere, quiete et honorifice, solvendo michi et heredibus meis sex denarios annuatim ad quatuor terminos, scilicet ad festum sancti Michaelis tres obulos et in festo sancti Andree tres obulos et in Pascha tres obulos et in festo sancti Iohannis Baptiste tres obulos pro omni servitio, consuetudine, exactione et demanda michi et heredibus meis pertinentibus, salvo servitio domini regis, scilicet ad scutagium obulum. Pro hac autem donatione et huius carte confirmatione et warantizatione dederunt michi predicti prior et canonici unam marcam argenti in gersumam, et ego huic scripto sigillum meum apposui. Hiis t(estibus): Hugone Talemasch, Willelmo de Brumford, Willelmo de Creping', Ermeiot de Wenham, Willelmo de Boitun', Mauricio et Thoma de Dodenes fratribus, Ricardo Godefrei, Warino Testard et multis aliis.

Geoffrey of Capel occurs 1227–28 (Rye, *Fines*, 26 no. 62). The witness list is identical to that of no. 95.

97. Grant by William of Waldingfield, knight, to the canons of all his wood called 'Dovelond' with appurtenances, saving a reasonable path for chase and carriage, also of three acres and three roods of land below the wood, lying lengthwise next to the land once held by Thuri and extending to the east into the parish of Capel, also of a parcel of land in 'Bromdune' adjacent lengthwise to Thuri's land, for an annual rent of 40d and payment of 12d towards scutage of 20s, and *pro rata*. The canons have paid ten marks as entry-fine. Warranty is granted.

[Early to mid thirteenth century, before 22 August 1230]

Cartulary no. 60; approx. 175 × 104 + 8 mm; endorsed: Willelmus de Waudingef', .iii.s .iv.d, iii'; vi.

Sciant presentes et futuri quod ego Willelmus miles de Waldigfeld concessi et dedi et hac presenti carta mea confirmavi priori et canonicis de Dodenes Deo servientibus et servituris totum boscum meum qui vocatur Dovelond cum pertinentiis, salva tamen una via rationabili ad caciandum et cariandum, et tres acras terre et tres rodas subtus boscum predictum iacentes de longo in longum iuxta terram quondam Thuri, et extendunt versus orientem in parochia de Capel', et unam peciam terre cum pertinentiis in Bromdone iacentem de longo in longum iuxta predicti Thuri terram, habenda et tenenda illis et eorum successoribus de me et heredibus meis libere et quiete, bene et in pace et honorifice, reddendo inde michi et heredibus meis quadraginta denarios ad duos terminos anni, scilicet ad Pascha viginti denarios et ad festum sancti Michaelis .xx. denarios pro omni servitio, consuetudine et demanda, salvo servitio domini regis, scilicet ad scutagium viginti solidorum .xii. denarios, et ad plus plus et ad minus minus. Pro hac autem concessione, donatione et huius carte mee confirmatione predictus prior et canonici dederunt michi .x. marcas argenti in gersumiam. Ego autem Willelmus et heredes mei warantizabimus sepedictis priori et canonicis prenominatum tenementum contra omnes homines qui mori possunt. Et ut hec mea donatio et concessio firmam optineant perpetuitatem, hoc scriptum sigilli mei appositione corroboravi. Hiis testibus: Hugone Thalemach', Ranulfo de Braham, Ermeiot de Wenham, Willelmo de Boitun' et Ricardo filio eius, Mauricio et Thoma de Doden(es) fratribus, Ysebardo de Braham, Galfrido de Capel clerico, Roberto de Boitun', Rogero Iuvencel, Warino Testard, Willelmo filio Thome, Herveo Quelp et multis aliis.

William of Waldingfield occurs in 1224–25 (17), attested a charter of the bishop of Ely on 20 Nov. 1228 (*CChR i, 1226–57*, 84–5), and was murdered in a field outside his gate at Purton in Stansfield on 22 Aug. 1230 (*CRR* xiv, no. 990; cf. *Close Rolls 1227–31*, 492–3). Ranulf of Brantham occurs 1227–30 (Rye, *Fines*, 29 no. 118; 30 no. 4), William of Boyton in 1227–28 (ibid., 25 no. 39), and Maurice and Thomas of Dodnash 1224–26 (16–17, 35).

98. Grant in perpetuity by William of Waldingfield to the prior and canons of two acres of land in 'Bromdune', lying between the land which they have previously received from him and his demesne in the parish of Capel [St Mary], for an annual rent of 8d and payment of 3d towards scutage of 20s, and *pro rata*. The canons have paid 16s as entry-fine.

[Early to mid thirteenth century, before 22 August 1230]

Cartulary no. 61; approx. 154 × 83+ mm; endorsed: De Willelmo de Waldingefeld, .viii.d, vi.

Sciant presentes et futuri quod ego Willelmus de Waldingefeld concessi et dedi et hac presenti carta mea confirmavi ecclesie beate Marie de Dodenes et priori et canonicis ibidem presentibus et futuris duas acras terre in Bromdune iacentes inter terram predictorum canonicorum quam de me prius receperunt et dominicum meum in parochia de Capele, habendas et tenendas predictis priori et canonicis de me et heredibus meis inperpetuum, libere, quiete et honorifice, reddendo inde michi et heredibus meis per annum octo denarios, scilicet ad festum sancti Michaelis quatuor denarios et ad Pascha quatuor denarios, pro omnibus serviciis, consuetudinibus et demandis, salvo servitio domini regis, scilicet ad scutagium viginti solidorum tres denarios, et ad plus plus et ad minus minus. Pro hac autem concessione et donatione et huius carte mee confirmatione et sigilli mei huic scripto appositione predictus prior et canonici dederunt michi sexdecim solidos sterlingorum in gersumiam. His testibus: Ermeiot de Wenham, Mauricio de Dodenes, Roberto filio Roberti le Barun, Roberto de Boitun', Galfrido clerico, Rogero Iuvencel, Rogero de Spina, Gileberto Claricie, Alano Bruning, Willelmo filio Thome de Hocholt, Iohanne de Hocholte, Henrico Bloman, Willelmo Cobat et aliis.

See no. 97; Roger Juvencal occurs 1224–26 (17, 35).

99. Quitclaim by William son of Robert of Waldingfield (*Waldingfeld*) of Capel [St Mary] to the prior and canons of an annual rent of 4s, paid in equal instalments at Easter and Michaelmas, which they used to render to him for the land called 'Doveland' in the parish of Capel [St Mary], which they hold of him in fee, so that neither he, his heirs nor assigns, nor anyone in his name, may henceforth make any claim to this rent. For this quitclaim they have given him 40s and a seam (*summam*) of corn, and they shall render each year at Michaelmas to him, his heirs or assigns a clove for all services *etc.*, saving scutage as is detailed in the charters of enfeoffment from his ancestors which they have in their possession. Warranty is granted against all persons in perpetuity. Sealed in testimony.

Hiis testibus: dominis Radulfo filio Willelmi, Iohanne de Wenham militibus, magistro Rogero de Holebroc, Rogero de Braham, Galfrido de Dodeneiss, Radulfo de Benetleya clerico, Ricardo de Bruar', Willelmo fratre suo, Roberto de Spina, Galfrido de la Mare et aliis.

[Late thirteenth century, probably before 1285]

Cartulary no. 77; approx. 253 × 95 + 7 mm; endorsed: relaxatio .iiii.s, vi.

Geoffrey de la Mare occurs 1252 × 57 (42), and was probably dead in 1285, when John de la Mare occurs (27). Geoffrey of Dodnash occurs 1252 × 57, 1276 and 1285 (27, 48, 63); Richard and William de Bruario occur in 1284 (206). Robert of Waldingfield had still been alive in 1250–51 (Rye, *Fines*, 52 no. 128).

100. Grant in perpetuity by Hervey Glanville of Capel [St Mary] to the prior and canons of a parcel of land in that parish called 'la grave Thuri', lying between the land called 'Duvelond' to the north and the grantor's land to the south, of which one headland abuts on the canons' land to the east and the other on that of Randulf son of William the steward, held of the fee of Richard of Boyton, to the west, with free chase and carriage when necessary with their ploughs and carts on a path of a perch's width, and with free entry and exit by another path which leads from Richard of Boyton's lane to 'Duvelond', to be held for an annual rent of ½d. The canons have paid him 7s as entry-fine. Warranty is granted.

[Mid thirteenth century]

Cartulary no. 89/2; approx. 210 × 132+ mm; endorsed: Carta Hervei de Glanvile, vii; seal, round, approx. 40 mm, natural wax, ornate fleur-de-lys, + S. . . . . . .EI D. GRANV. . .

Sciant presentes et futuri quod ego Herveius Glanvile de Capele concessi, dedi et hac presenti carta mea confirmavi priori et canonicis de Dodenes presentibus et futuris inperpetuum unam peciam terre in parochia de Capeles que vocatur la grave Thuri iacentem inter terram que vocatur Duvelond ex aquilonali parte et inter terram meam ex australi parte, cuius unum capud abutat super terram dictorum prioris et canonicorum versus orientem et aliud capud super terram Randulfi filii Willelmi dispensatoris de feodo Ricardi de Boytun' versus occidentem, cum libera chascia et etiam cum libero cariagio quandocumque opus fuerit cum aratris et quadrigis in una via habente in se latitudinem unius pertice, et cum libero introitu et exitu in una altera via que tendit de la lane Ricardi de Boyt(un) versus terram de Duvelond, et cum omnibus pertinentiis, tenendam et habendam de me et de heredibus meis dictis canonicis et successoribus suis inperpetuum libere, quiete et hereditarie, bene et in pace, reddendo inde michi et heredibus meis dicti prior et canonici et successores sui annuatim unum obulum ad unum terminum, scilicet ad Pascha, pro omnibus servitiis, consuetudinibus, releviis, homagiis, sectis, querelis et secularibus demandis. Pro hac autem concessione, donatione et presentis carte mee confirmatione dederunt michi predicti prior et canonici septem solidos sterlingorum in gersumam. Et ego dictus Herveus et heredes mei warantizabimus, acquietabimus et defendemus dictam terram cum libera chascia et cariagio in viis prescriptis et cum omnibus pertinentiis dictis priori et canonicis et successoribus suis per predictum servitium contra omnes tam Iudeos quam Cristianos inperpetuum. Ut autem hec mea concessio, donatio et presentis carte mee confirmatio firma et stabilis permaneat inperpetuum, presenti scripto sigillum meum apposui. Hiis testibus: domino Ricardo de Braham, domino Waltero fratre eius militibus, Willelmo de Wenham, Eadmundo de Chapel', Ricardo filio Roberti de Boyt(un), Iohanne Bolle, Roberto de Capel, Willelmo de Capele, Hugone fabro, Iohanne Bruning et aliis.

Hervey Glanville, Sir Richard of Brantham and Edmund of Capel occur in 1250 (25); William of Wenham occurs 1252 × 57 (42), and Richard of Boyton 1233–34 (Rye, *Fines*, 32 no. 47).

COPDOCK

101. Grant in fee and heredity by Alan Bernard of Tattingstone to the canons of all the land which is the right of Wimarc his wife, held of the fee of Hugh Tollemache in Copdock, which is called 'Hunemaneslond' and lies between the land of Roger son of Humphrey of 'Knuttewod' and 'Suthei' and abuts on the land of Roger Bunehard, to be held for an annual rent of 9d. The canons have given 5s entry-fine.   [Early to mid thirteenth century]

Cartulary no. 47; approx. 160 × 72+ mm; endorsed: Alanus Bernard de Hunemenislond, xvi.

Sciant presentes et futuri quod ego Alanus Bernard de Tatingest(un) dedit et concessi et hac presenti carta mea confirmavi Deo et ecclesie beate Marie de Dodenes et canonicis ibidem Deo servientibus totam terram de iure Wimarce uxoris mee que est de feudo Hugonis Talemasche in Coppedoch que vocatur Hunemaneslond, que iacet inter terram Rogeri filii Hunfridi de Knuttewod et Suthei et abutat terre Rogeri Bunehard, tenendam et habendam in feudo et in hereditate de me et de heredibus meis illis et eorum successoribus iure hereditario, reddendo inde michi et heredibus meis per annum novem denarios ad quatuor terminos, scilicet ad festum sancti Michaelis duos denarios et quadrantem, et ad festum sancti Andree ii d. et qu., et ad Pascha ii d. et qu. et ad festum sancti Iohannis Baptiste ii d. et qu., pro omni servitio et seculari exactione. Pro hac donatione et carte mee confirmatione predicti canonici quinque solidos argenti de gersuma michi dederunt. His t(estibus): Willelmo de Bromford, Roberto de Coppedoch, Mauricio de Dodenes, Thoma fratre eius, Willelmo clerico de Thatingest(un), Ricardo de Kattewade, Rogero de Coppedock, Gileberto filio Claricie, Rogero fratre eius, Roberto filio Ordmari de Simundesford.

William, clerk of Tattingstone, attests late twelfth-century charters (7, 9). William of Bramford occurs in 1202 and 1211 (*Fines* ii, nos 345, 553), and was probably still alive in 1224–25 (17). Maurice and Thomas of Dodnash occur 1224–26 (16–17, 35). For variations of the toponymic 'Knuttewode', see nos 102–7; despite 'Chittewode' of no. 104, the probability is that these are variations of 'knight's wood'.

102. Grant in perpetuity by Alan Bernard of Tattingstone to the prior and canons of the land called 'Hunemanneslond' in Copdock, lying between the land of Roger of 'Knithewde' and that of Ivo, to be held for the annual rent of a penny. The canons have paid three marks as entry-fine. [Early to mid thirteenth century]

Cartulary no. 49; approx. 180 × 84 mm; endorsed: Carta Alani Bernard de Tatingestone, Coppedok, v; xvi; seal, round, approx. 42 mm, natural wax varnished brown, star nesting in crescent moon, + SIGILL ALANI BERNARD.

Sciant presentes et futuri quod ego Alanus Bernard de Thatingestun concessi et dedi et hac presenti carta mea confirmavi Deo et ecclesie beate Marie de Dodenes et priori et canonicis ibidem Deo servientibus et servituris illam terram que vocatur Hunemanneslond iacentem in Koppedoc inter terram Rogeri de Knithewde et terram Yvonis, habendam et tenendam prenominatis priori et canonicis et eorum successoribus inperpetuum libere et quiete de me et heredibus meis, reddendo inde nobis per annum unum denarium ad duos terminos, scilicet ad festum sancti Michaelis unum obolum et ad Pascha unum obolum pro omnibus servitiis, consuetudinibus et demandis. Pro hac autem concessione, donatione et huius carte confirmatione sepedicti prior et canonici dederunt michi tres marcas argenti in gersumiam. Et ad maiorem autem securitatem ego huic scripto sigillum meum apposui in testimonium. His testibus: Radulfo de Chevrevill, Willelmo filio Roberti de Reindun', Willelmo de Waldingefeld', Roberto de Aldewartun, Roberto de Ramis, Roberto de Alneto, Ricardo de Hintlesham, Mauricio et Thoma de Dodenes, Edmundo Bernard, Gilberto de Spina, Ysenbardo filio Hugonis, Alano filio Rogeri de Braham, Warino Testard et multis aliis.

William son of Robert of Raydon occurs 1223–24 (16); William of Waldingfield and Isembard son of Hugh in 1224–25 (17) and Robert of the Aldergrove and Maurice and Thomas of Dodnash in 1226 (35).

103. Grant in perpetuity by Robert Predican of Stutton to the prior and canons of the land called 'Hunemanneslond' in Copdock, lying between the land of Roger of 'Knithewde' and that of Ivo, to be held for the annual rent of a penny. The canons have paid three marks as entry-fine.   [Early to mid thirteenth century]

Cartulary no. 50; approx. 145 × 79+ mm; endorsed: Carta Roberti Predican de Stutton.

Sciant presentes et futuri quod ego Robertus Predican de Stuttun concessi et dedi et hac presenti carta mea confirmavi Deo et ecclesie beate Marie de Dodenes et priori et canonicis ibidem Deo servientibus et servituris illam terram que vocatur Hunemanneslond iacentem in Coppedoc inter terram Roggeri de Knithewde et terram Yvonis, habendam et tenendam prenominatis canonicis et eorum successoribus inperpetuum libere et quiete de me et heredibus meis, reddendo inde nobis per annum unum denarium ad duos terminos, scilicet ad festum sancti Michaelis unum obolum et ad Pascha unum obolum pro omnibus servitiis, consuetudinibus et demandis. Pro hac autem concessione, donatione et huius carte confirmatione predicti prior et canonici dederunt michi tres marcas argenti in gersumiam. Et ad maiorem autem securitatem ego huic scripto sigillum meum apposui in testimonium. His tesibus: Roberto de Chevrevill, Willelmo filio Roberti de Reindun', Willelmo de Waldingefeld, Roberto de Aldewartun, Roberto de Ramis, Roberto de Alneto, Ricardo de Hintlesham, Willelmo de Kenebroc, Mauricio et Thoma de Dodenes, Edmundo Bernard, Gilberto de Spina, Ysenbarto filio Hugonis, Alano filio Rogeri de Braham, Warino Testard et multis aliis.

All witnesses except William of Kembroke attest no. 102.

104. Grant in fee and heredity by Denise daughter of Fulkelove to the canons of all her portion of the land of Huneman, which is of the fee of Hugh Tollemache in Copdock, with all appurtenances, as it lies between the land of Roger son of Humphrey of 'Chittewode' and 'Suthei', and abuts on the land of Roger Bunehard, to be held for an annual rent of 9d. Warranty is granted. The canons have paid 5s as entry-fine.   [Early thirteenth century, before 1223]

Cartulary no. 69; approx. 175 × 87+ mm; endorsed: Dionisia filia Fulkelove, xvi.

Sciant presentes et futuri quod ego Dionisia filia Folkelove dedi et concessi et hac presenti carta mea confirmavi Deo et ecclesie beate Marie de Dodenes et canonicis ibidem Deo servientibus totam partem meam de terra Huneman que est de feudo Hugonis Thalemasch in Coppedoch cum omnibus pertinentiis, habendam et tenendam in feudo et hereditate libere et quiete de me et de heredibus meis illis et eorum successoribus inperpetuum, scilicet illam que iacet inter terram Rogeri filii Humfridi de Chittewode et Suthei, et abuttat super terram Rogeri Bunehard, reddendo inde michi et heredibus meis per annum novem denarios ad quatuor terminos, scilicet ad festum sancti Michaelis .ii. d et quadrantem, et ad festum sancti Andree .ii. d. et quadrantem, et ad Pascha .ii. d. et quadrantem, et ad festum sancti Iohannis Baptiste .ii. d. et quadrantem, pro omnibus servitiis et exactionibus secularibus. Ego vero et heredes mei debemus warantizare predictam terram predictis canonicis contra omnes homines. Pro hac donatione et concessione predicti canonici quinque solidos de gersuma michi dederunt. T(estibus): Rogero de Braham, Willemo de Bromford, Ada Malveisin, Roberto Baro, Roberto de Coppedoch, Willelmo clerico de Tating(eston), Mauricio de Dodenes, Thoma fratre eius, Ricardo filio Godefridi, Rogero de Chittew', Mauricio de Fram(esden), Rogero de Spin', Ricardo de Chatew(ade).

William, clerk of Tattingstone, attests late twelfth-century charters (7, 9). Roger of Brantham, son of Eustace, was active by 1195 and dead by 1223 (*PR 7 Richard I*, 76; *CRR* xi, no. 738). For confirmation by her husband, see no. 105.

105. Grant in fee and heredity by Simon son of Roger of Bury to the canons of all the land held by right of his wife Denise of the fee of Hugh Tollemache in Copdock, which is called 'Hunemaneslond' and lies between the land of Roger son of Humphrey of 'Knutecchewod' and 'Suthei' and abuts on the land of Roger Bunehard, to be held for an annual rent of 9d. The canons have paid 5s as entry-fine.   [Early to mid thirteenth century]

Cartulary no. 80; approx. 187 × 75+ mm; endorsed: Simon de Beri, xvi.

Sciant presentes et futuri quod ego Symon filius Rogeri de Biri dedi et concessi et hac presenti carta mea confirmavi Deo et ecclesie beate Marie de Dodenes et canonicis ibidem Deo servientibus totam terram de iure Dionisie uxoris mee que est de feudo Hugonis Talemasche in Coppedoch que vocatur Hunemaneslond, que iacet inter terram Rogeri filii Humfridi de Knutecchewod et Suthei et abutat terre Rogeri Bunehard, tenendam et habendam in feudo et hereditate de me et de heredibus meis illis et eorum successoribus iure hereditario, reddendo inde michi et heredibus meis annuatim novem denarios ad quatuor terminos, scilicet ad festum sancti Michaelis duos denarios et quadrantem et ad festum sancti Andree .ii. d et qu. et ad Pascha .ii. d et qu. et ad festum sancti Iohannis Baptiste duos denarios et qu. pro omni servitio et seculari exactione. Pro hac donatione et concessione et carte mee confirmatione predicti canonici quinque solidos de gersuma michi dederunt. His testibus: Willelmo de Bromford, Roberto de Coppedoch, Mauricio de Dodenes, Thoma fratre eius, Willelmo clerico de Thatingest(un), Ricardo de Kattewad, Rogero de Coppedethorn, Gileberto filio Claricie, Rogero fratre eius, Roberto filio Ordmari de Simundesford.

See no. 104.

106. Quitclaim by Robert and Roger, sons of Ivo of Copdock, to the prior and canons, for 20s which they gave in cash, of all right and claim in the field called 'Hunemanneslond' in Copdock, of which they are and previously were seised, which lies between the land of Robert of 'Cnicktewde' and that of the said Robert Yve, of which one headland abuts on the fee of William of Wenham and the other on that of Richard Lucas, to be held in perpetuity and freely for an annual rent of 2d. Warranty is granted to the canons for the old tenement in the said field.
                                                                          [Mid thirteenth century]

Cartulary no. 89/1; approx. 160 × 110 + 15 mm; endorsed: Carta Roberti et Rogeri filiorum Yvonis, xvi; slits for three seals; centre, seal, round, approx. 38 mm, brown wax, cinquefoil flower, + SIGILLUM ROG... ENC.

Omnibus Cristi fidelibus ad quos presens scriptum pervenerit Robertus et Rogerus filii Yvonis de Coppedoc salutem. Noveritis nos concessisse, remisisse et omnino

quietumclamasse pro nobis et pro heredibus nostris priori et canonicis de Dodenes presentibus et futuris inperpetuum, pro viginti solidis sterlingorum quos dicti
prior et canonici nobis dederunt pre manibus, totum ius et clamium quod
habuimus vel habere potuimus in campo qui vocatur Hunemanneslond in
Coppedoc, unde dicti prior et canonici sunt in saisina et antea fuerunt, iacente
inter terram Rogeri de Cnicktewde et terram dicti Roberti Yve que est de eodem
feodo, cuius unum capud abutat super feodum Willelmi de Wenham et aliud
capud super terram Ricardi Lucas, tenendum et habendum de nobis et heredibus
nostris illis et successoribus suis vel suis assignatis inperpetuum libere, quiete et
hereditarie, bene et in pace, reddendo inde nobis et heredibus nostris annuatim
duos denarios ad duos anni terminos, scilicet ad festum sancti Michaelis unum
denarium et ad Pascha unum denarium, pro omnibus servitiis, homagiis, releviis,
sectis et secularibus demandis. Et nos dicti Robertus et Rogerus et heredes nostri
warantizabimus, acquietabimus et defendemus dictis priori et canonicis presentibus et futuris vel eorum assignatis vetus tenementum quod de nobis tenent in predicto campo cum pertinentiis contra omnes tam Iudeos quam Cristianos. In huius
rei testimonium huic scripto sigilla nostra apposuimus. Testibus: domino Ricardo
de Braham, domino Waltero fratre eius, domino Willelmo de Holebroc militibus,
Willelmo de Wenham, Roberto de Cniktewde, Ricardo filio suo, Willelmo de
Capele, Eadmundo de Capele et aliis.

Richard of Boyton occurs 1233–34 (Rye, *Fines*, 32 no. 47); Richard of Brantham, William of Holbrook and Edmund of Capel in 1250 (25), and William of
Wenham 1252 × 57 (42).

107. Quitclaim by Roger Yve, son of Robert Yve, of Copdock (*Coppedoc*) to the
canons, for his heirs and assigns in perpetuity, of an annual rent of one penny
which they used to pay him for the field called 'Hunemaneslond' in Copdock,
lying between the land of Roger of 'Knitwode' and his own, so that neither he,
his heirs nor anyone in their name may henceforth make any claim therein. For
this quitclaim the canons have given him 12d in cash, and they shall render to
him and his heirs each year at Easter a clove. Warranty is granted against all
persons. Sealed in testimony.
Hiis testibus: domino Radulfo filio Willelmi, Iohanne de Wenham militibus,
Rogero de Braham, magistro Rogero de Holebroc, Willelmo de Wudingfeud,
Roberto de Coppedoc, Roberto Stepman, Willelmo de Bruer' et aliis.
[Late thirteenth century, probably 1270s–1280s]

Ipswich, SRO, q s 271 (Fitch's *Monasticon*), vol. ii, at p. 186; approx. 190 × 89
mm, no turn-up; endorsed: Carta Roger Ywe xii; ii; xvi; two slits for seal, tag
and seal missing.

Roger of Brantham occurs 1276 (48); William de Bruario, 1284 (206); Robert of
Copdock, 1285–86 (Rye, *Fines*, 86 no. 25).

108. Grant in pure and perpetual alms by Sewal son of Richer of Copdock to the
prior and canons, for his soul and the souls of his ancestors, of an annual rent of

8d which he used to receive from Simon of Bury and Alan Bernard from Pinell's land. [Early to mid thirteenth century]

Cartulary no. 39; approx. 130 × 85+ mm; endorsed: Carta Sewalli filii Richeri de Coppedok, xvii; relaxatio .viii.d.

Omnibus matris ecclesie filiis ad quos presens scriptum pervenerit Sewale filius Richeri de Copedoch salutem. Sciatis me concessisse, dedisse et hac carta mea confirmasse Deo et ecclesie beate Marie de Dodenes et priori et canonicis ibidem Deo servientibus et servituris octo denarios de redditu annuos quos ego solebam percipere de Simone de Biri et Alano Bernard de terra Pinelli in Copedach ad quatuor terminos censuales et omnia alia predicte terre servitia sine aliquo retenemento, habendos prenominatis canonicis et eorum successoribus inperpetuum, in puram et perpetuam elemosinam pro salute anime mee et antecessorum meorum. Ego autem Sewale in testimonium huic scripto sigillum meum apposui. His testibus: domino Ricardo de Kodeham decano, Thoma persona de Reidun', Willelmo de Brumford persona de Holetun', Ranulfo de Braham, Ermeiot de Wenham, Willelmo de Waudingefeld, Willelmo de Boitun', Roberto de Alneto, Mauricio de Dodenes et Thoma fratre eius et Galfrido et Hugone filiis eorum, Rogero Iuvencel, Roberto filio Ricardi de Boitun', Willelmo filio Agnetis et aliis.

Richard, dean of Coddenham, and Thomas, parson of Raydon, occur 1223–24 (16); Roger Juvencal and William of Waldingfield, 1224–25 (17); Maurice and Thomas of Dodnash, 1223–26 (16–17, 35). For Simon of Bury, see no. 104.

109. Grant in fee and heredity by Wimarc, widow of Alan Bernard, to Prior J. and the canons, of all her part of the land called 'Pinel's land' in Copdock, with appurtenances, to be held of her and her heirs for an annual rent of ½d at Easter. They have paid her one mark as entry-fine. [Probably 1220s–1230s]

Helmingham, T/Hel/98/2 (A2/11); approx. 154 × 51 + 5 mm; endorsed: Redditus .i. ob., xvii; parchment tag, seal missing.

Sciant presentes et futuri quod ego Wimark quondam uxor Alani Bernard concessi, remisi et hac presenti carta confirmavi I. priori et canonicis ecclesie beate Marie de Dodenes ibidem Deo servientibus et servituris, pro una marca argenti quam michi dederunt in gersumam, totam partem meam terre cum omnibus pertinentiis suis que vocatur terra Pinel in Coppedoc, habendam et tenendam dictis I. et canonicis de me et heredibus meis libere, quiete, bene et pacifice in feodo et hereditate, reddendo inde michi et heredibus meis per annum unum obulum ad Pascha pro omnibus serviciis, consuetudinibus et demandis. Et ego predicta Wimark et heredes mei aquietabimus et warantizabimus dictis I. et canonicis predictam terram cum pertinentiis per prenominatum servitium contra omnes homines. Hiis testibus: Willelmo de Holebrok, Mauricio de Dodenes et Galfrido et Mauricio filiis suis, Thoma de Dodenes et Hugone filio suo, Thoma filio Hugonis, Thoma filio Radulfi, Iohanne Cobelot, Henrico Bloman, Iordano filio eius, Iohanne le Templer et aliis.

After no. 108, where Alan Bernard is still alive. The prior is probably Jordan, who occurs between 1228 and 1234. The father of Jordan son of Henry Bloman, who attests in 1250 (25), is still alive.

110. Grant in pure and perpetual alms by Hugh Husbonde of Copdock to the prior and canons, for the salvation of his and his ancestors' souls, of an annual rent of 8d from the land once Pinel's. [Early to mid thirteenth century]

Helmingham, T/Hel/98/6 (A2/17); approx. 188 × 58 + 13 mm; endorsed: Carta Hugonis Husbond, i; xvvii (*sic*); parchment tag, seal missing.

Sciant presentes et futuri quod ego Hugo Husebonde de Coppedoc concessi et dedi et hac presenti carta mea confirmavi Deo et ecclesie beate Marie de Dodenes et priori et canonicis ibidem Deo servientibus et servituris octo denarios de redditu quos solebam percipere de terra quondam Pinel iacente inter terram Rogeri Iuvencel et terram Yvonis in Coppedoc, habendos prenominatis priori et canonicis in puram et perpetuam elemosinam pro salute anime mee et antecessorum meorum in perpetuum. Ut autem hec mea donatio, concessio et huius carte confirmatio perpetuam optineant firmitatem, huic scripto sigillum meum apposui. Hiis testibus: Willelmo de Waldingefeld, Mauricio et Thoma de Dodenes, Roberto filio Ricardi de Boytune, Osberto de Stuttona clerico, Alexandro filio suo, Warino Testard, Ysebard de Braham, Galfrido clerico de Capell', Alano Bruning, Rogero Talleburg, Roberto de Hulenhey et Hugone fratribus et aliis.

Five of the witnesses occur in documents dated 1223–26 (16–17, 35).

FALKENHAM AND STREWSTON (IN KIRTON)

111. Confirmation by Pope Honorius III to the prior and canons of their possessions, and especially of the church of Strewston [in Kirton] and the land and church of Falkenham. They are not to be required to pay tithes on lands newly cultivated or on the nutriments of animals, and they may receive and profess clerks and laymen fleeing from the world. Lateran, Rome, 17 January 1218.

Cartulary no. 15; approx. 327 × 217 + 24 mm; on *plica* (turn-up), scribal mark: al; endorsed: elaborate *signum* (Sayers, as below, fig. 4); Sterstone et Falcenham; lead *bulla* on cords, chamois pouch.

Calendared in J.E. Sayers, *Calendar of Original Papal Letters in England and Wales, 1198–1304*, Oxford forthcoming, no. 65 (with analysis).

HONORIUS episcopus servus servorum Dei dilectis filiis priori et canonicis de Dodenes salutem et apostolicam benedictionem. Cum a nobis petitur quod iustum est et honestum tam vigor equitatis quam ordo exigit rationis ut id per solicitudinem officii nostri ad debitum perducatur effectum. Eapropter, dilecti in

Domino filii, vestris iustis precibus inclinati, monasterium vestrum, personas et possessiones vestras cum omnibus pertinentiis vestris quas[a] in presentiarum rationabiliter possidetis aut in futurum iustis modis, prestante Deo, poteritis adipisci, sub beati Petri et nostra protectione suscipimus, specialiter autem ecclesiam de Sterstone, terram de Fauceham et ecclesiam de Fauceham cum omnibus pertinentiis devotioni vestre auctoritate apostolica in proprios usus confirmamus et presentis scripti patrocinio communimus, statuentes etiam ut de terris vestris noviter ad culturam redactis et ortis quas sumptibus colitis sive de nutrimentis animalium vestrorum nulli teneami decimas exhibere. Liceat quoque vobis clericos vel laicos e seculo fugientes liberos et absolutos ad conversionem recipere et eos absque contradictione aliqua retinere. Nulli omnino hominum liceat hanc paginam nostre protectionis, confirmationis et concessionis infringere vel ei ausu temerario contraire. Si quis autem hoc attemptare presumpserit, indignationem omnipotentis Dei et beatorum Petri et Pauli apostolorum ei se noverit incursurum. Dat' Lateran' .xvi. kalendas Februarii pontificatus nostri anno secundo.

[a] MS: qui

The diplomatic form of this document is highly suspect. In several ways it differs from the norm produced by Pope Honorius III's chancery – for example, the distinctive initial H of the pope's name, the use of superscript abbreviations for *quam* and *quas*, the use of initial abbreviation for the *con* of *confirmamus* et *communimus*, the absence of capitals for *Petri* and *Pauli*. This is unlikely to be the scribe 'al' of Sayers, nos 1, 22. It is either a highly unorthodox product of the papal chancery, or a forgery to which a genuine *bulla* has been attached.

The usefulness of such a papal document to the canons of Dodnash may be appreciated in the context of the litigation between them and their brethren of Holy Trinity, Ipswich, in 1216 and 1232 (15, 19), particularly in relation to tithes in the parish of Bentley. On the dorse of the late medieval memorandum which is in effect a commentary on the decision of the papal judges-delegate in 1216, and which may indeed be an English translation of a much earlier document (15A), is transcribed the decretal *Ex parte* of Pope Alexander III (X, III. 30. 10; J–L 14117), addressed to various diocesans, which concludes: 'he (Adrian IV), however, allowed other religious to pay no tithes from their new lands which they cultivated by their own hands and for their own use, from the food of their animals and from their gardens, and in these matters we have imitated him'. For discussion, see G. Constable, *Monastic Tithes from their Origins to the Twelfth Century*, Cambridge 1964, 298–9, 306. Following the Fourth Lateran Council the Benedictines and the canons regular were normally freed only from payment of tithes of the produce of newly-cultivated lands. For the policy of Honorius III on this matter, see J.E. Sayers, *Papal Government and England during the Pontificate of Honorius III (1216–1227)*, Cambridge 1984, 115–17.

The canons apparently enjoyed uninterrupted possession of the church of Falkenham from its acquisition some time between 1188 and 1218 until the priory's dissolution (see Introduction, p. 19). For the identification of 'Sterstone' as Strewston in Kirton in Colneis hundred, see no. 123n., also no. 4.

112. Notification by Prior Richard Whytyng of St Mary at Dodnash, patron of the parish church of Falkenham (*Falcynham*) in the hundred of Colneis (*Colneyse*) in Norwich diocese, Richard Clark, perpetual vicar of the same church, and William Scroton, Thomas Walden and John Bryghtles, parishioners and wardens of the fraternity in that church founded in honour of St Mary Magdalen, that because they cannot attend personally to all matters pertaining to the foresaid church, they have ordained and constituted as their true and legitimate proctor and special messenger in the vills and all other places in the county of Essex their beloved in Christ Walter Parker of Wickham St Pauls (*Wykham Powle*) that he should seek, collect and receive in their name and that of the said parish church and fraternity the alms of the faithful given to God, the parish church and fraternity, with full authority to declare the indulgences and business of the church and fraternity and to grant the benefits conceded to the benefactors of church and confraternity and to constitute such benefactors participators in all the masses, prayers, canonical hours, alms, seven works of mercy and all other spiritual works in the said church in perpetuity, and also to execute all other business of the church and confraternity as the law demands and requires, for a full year from the date of these presents. Sealed in testimony. 1 September 1472.

Helmingham, T/Hel/98/38 (A3/3); approx. 388 × 155 + 30 mm; no medieval endorsement; tag and seal missing.

FRAMSDEN

113. Grant in pure and perpetual alms by Warin son of Philip of Framsden to the canons, for the salvation of his soul and those of his father, mother and all his ancestors, of all the land which Godwin Potter held of his fee in Framsden, with all appurtenances, free from secular exaction. Warranty is granted against all men and women.   [Late twelfth to early thirteenth century]

Cartulary no. 20; approx. 145 × 90+ mm; endorsed: Warinus filius Philippi de Framisden; Fraemisden, xiii; seal, round, approx. 30 mm, natural wax varnished brown, radiating device of eight petals.

Universis sancte matris ecclesie filiis et omnibus hominibus suis et amicis presentibus et futuris Warinus filius Philippi de Framesdenia salutem. Noverit universitas[a] vestra me dedisse et concessisse et hac carta mea confirmasse Deo et beate Marie de Dodenes et priori et canonicis ibidem Deo servientibus in puram et perpetuam elemosinam pro salute anime mee et patris et matris mee et omnium antecessorum meorum totam terram quam Godwinus le Poter tenuit de feudo meo in Framesd(en) cum omnibus pertinentiis. Hanc elemosinam ego predictus Warinus et heredes mei debemus warantizare predicte religioni et prenominatis canonicis contra omnes homines et contra omnes feminas. Unde volo et firmiter precipio quod predicta religio et predicti canonici teneant et habeant predictam terram cum omnibus pertinentiis ab omni exactione seculari absolutam. Hiis testibus: domino Rogero comite, Roberto capellano, Eustachio de Braham, Rogero filio eius, Mil(one) Lenveise, Willelmo Lenveise, Gileberto de Lindesh', Bertram de Verdun, Willelmo de Manent, Mauricio de Doden(es), Thoma fratre eius, Willelmo de Raimes, Willelmo Malkael, Eadwardo de Alneto, Hugone filio Edild', David de Berch(olt) et pluribus aliis.

a MS: universa

Roger Bigod, earl of Norfolk, 25 Nov. 1189–1221. Edward of the Aldergrove occurs before November 1196 (11). Eustace of Brantham occurs from 1165 to 1202, and not thereafter (71n.), although Maurice and Thomas of Dodnash occur as late as 1226 (35). Warin of Framsden attested an actum of papal judges-delegate in 1205–6 (*Leiston Cartulary*, no. 131).

114. Grant in pure and perpetual alms by William son of William of Cretingham to the canons, made through the promptings of charity and from his salvation and that of his predecessors and successors, of 18d annual rent from the land which William Potter held of his fee in the vill of Framsden, adjoining the land of Robert Hare and abutting on that of Roger del Hacche, to be received from whoever holds that land of William and his heirs. Warranty is granted against all men.

[Early thirteenth century, before August 1221]

Cartulary no. 19; approx. 145 × 84+ mm; endorsed: Willelmus de Cretingham; seal, round, approx. 35 mm, dark green wax, armorial shield, bird displayed under hatchment, +. . .LE WILE. . . . . .INGHAM.

Omnibus sancte matris ecclesie filiis presentibus et futuris Willelmus filius Willelmi de Cretingham salutem. Noverit universitas vestra me caritatis intuitu et pro salute anime mee et predecessorum et successorum meorum dedisse et hac carta mea confirmasse Deo et ecclesie beate Marie de Dodenes et canonicis ibidem Deo famulantibus octodecim deneratus redditus annuatim de terra quam Godwinus Poter tenuit de meo feodo in villa de Framesdene, iacente de longo in longum iuxta terram Roberti Hare, et abutat super terram Rogeri del Hacche, ad duos terminos percipiendos de illo vel de illis qui tenebunt predictam terram de predicto Willelmo vel de heredibus suis, scilicet ad Pascha novem denarios et ad festum sancti Michaelis novem denarios, habendos de me et heredibus meis inperpetuum pacifice, integre et quiete, in puram et perpetuam elemosinam. Ego autem et heredes mei warantizabimus predictum redditum prenominatis canonicis contra omnes homines. Hiis testibus: Rogero Bigoth comite Norfolch, Hugone filio eius, Ricardo de Seinges, Rogero de Braham, Roberto de Burnaville, Roberto de Neude, Willelmo de Blumvile, Thoma de Blumvile, Ada de Bedingefeld, Willelmo del Bois, Ricardo de Bromtun, Hugone de Rikinghale, Ricardo filio Eustachii de Braham, Armeiot de Wenham, Roberto Barun et multis aliis.

Roger Bigod, earl of Norfolk. Thomas Blundeville, from an East Anglian family, was active in royal administration in the region from 1205–16 (*Rot. Litt. Claus.* i, 59b, 60b, 244, 256b); he became bp of Norwich in December 1226.

HOLBROOK

115. Grant in perpetual alms by Hugh son of Eustace of Brantham to the canons of four acres of land in Holbrook, of which the headland to the north abuts on the land of Geoffrey Stainere and that to the south on the path from Alton [in Stutton], for an annual rent of 4d and payment of a penny towards scutage of 20s, and *pro rata*. Warranty is granted. [Early to mid thirteenth century]

> Cartulary no. 59; approx. 158 × 62+ mm; endorsed: Holbrok, Hugo de Braham, i; fragment of seal, round, approx. 35 mm, natural wax varnished brown, standing bull facing to left, . . .BRAHA.

Omnibus sancte matris ecclesie filiis ad quos presens scriptum pervenerit Hugo filius Eustachii de Braham salutem. Sciatis me concessisse et dedisse et presenti carta mea confirmasse Deo et ecclesie beate Marie de Dodenes et canonicis ibidem Deo servientibus et servituris quatuor acras terre in Holebroch, cuius terre unum capud lanceat versus north iuxta terram Galfridi Stainere et aliud capud versus suth abuttat super cheminum de Altune, in perpetuam elemosinam, tenendas et habendas de me et heredibus meis pro libero servitio quatuor denariorum michi et heredibus meis ad duos terminos per annum solvendorum, scilicet ad festum sancti Michaelis duos denarios et ad Pascha duos denarios pro omni servitio, consuetudine, exactione et demanda michi et heredibus meis pertinentibus, salvo servitio domini regis, scilicet ad scutagium viginti solidorum unum denarium, et ad plus plus et ad minus minus. Et ego et heredes mei warantizabimus prenominatis canonicis predictam terram contra omnes homines. Et ego huic scripto sigillum meum apposui. Hiis testibus: Willelmo et Radulfo de Brumford fratribus, Willelmo de Boitune, Ermeiot de Wenham, Mauricio et Thoma de Dodenes fratribus, Radulfo filio Roberti, magistro Walkelino de Brumford, Thoma de Reindun clerico, Willelmo de Hildercle et multis aliis.

> Eustace of Brantham does not occur after 1202 (71n.); Hugh of Brantham occurs 1219–20 (Rye, *Fines*, 21 no. 101); William of Bramford occurs 1202, 1211 (*Fines* ii, nos 345, 543) and 1228 (*CRR* xiii, no. 1201). Maurice and Thomas of Dodnash occur 1223–26 (16–17, 35).

IPSWICH

116. Grant by Thomas Bonde and Lora Bretun of Harkstead (*Herkystede*) to Prior Roger and the canons of a parcel of a messuage in the parish of St Nicholas, Ipswich (*Gyppwyci*), lying between the messuage of Thomas and Lora on one side and that of Thomas Love on the other, of which one headland abuts on the common road leading from Stoke Bridge (*Stokebregg*) to the marketplace of Ipswich and the other on the messuage of Thomas Love, to have and to hold of the capital lords of the fee by the due and legally accustomed services. Warranty is granted against all persons in perpetuity. Sealed in testimony.

Hiis testibus: Ricardo Havirlond, Roberto Prestone, Gilberto Mayster, Iohanne Eyk, Thoma Love et aliis.   Ipswich, Friday 3 November 1368

> Cartulary no. 144; approx. 226 × 84+ mm; endorsed: Carta Thome Bonde et Lore sororis sue facta nobis super .i. pecia mesuagii iacente in villa Gipp'; licentia domini regis de (? alienatione) inter cartas de ten' in Tatingston, xi; fragment of seal, probably round, red wax, shield with a fess, with scrollwork border, legend indecipherable.
>
> For the royal licence, see no. 155.

117. Quitclaim in perpetuity by Thomas Love and Margery his wife, of Ipswich (*Gippewico*) to the prior and convent of all right, title and claim which they had, have or in any way might have in a messuage in the same town with appurtenances, sited between their messuage to the south and that of John Fullere to the north, so that neither they, their heirs nor anyone in their name may henceforth in perpetuity make any claim to it or any part of it. They have also remitted and relaxed in perpetuity all manner of actions, suits and demands which they have or may have against the prior and convent by reason of a gutter running down the houses on the canons' messuage towards the site of their own. Sealed in testimony.

Hiis testibus: Petro Seman de Gipp', Nicholao Dykeman de Estbergholt, Thoma Walays de eadem, Iohanne Drivere de Benteleya, Stephano Masoun de Gipp' et aliis.   Ipswich, Monday 30 May 1384.

> Cartulary no. 150; approx. 214 × 130+ mm; endorsed: Quietaclamatio Thome Love de Gipp' et Margerie uxoris sue super omni iure et clamea et calumpnia, querela vel demanda quod habuerunt contra nos ratione mesuagii nostri quod perquisivimus in eadem villa de Thoma Bonde et Lora sorore sua, xi
>
> Two seals, both round, approx. 24 mm, red wax, both shield of arms hanging by cords, but different.

SHIPMEADOW

118. Grant in pure and perpetual alms by Bartholomew of Shipmeadow to the canons, for his soul and those of his ancestors, of the homage of Henry son of Hervey Sired with his tenement, suit and service of 5s a year in two instalments; and also of the land which was held by William Cristemasse, which is to be held in heredity by Matilda daughter of Simon Sauvage of the priory for the annual service of 2s; and also of Bartholomew's part of 'Westfen' in Shipmeadow, to be held in heredity by Margaret, his first-born daughter, of the priory for the annual service of 16d; and also 'Suetemanescroft' and 'Haurecroft', for the annual service of 20d. Warranty is granted against all persons.

[Early to mid thirteenth century, before 1232]

113

Ipswich, SRO, HD 1538/278/1; approx. 190 × 90 mm, no turn-up; endorsed: Bartolomeus de Sipmed'; one slit, tag and seal missing.

Universis sancte matris ecclesie filiis ad quos presens scriptum pervenerit Bartholomeus de Sipmede salutem. Noverit universitas vestra me concessisse, dedisse et hac presenti carta mea confirmasse Deo et ecclesie beate Marie de Dodenes et canonicis ibidem Deo servientibus et servituris homagium Henrici filii Hervei Sired cum toto tenemento suo quod de me tenuit et tota secta sua et toto servitio suo quod michi debuit, scilicet quinque solidos annuos ad duos terminos percipiendos, scilicet ad festum sancti Michaelis triginta denarios et ad Pascha triginta denarios; et totam teram que fuit Willelmi Cristemasse quam Matildis filia Simonis Sauvage tenebit hereditarie de predicta domo per servitium duorum solidorum annuorum ad dictos terminos percipiendorum; et totam partem meam de Westfen in villa de Sipmed quam Margareta filia mea primogenita tenebit de predicta domo hereditarie per servitium sexdecim denariorum; et Suetemanescroft et Haurecroft per servitium viginti denariorum ad eosdem terminos percipiendorum, habenda et tenenda in puram et perpetuam elemosinam pro salute anime mee et antecessorum in perpetuum. Ego vero et heredes mei predictam elemosinam contra omnes homines protegemus, warantizabimus, defendemus et aquietabimus. Et ut hec mea concessio et donatio stabilis et firma permaneat, eam presenti scripto et sigilli mei appositione corroboravi. His testibus: Thoma filio Gileberti, Hamone Lenveise, Roberto de Ponte, Radulfo de Barsham, magistro Alexandro de Munci, magistro Michaele de Ringefeld, Thoma de Reindun, Radulfo de Berchout, Luca persona de Wlferest', Thoma persona de Elingham, Henrico de Yketleshal' capellano, Roberto filio Ade, Willelmo filio Herberti, Michaele de Bungeie et multis aliis.

Hamo Lenveise first occurs in 1210, and died between Easter 1231 and Easter 1232 (*Sibton Cartularies* ii, no. 390n.). For mr Alexander de Muncy, see ibid., i 75–76; he, like mr Michael of Ringsfield, attested several acta of bp Thomas Blundeville.

119. Confirmation by Thomas son of Gilbert [of Ilketshall] to the canons of the grant made to them by Bartholomew of Shipmeadow of 'Suetemanescroft' and 'Haurecroft' in Shipmeadow. [Early to mid thirteenth century]

Ipswich, SRO, HD 1538/278/2; approx. 155 × 62 mm, no turn-up; no endorsement; one slit, tag and seal missing.

Omnibus sancte matris ecclesie filiis ad quos presens scriptum pervenerit Thomas filius Gilberti salutem. Sciatis me concessisse et confirmasse Deo et ecclesie beate Marie de Dodenes et canonicis ibidem Deo servientibus et servituris concessionem et donationem quam Bartholomeus de Sipmede fecit prenominatis ecclesie et canonicis de Suetemanescroft et de Haurecroft in Sipmede, sicut carta quam ipsi habent de predicto Bartholomeo testatur. Et ut hec mea concessio et confirmatio firma sit et stabilis, huic scripto sigillum meum apposui. His testibus: magistro A(lexandro) de Munci decano, magistro Michaele de Ringesfeld, Roberto filio Warini, Rogero de Metingham, Thoma Latimer, Roberto filio Adam, Henrico de Rode, Adam Sauvage, Sewale de Rothenhale, Roberto de Barsham, Willelmo filio Herberti et multis aliis.

Thomas son of Gilbert of Ilketshall was active by 1196 and still alive in 1230 (*Sibton Cartularies* i, 65); the family held lands of the honour of Chester which came to be held of Bigod by the marriage of Countess Gundreda to Hugh Bigod (W. Farrer, *Honours and Knights' Fees* iii, 230).

120. Confirmation by Thomas son of Gilbert of Ilketshall for the canons of the grant to them by Bartholomew of Shipmeadow of annual rents of 10s from the men of his fee which have been assigned to them, as specified in his charter [118].

[Early to mid thirteenth century]

Ipswich, SRO, HD 1538/278/4; approx. 162 × 70 + 14 mm; no endorsement; seal, round, approx. 48 mm, damaged, equestrian figure, drawn sword in right hand, facing right, + SIG. . ..

Sciant presentes et futuri quod ego Thomas filius Gileberti de Ylketeshale concessi et hac presenti carta mea confirmavi Deo et ecclesie sancte Marie de Dodenes et canonicis ibidem Deo servientibus et servituris donum quod Bartholomeus de Sipmedue eis fecit de decem solidatis redditus de hominibus de feodo suo de Sipmedue eis assignatis, prout carta predicti Bartholomei quam ab eo habent testatur. Et ut hec mea concessio stabilis et rata permaneat, eam presenti scripto et sigilli mei appositione corroboravi. Hiis testibus: magistro Simone de Risinge, Radulfo de Barsham, magistro Alexandro de Munci, magistro Michaele de Ringesfelde, Bartholomeo persona de Holebroc, Luca fratre suo, Radulfo de Bercholt, Thoma de Reidun, Thoma persona de Elingham, Henrico capellano de Ylketeleshal, Ada le Sauvage, Willelmo filio Herberti, Michaele de Bung' et multis aliis.

See no. 119.

STRATFORD ST MARY

121. Quitclaim by William of Bramford to Prior J. and the canons of the homage and service of Thomas Locun for the meadow which he holds of him in 'Sturmede' which is called 'Hauckesmede', that is, 4d p.a. Thomas has returned to him the charter which he had concerning this meadow.

[Early to mid thirteenth century, probably after 13 October 1228]

Cartulary no. 65; approx. 190 × 55 mm; endorsed: Carta Willelmi de Brumford de Sturmedue, Straffords, xiii.

Sciant presentes et futuri quod ego Willelmus de Brumford reddidi et quiete clamavi pro me et pro heredibus meis I. priori de Dodenes et canonicis suis presentibus et futuris homagium et servitium Thome Locun de prato quod tenuit de me in Sturmede quod vocatur Hauckesmede, scilicet duos denarios at festum sancti Michaelis et duos denarios ad Pascha, habendum et tenendum prenominatis canonicis inperpetuum, libere et quiete et honorifice pro me et pro heredibus meis. Pro hac autem concessione et quieteclamatione reddidit michi predictus Thomas Locun cartam quam habuit de me de predicto prato. His t(estibus): Willelmo filio Roberti, Radulfo de Chevereville, Willelmo et Huberto filiis eius, Iohanne filio Edmundi, Huberto de Dentun, Roberto Ascelun, Radulfo de Berholt, Roberto de Lasham, Galfrido de Brumford et Huberto fratre eius, Mattheo de Stanfeld, Iohanne de Holetun et multis aliis.

> The prior is probably Jordan, who occurs in 1228 and 1234 (38, 62). William of Bramford occurs before 1196 (9) until 1228 (*CRR* xiii, no. 1201). This quitclaim probably follows the court case brought by Roger de Akeni against the prior, William of Bramford and others at Michaelmas 1228 (see 60n.).

122. Confirmation and quitclaim by Ralph Locun of Raydon (*Reydon*) to the prior and canons of an annual rent of 4d which he and his ancestors have paid for the meadow called 'Haukemedwe' in 'Sturmedwe' in Stratford St Mary (*Stratford*). Grant to them also, in pure and perpetual alms, for his soul and those of his ancestors, of 4d annual rent which he has been accustomed to receive for the said meadow of 'Haukemedwe' in the meadow of Stratford, which the canons shall receive annually in equal instalments at Easter and Michaelmas from William son of Robert the shepherd, his heirs and assigns; they shall also receive 4d a year at the same terms from John Frivel of Holton (*Holeton'*), his heirs and assigns, together with the homage of both of them. Ralph, his heirs and assigns may henceforth make no claim thereto. Sealed in testimony.

Hiis testibus: domino Iohanne de Wenham milite, Iohanne de Reymes de Heyham, Waltero de Bercholt, Waltero Baudewyn, Iacobo de Wallibus, Hamone de Stratford, Galfrido de Dodeness, Roberto de Braham de Capeles, Mauricio de Suthflet de Bercholt, Roberto de Spina de Capeles, Ricardo de Bruar', Willelmo de Bruar' de Capele et aliis.   [Late thirteenth century]

> Cartulary no. 95; approx. 225 × 114 + 12 mm; endorsed: Stratforde, xiii, Locoun de Reydon.
>
> Geoffrey of Dodnash attests from 1252 × 57 (42) to 1285 (27); Richard and William de Bruario in 1284 (206) and Walter Baldwyn in 1301 (127).

STREWSTON (IN KIRTON)

123. Notification by Thomas [of Brotherton], earl of Norfolk and Marshal of England, that since once Robert de Bosco, Richard son of Ranulf of 'Stirstone', Hervey son of Hugh of 'Stirstone' and Henry son of Hamo of 'Stirstone', true patrons of the four parts of the church of 'Stirstone', by their separate charters

which the earl has inspected, conceded, granted and confirmed that church to the prior of Dodnash and the canons there serving God and their successors in pure, free and perpetual alms and, as far as they might, to their own use (*in proprios usus*), which concessions, grants and confirmations John, then bishop of Norwich, accepted, ratified and confirmed by letters which the earl has also inspected; and since the earl's predecessors or ancestors, not sufficiently informed of the right of the prior and canons, injuriously and violently ejected them from the church and its revenues after long and peaceful possession in the form aforesaid, claiming to be the true patrons of the church and appropriating to themselves its advowson, and they presented several parsons to the diocesan, who were admitted; and since the earl truly believed that the advowson of the church pertained to his comital office, because his ancestors had, as foresaid, presented injuriously thereto, completely ignoring the right of the prior and canons, and therefore had himself presented the present incumbent; and since thereafter he considered the rights of the prior and canons and their foresaid legitimate and peaceful possession, and became fearful for the souls of his ancestors set on a perilous path by their actions and wished to seize them from it, and wished to avert peril to his own soul and those of his successors; considering also the sentences of the holy father Honorius, at that time pope of the apostolic see, promulgated against spoliators and disturbers, which bull he has also inspected and understood; by these presents, insofar as in him lies, he concedes, restores and confirms to the prior and convent of Dodnash the church of 'Stirstone' *in proprios usus*, with all its rights and appurtenances, freely, quit and absolutely, and insofar as in him lies he restores the prior and convent to their former status, according to the form of the concessions, grants and confirmations aforesaid, all of which he confirms, ratifies and approves, so that he and his heirs are hereby excluded henceforth from any right in or claim to the said church or its advowson, rights and appurtenances. Sealed in testimony.

Hiis testibus: dominis Iohanne Tibbetot, Roberto de Ufford, Willelmo Giffard, Radulpho de Bockyngge militibus, domino Iohanne de Goldyngham clerico, Thoma de Holbrok, Roberto de Wachesham, Iohanne Talemache, Thoma de Visdelou, Iohanne de Frestone et aliis.

Hollesley (Holeslegh), Thursday 29 June 1335.

Cartulary no. 127; approx. 285 × 224 mm; endorsed: Dodenasch, carta domini Thome comitis Norf'; seal, round, approx. 32 mm, red wax, shield of arms, three leopards, SECRETUM. . .

For the bull of Pope Honorius III, see no. 111; for the confirmation of bp John of Oxford, no. 4. Of the patrons of the four quarters of the church mentioned above, Richard son of Ranulf is presumably Richard the parker of no. 4, and Hervey son of Hugh is identical with Hervey the clerk; note the discrepancy, for the fourth patron, between Henry son of Hamo of 'Stirstone' above and Bartholomew de Everols in no. 4.

The identification of the church of 'Stirstone' has proved very problematic, but it seems almost certain that it represents Kirton, in Colneis hundred, a parish adjoining Falkenham, which was certainly held by the canons *in proprios usus*. In bp John's confirmation charter of 1188 (4) the church is called 'Terston', in the bull of Honorius III 'Sterstone' (111). The lost hamlet of Strewston (DB 'Struu-stuna', variant spellings 'Strusten' (1395), 'Sturston' (1528) (see W.G. Arnott, *The Place-Names of the Deben Valley Parishes*, Ipswich 1946, 32) lay in the north part of Kirton parish (*DB* ii, 340b, 341b). 'Terston' is probably the unidentified DB 'Thurstanestuna' in Colneis hundred (*DB* ii, 340a). Both these places were in 1086 within the honor of Roger Bigod, held by various freemen. Of Kirton, Arnott (p. 31) writes: 'Here, the names indicate that the parish formerly consisted of three important settlements, Guston, Strewston and Croxton. Kirton itself must have been a small hamlet lying around the church.' If 'Terston' or Thurston was a fourth such settlement, the division of the advowson into four parts is explained. In 1254 Dodnash priory is credited with a portion of 4s 8d in Kirton church (*VN*, 458).

The confusion experienced by the present editor in identifying this church is a reflection of that of the canons and the earl's clerks in the fourteenth century. No. 125 demonstrates that the prior and convent had impleaded the earl for the advowson of the church of 'Sterstone in the county of Norfolk'. This is almost certainly Starston in Earsham hundred (DB 'Sterestuna', 'Stirston' in 1205; see E. Ekwall, *Concise Oxford Dictionary of English Place-Names*, Oxford 1936, 419). For the Bigod holding there, see *DB* ii, 139a, 186a, 210b). The advowson of Starston remained in the hands of Brotherton's heirs (F. Blomefield and C. Parkin, *An Essay towards a Topographical History of the County of Norfolk*, 11 vols, London 1805–10, v, 348–9). Other, although unlikely, possibilities, are Tharston in Depwade hundred (both 'Therstuna' and 'Sterstuna' in DB), held in 1086 by Robert de Vaux of Roger Bigod – but the advowson here was granted in the twelfth century to Pentney priory and remained with it until the Dissolution (Blomefield, *Norfolk* v, 303–8); and Sturston, in Grimshoe hundred, where there was a small Bigod holding, but the main estate was held in 1086 by Ralph Baynard, and the church was subsequently granted to Dunmow priory (*DB* ii, 183a, 235b, 251b; Blomefield, *Norfolk* ii, 248–50).

It is doubtful if the canons ever obtained the appropriation of the church of Kirton either. Certainly in 1499 Kirton still had a secular rector (*Register of John Morton, Archbishop of Canterbury, 1486–1500* iii, no. 469), and no revenues from the church are recorded in any of the documents relating to the dissolution of Dodnash. Indeed, since the tiny community failed to maintain the chantry of one priest for William le Newman (158), it is very unlikely that it could have provided two priests for the Brotherton chantry.

124. Indenture made between Thomas of Brotherton (*Brothertone*), son of the illustrious King Edward, earl of Norfolk and Marshal of England on the one part, and the religious men the prior and canons of St Mary of Dodnash on the other. The predecessors of the prior and canons for many years in the past held the church of 'Stirstone' in Norwich diocese with all its rights and appurtenances, and had peacefully and legitimately obtained its appropriation to themselves and their successors in the church of Dodnash in perpetuity. After long and peaceful possession they were violently and injuriously ejected by the ancestors or predecessors of the earl who, insufficiently informed of the canons' rights, unjustly claimed the advowson of 'Stirstone', which for some long time they held, un-

justly presenting certain parsons who were admitted by the diocesan, to the prejudice of the prior and convent, and the church was now occupied at the earl's own
presentation. The earl, having inspected the charters, muniments, bulls, confirmations and ratifications which the predecessors of the prior and convent had re-
quested with regard to the appropriation of the church, and now sufficiently
informed of their right and possession and also of the immense injury done to
their church, was anxious to avert as far as possible danger to his own soul and
those of his predecessors and successors, but rather to provide wisely for their
salvation by the pious provision of anniversaries in perpetuity. Therefore, having
deliberated diligently and taken counsel as to the canons' right, for the salvation
of his soul and those of his ancestors, predecessors and successors, he has conceded and confirmed to the foresaid prior and canons the church of 'Stirstone'
with all rights and appurtenances, to be held by them and their successors in perpetuity *in proprios usus*, and as far as in him lay restored them to their former
status, as is evident from his charter. Wherefore the prior and canons have conceded to the earl that, when they have recovered the said church of 'Stirstone'
with its rights and appurtenances as formerly *in proprios usus* and hold it peacefully, then they and their successors shall be bound and obliged by these presents
to find in their priory of Dodnash two canons there living the regular life and
every day celebrating divine office for the souls of the said lord earl and Alice his
late wife and Mary his present wife, of his sons and daughters, his parents, ancestors and successors and of others for whom the lord earl shall be disposed to do
acts of mercy. The choice, admission and ordination of these two canons the earl
has conceded by these presents to the prior and canons and their successors in
perpetuity. The prior and canons obligate themselves and their successors by
these presents faithfully to perform the celebration and other things as aforesaid,
so that if they or their successors, after recovery of the church of 'Stirstone', are
removed therefrom by the earl or his successors, or are molested or vexed therein,
then they shall be exonerated from providing the said canons and from the said
celebration in perpetuity. In testimony and to the perpetual memory whereof the
earl and the prior and convent have sealed each other's copy of this indenture.
Hiis testibus: dominis Iohanne Tibbetot, Roberto de Ufford, Willelmo Giffard,
Radulfo de Bokkinge, Thoma de Holebrok militibus, domino Iohanne de Goldingham clerico, Roberto de Wachesham, Thoma de Visdelou, Iohanne Talmache,
Iohanne de Freston et aliis.   Dodnash, Thursday 4 April 1336

> Cartulary no. 128; a transcript, two strips of parchment sewn together, upper: 80
> × 298 mm, lower, 162 × 440 mm, different hands.
>
> For discussion, see no. 123.

125. Notification by Thomas, the king's son, earl of Norfolk and Marshal of
England, that whereas Prior John of Gusford (*Godellesford*) and the canons of
Dodnash (*Dodenassch*) are bound and obligated by a writing sealed with their
common seal to the earl in the sum of £80 in silver to be paid at a certain date and
place, as contained in the said writing, which is dated at Dodnash in their chap-

terhouse, 21 April 1337, he wills and concedes by these presents that if the present or future prior and the canons shall pay to the king on behalf of him or his heirs the amercements which he has incurred to the king for certain defaults made in a certain writ of right concerning the advowson of the church of 'Sterstone' in the county of Norfolk sued out by the prior against the earl and brought to a hearing at the grand assize, and if the prior and canons acquit the earl and his heirs for the said amercements and save them harmless, then the said letter obligatory for £80 should be of no account or force, but should entirely lack effect; otherwise the said letter obligatory shall remain in force. In testimony whereof the parts of this indenture have been sealed alternately by the parties.

Dodnash, 24 April 1337

Cartulary no. 130; approx. 220 × 140 mm, chirograph indented at top margin; no medieval endorsement.

For discussion, see no. 123.

STUTTON

126. Grant in perpetuity by Ralph del Breggs, son of Thomas del Breggs the chaplain, to the canons, for the salvation of his soul and those of his ancestors and successors, of all his tenement in the vill of Stutton (*Stuttun'*), which was once held by Agnes daughter of Reginald of Stanhoe (*Stanho*), including messuages, arable, meadows, grazing land, pastures and woods, as they are enclosed by hedges and embankments, waters, roads, paths and all other revenues and appurtenances in any way thereto pertaining, with no retention, to have and to hold in perpetuity, rendering therefrom annually to the capital lords of the fee the due and accustomed services owed for this land and woods, and forinsec service when it may occur, as is more fully contained in the charters of enfeoffment of his predecessors, and to the lord John of Holbrook (*Holebrok*), his heirs and assigns, a pair of white gloves worth ½d at Easter. Warranty is granted against all persons in perpetuity. Sealed in testimony.

Hiis testibus: domino Rogero Reymes milite,[a] domino Willelmo Visdelou milite,[a] domino Bartholomeo Daunclers milite, Willelmo Argent, Radulfo Quereme, Iohanne de Stoke, Iohanne Hardy, Iohanne Rodlond, Rogero Fraunceys et multis aliis.   [Shortly before 29 September 1301]

[a] MS: melite

Cartulary no. 117/1; approx. 264 × 130+ mm; endorsed: vi[ta] carta Radulfi de Brigg; seal, round, approx. 30 mm, red-brown wax, radiating device of four petals.

Shortly before no. 127. William Argent occurs 1309 (162), William Visdelou 1312–13 (Rye, *Fines*, 126 no. 41), and Roger Reymes 1314–15 (ibid., 133 no. 32).

127. Quitclaim in perpetuity by John of Holbrook (*Holebrok*), for himself and his heirs, to the canons and their successors, of all right and claim which he had or in any way might have in all the lands and tenements which were once held by Ralph son of *dominus* Thomas de Ponte and by Thomas himself, which tenements are of the fee of the prior and church of Dodnash, so that neither he, his heirs nor anyone in their name may henceforth demand or claim any right therein. Sealed in testimony.

Testibus: domino Roberto de Reydon, Waltero Baldewyne, Willelmo de Crepy-pyngg', Edmundo de Boyton et aliis.   Stutton, Friday 29 September 1301.

> Cartulary no. 114; approx. 217 × 68+ mm; descriptive endorsement, iiii.

TATTINGSTONE

128. Grant in pure and perpetual alms by William, clerk of Tattingstone, to the prior and canons, for his salvation and that of his ancestors, of three parcels of land in 'Redigge' towards 'Baldrikebroc' in Tattingstone, which were held by William son of Thedewe.   [Late twelfth – early thirteenth century]

> Cartulary no. 24; approx. 151 × 76 + 20 mm; endorsed: Willelmi clerici, xx; seal, round, approx. 42 mm, natural wax varnished brown, ? dragonfly, + SIGILLUM WILLMI CLI DE TATIGES.

Willelmus clericus de Thatingest(on) omnibus hominibus et amicis suis tam presentibus quam futuris salutem. Sciatis me dedisse et concessisse et hac presenti carta mea confirmasse Deo et ecclesie beate Marie de Dodenes et priori et canonicis ibidem Deo servientibus tres pecias terre in Redigge versus Baldrikesbroc in Tatingestonia quas Willelmus filius Thedewe tenuit, pro salute anime mee et antecessorum meorum in puram et perpetuam elemosinam. Et ut hec donatio mea et confirmatio firma sit et stabilis permaneat, sigilli mei appositione corroboravi. T(estibus): Rogero comite Norfolch(ie), Eustachio de Braham, Rogero filio eius, Roberto capellano, Mil(on)e Lenveise, Willelmo de Manent, Bertram de Veredun, Bartolomeo de Braham, Hugone fratre eius, Willelmo de Sadenesfeld, Willelmo de Raimes, Eadwardo de Alneto, Herberto de Witlesham, Mauricio de Framesd(en) et multis aliis.

> William the clerk attests late twelfth-century charters (7, 9). Eustace of Brantham does not occur after 1202 (71n.).

129. Grant in pure and perpetual alms by Michael of Freston to the prior and canons, for his salvation and that of Isabelle his wife, of an annual rent of 6d from Walter son of Roger Ketlebern and his heirs in Tattingstone from the land called 'Putforke'. Warranty is granted against all Christians and Jews, free from all secular service. Right of distraint upon goods found on the land is conceded in event of non-payment.   [Mid thirteenth century]

Cartulary no. 96; approx. 182 × 120 mm; endorsed: Tatyndston, i, Michael de Frestune; seal, round, approx. 36 mm, natural wax varnished brown, fleur-de-lys, + S. . . . . .T.

Sciant presentes et futuri quod ego Michael de Frestun' concessi, dedi et hac presenti carta mea confirmavi Deo et ecclesie sancte Marie de Dodenes et canonicis ibidem Deo servientibus et inperpetuum servituris in puram et perpetuam elemosinam, pro salute anime mee et uxoris mee Isabel', annuum redditum sex denariorum recipiendum de Waltero filio Rogeri Ketlebern et heredibus suis in Tatingestun' de illa terra que vocatur Putforke ad duos terminos anni, scilicet ad festum sancti Michaelis tres denarios et ad Pascha tres denarios. Et ego dictus Michael et heredes mei warantizabimus ac defendemus dictis canonicis presentibus et futuris predictum redditum absque omni seculari servitio et demanda contra omnes homines et feminas inperpetuum, tam Iudeos quam Cristianos. Si autem forte contingat quod dictus Walterus vel heredes sui a solutione dicti redditus ad aliquem prefixum terminum cessaverint, liceat dictis canonicis distringere per averia capienda illam predictam terram que vocatur Putforke quousque redditum persolverint. In huius rei testimonium huic scripto sigillum meum apposui. Hiis testibus: Iohanne Chobelot, Ricardo filio Roberti de Boytun, Eadmundo de Chaepel', Iurdano filio Henrici, Roberto de Chaepel', Willelmo dispensatore de Berchowte, Randulfo filio eius, Roberto de Hulneye et aliis.

The grantor and three witnesses occur in 1250 (25); Robert of Hulney occurs 1223–24 (16).

130. Recognition by Adam de Gardino that he and his heirs are bound to discharge all suit of court and to render an annual rent of 10d in the court of Chelmondiston on behalf of the prior and convent of Dodnash, and also to pay to the canons an annual rent of 14d, for a tenement once held by the late Maurice of Dodnash, which Adam now holds of the canons in Tattingstone; for this warranty is granted. He conceded that if he or his heirs should default in any way, the royal bailiff of Chelmondiston may distrain upon their chattels until satisfaction is made, and he renounces all legal action in ecclesiastical or civil courts which might be taken to avert such restraint.

[Later thirteenth century, possibly soon after 1279]

Cartulary no. 83; approx. 155 × 142+ mm; endorsed: xxx, carta Ade de Gardino quod debet facere sectam pro priore ad Chelmond'; seal, round, approx. 38 mm, green wax, fleur-de-lys, + S. ADE DE LE GARDIN.

Omnibus Cristi fidelibus ad quos presens scriptum pervenerit Adam de Gardino salutem in Domino. Noverit universitas vestra me teneri pro me et pro heredibus meis ad faciendum omnes sectas et decem denarios annui redditus de anno in annum ad curiam de Chelmondestone pro priore de Dodenes et canonicis eiusdem loci, et eisdem quatuordecim denarios annui redditus de anno in annum pro quodam tenemento quondam Mauricii de Dodenes defuncti, quod ab eisdem teneo in villa de Tatingestone, et ad warantizandum et acquietandum et defendendum dictum priorem et dictos canonicos et successores suos de dictis sectis et de dictis decem denariis annui redditus et de omnibus secularibus demandis que pro predicto tenemento exigi poterint inperpetuum. Et si ita contingat quod dictus prior vel dicti canonici vel successores sui in aliquo dampno vel gravamine vel molestia per defaltam meam vel heredum meorum incurrerint, volo et concedo pro me et pro heredibus meis quod ballivus domini regis de Chelemondestone qui pro tempore fuerit habeat potestatem me distringere per omnia catalla mea mobilia et immobilia ubicumque fuerint inventa quousque eisdem plenarie fuerit satisfactum, renuntiando in hac parte omne cavillationi, exceptioni, regie prohibitioni et omne iuris remedio tam ecclesiastico quam civili; et ad maiorem securitatem huic presenti scripto sigillum meum apposui. Hiis testibus: domino Hugone Talemache milite, Ricardo de Holebrok, Galfrido de Dodenes, Willelmo Gubyun, Rogero de Braham, Bartholomeo de Alneto, Galfrido de Mara, Radulfo de Braham, Mauricio de Braham, Ricardo Andreu, Roberto de Faucenham, Ricardo de Bruera, Radulfo clerico et aliis.

> Geoffrey of Dodnash occurs from 1252 × 57 (42) to 1285 (27); Geoffrey de la Mare 1252 × 57 (42); Roger of Brantham 1276 (48); Richard de Bruera 1284 (206); Ralph the clerk 1276–85 (27, 48).

> For 10d rent due to the soke of Chelmondiston, see no, 14. In the Hundred Rolls of 1279 it is recorded that the prior of Dodnash has the land of Maurice of Dodnash, whereby the king has lost the reliefs which pertain to the soke of Chelmondiston (*RH* ii, 177b), and similarly that Hugh Tollemache and the prior had subtracted from the court of Chelmondiston suit due from the tenement once held by Thomas and Maurice of Dodnash (ibid., 190). It may be that this charter represents the attempt to remedy this situation.

130A. Grant in perpetual alms by [? Richard] of Holbrook to the canons of the site of his mill of [? Tattingstone] with millsoke, to be held freely, well and in peace, in fee and heredity, rendering to him, his heirs and assigns a penny each year at Michaelmas, and to Richard [. . .] for the millsoke, for all service, suit of court, custom and demands. Warranty is granted. Sealed in testimony.
Testibus [. . .], Roberto de Vallibus militibus, Egidio de Wachesham, Willelmo Gubioun, [. . .], Roberto de Boitun', Willelmo Bertelmen, Galfrido de la Mare, Willelmo [. . .] et aliis.   [Late thirteenth century, probably 1280s]

> Helmingham, T/Hel/98/3 (A23/14); one third missing, right-hand two-thirds = 118 × 125 + 28 mm; no medieval endorsement; tag and seal missing.

> At its dissolution the priory held watermills in Bentley, East Bergholt and Tattingstone (PRO, C142/76/42). Flatford mill in East Bergholt was acquired early in the thirteenth century by the gift of Edward of the Aldergrove (55–7), and the fuller's mill at Bentley called 'Charlismelle' (176) was almost certainly acquired with the lands of William Charles in the 1330s. Richard of Holbrook was the son of William of Holbrook, who attests charters of the mid thirteenth century and who occurs in 1246 (BL Add. ch. 9485); Richard himself attests a charter of 1256 (BL Add. ch. 9480). In 1253 Richard held one of the three manors in the vill of Tattingstone, where he received a grant of free warren; he was still alive in 1286 (Coppinger, *Manors* vi, 12, 104, with references). Of the witnesses,

William Gubioun occurs shortly after 1279 and in 1286 (64, 130), and Geoffrey de la Mare was still alive in 1283 (BL Add. ch. 9519).

GREAT WENHAM

131. Grant in perpetuity by Warin Testard to the prior and canons of one and a half acres and a rood of land lying between the land of the lady Cecily de Alno and that of Walter the miller in 'Aspelond', to be held of him and his heirs for an annual rent of 8d for all services etc. The canons have paid one mark as entry-fine.

[Early to mid thirteenth century]

Cartulary no. 44; approx. 168 × 74+ mm; endorsed: De Warino Testard, Wenham, xiiii; seal, round, approx. 33 mm, natural wax varnished brown, fleur-de-lys, + SIGILL WARI. . . . . . .STARD.

Sciant presentes et futuri quod ego Warinus Testard concessi et dedi et hac presenti carta mea confirmavi Deo et ecclesie beate Marie de Dodenes et canonicis ibidem Deo servientibus et servituris unam acram terre et dimidiam et unam rodam iacentes inter terram domine Cecilie de Alno et terram Walteri molendinarii in Aspelond, habendas et tenendas prenominatis canonicis de me et heredibus meis inperpetuum libere et quiete et honorifice, reddendo nobis singulis annis octo denarios ad quatuor terminos, scilicet ad festum sancti Michaelis duos d., ad festum sancti Andree duos d., ad Pascha duos d., ad nativitatem sancti Iohannis Baptiste duos d., pro omnibus consuetudinibus, exactionibus et demandis. Pro hac autem concessione et donatione et huius carte mee confirmatione et warantizatione dederunt michi sepedicti canonici unam marcam argenti in gersumam. Hiis t(estibus): Willelmo de Brumford, Willelmo filio Roberti, Willelmo de Waudingefeld, Rogero de Horshae, Ermeiot de Wenham, Willelmo de Boitun', Mauricio et Thoma de Dodenes fratribus, Waltero filio Hugonis de Braham et Alano filio eius, Rogero Iuvencel, Iohanne de la Mare et aliis.

Warin Testard attests many early thirteenth-century charters. Many of the witnesse occur 1223–26 (16–17, 35).

132. Quitclaim by Matthew son of Warin Testard to the prior and canons of the annual rent of 8d which he used to receive from them for 'Aspelond' in [Great] Wenham. For this quitclaim they have given him 2s.

[Early to mid thirteenth century]

Cartulary no. 45; approx. 130 × 70+ mm; endorsed: Wenham Combust'.

Sciant presentes et futuri quod ego Mattheus filius Warini Testard remisi et inperpetuum quiete clamavi pro me et pro heredibus meis priori et canonicis de Dodenes presentibus et futuris illos octo denarios quos annuatim ab eisdem percipere solebam de terra de Aspelond in villa de Wenham, pro duobus solidis esterlingorum quos michi dederunt. Et ut hec mea remissio et quiete clamantia firma sit et stabilis, huic scripto sigillum meum apposui. Testibus hiis: domino Ermengot de Wenham, Ricardo de Boytun, Herveio de Glanvill', Galfrido Tailleburg, Rogero Iuvencel, Rogero de Spina et multis aliis.

Roger Juvencel occurs in 1226 (35), Richard of Boyton 1233–34 (Rye, *Fines*, 25 no. 39), Hervey Glanvill in 1250 (25).

133. Grant in perpetuity by William of Bramford to the prior and canons of three acres and a rood of land, with appurtenances, called 'Aspelond', in the vill of [Great] Wenham, to be held for an annual rent of 22d. The canons have paid a mark as entry-fine. [Early to mid thirteenth century]

Cartulary no. 67; approx. 147 × 90+ mm; endorsed: Wenham, de Willelmo de Bromford milite, xiiii.

Sciant presentes et futuri quod ego Willelmus de Brumford concessi et dedi et hac presenti carta mea confirmavi priori de Dodenes et canonicis ibidem Deo servientibus et servituris tres acras terre et unam rodam cum pertinentiis que vocatur Aspelond in villa de Wenham, habendas et tenendas illis de me et heredibus meis inperpetuum libere et quiete, bene et in pace, reddendo inde nobis singulis annis viginti et duos denarios ad quatuor terminos, scilicet ad festum sancti Michaelis quinque denarios et obulum, ad festum sancti Andree quinque denarios et obulum, ad Pascha quinque denarios et obulum, ad festum sancti Iohannis Baptiste quinque denarios et obulum, pro omnibus servitiis, consuetudinibus, exactionibus et demandis. Pro hac autem concessione et donatione et huius carte mee confirmatione et huic scripto sigilli mei appositione dederunt michi prenominati prior et canonici unam marcam argenti in gersumiam. His t(estibus): Willelmo de Waudingefeld, Ermeiot de Wenham, Willelmo de Boitun', Willelmo Angot, Rogero Iuvencel, Galfrido de Capele clerico, Roberto de Boitune, Mauricio de Dodenes, Ricardo filio Roberti, Ricardo filio Warini et multis aliis.

William of Bramford made a grant before 1196 (9), but it is probably the same man who was alive in 1228 (*CRR* xiii, no. 1201). William of Waldingfield, Roger Juvencel and Maurice of Dodnash occur 1224–26 (17, 35). William of Boyton occurs 1227–28 (Rye, *Fines*, 25 no. 39) and Robert of Boyton from 1223–24 (16) to 1243–44 (Rye, *Fines*, 47 no. 16).

134. Quitclaim by Richard son of William of Bramford to the prior and canons of an annual rent of 22d which he used to receive from them for 'Aspelond' in [Great] Wenham. For this quitclaim they have given him 2s.

[Early to mid thirteenth century]

Cartulary no. 46; approx. 135 × 68+ mm; endorsed: Ric' filius Willelmi de Brumford; Mattheus Warini Testard; Wenham; carta relaxationis redditus xxii.d per Ric' fil' Will' de Bromford; item relaxatio .viii. d redditus per Mattheum filium Warini Testard.

Sciant presentes et futuri quod ego Ricardus filius Willelmi de Brumford remisi

125

et inperpetuum quiete clamavi pro me et pro heredibus meis priori et canonicis de Dodenes presentibus et futuris illos viginti et duos denarios quos annuatim ab eisdem percipere solebam de terra de Aspelond in villa de Wenham, pro duobus solidis esterlingorum quos michi dederunt. Et ut hec mea remissio et quiete clamantia inperpetuum firma sit et stabilis, presenti scripto sigillum meum apposui. Testibus hiis: domino Ermengot de Wenham, Ricardo de Boytun, Herveio Glanvill', Galfrido Tailleburg', Rogero Iuvencel, Rogero de Spina, Iurdano filio Henrici et multis aliis.

> Roger Juvencel occurs 1224–26 (17, 35); Hervey Glanvil and Jordan son of Henry in 1250 (25).

135. Confirmation in perpetuity by Vinnais de Alno to the canons of five acres of land with the adjacent pasturage-track and other appurtenances in [Great] Wenham, called 'Aspelond', which they hold of Richard son of William of Bramford and Matthew son of Warin Testard and of their ancestors, to have and to hold of him and his heirs for an annual rent of 30d which they used to pay to Richard and Matthew and their ancestors, as is witnessed by their charters. He has also conceded to them liberty of carriage and chase through his pond of 'Cherecheford' when they so wish. For this confirmation and concession they have given one mark. [Mid thirteenth century]

> Cartulary no. 68; approx. 165 × 95+ mm; endorsed: Carta Vinnays de Alno, Wenham, xiii.

Sciant presentes et futuri quod ego Vinnais de Alno concessi et hac presenti carta mea confirmavi Deo et canonicis de Dodeneys presentibus et futuris quinque acras terre cum p(as)tura,*a* chemini eidem adiacenti et aliis pertinentiis in villa de Wenham Aysse que vocatur Aspelond, quas ipsi tenuerunt de Ricardo de Bromford filio Willelmi de Bromford et M(attheo Tes)tard*a* filio Warini Testard de Berholt et antecessoribus eorum, habendas et thenendas eas inperpetuum libere et quiete de me et heredibus meis, reddendo inde nobis triginta denarios ad quatuor terminos anni quos solebant reddere predicto Ricardo de Bromford et Mattheo Tastard et eorum antecessoribus sicut in cartis suis continetur, scilicet ad festum sancti Michaelis septem denarios et obulum et ad festum sancti Andree septem denarios et obulum et ad Pascha septem denarios et obulum et ad festum sancti Iohannis Baptiste septem denarios et obulum, pro omnibus consuetudinibus, demandis et releviis. Concessi etiam prenominatis canonicis pro me et heredibus meis libertatem ad cariendum et casiendum per stangnum meum de Cherecheford cum voluerint. Pro hac autem concessione et huius presentis carte*b* confirmatione dederunt michi sepedicti prior et canonici unam marcham argenti. In huius rei testimonio presenti scripto sigillum meum apposui. Hiis testibus: domino Hermingot de Wenham, Willelmo de Holebroc, Ricardo de Boitun', Iohanne Godsuain, Roberto de Boitune et Ricardo filio eius, Willelmo Angot, Willelmo Anneis et aliis.

> *a* hole in MS.   *b* MS: huic presenti carta

Robert of Boyton occurs 1223–24 (16) to 1243–44 (Rye, *Fines*, 47 no. 16); William of Holbrook occurs 1250 (25).

136. Grant in fee and perpetuity by Agnes, widow of William of Pebmarsh, to the canons, for her salvation and that of her ancestors and successors, of a parcel of land in Great Wenham with appurtenances, lying between the canons' land to the west and that of Robert the smith to the east, of which one headland abuts on the road which leads from 'Cherchesford' towards 'Selfleye' and the other on the house of Robert the smith. In return for this grant the prior and convent shall in perpetuity keep a candle burning every day at high mass before the image of the Blessed Virgin Mary at the high altar; saving to the grantor and her heirs the great ash tree standing on this land. The canons shall render to the grantor and her heirs ½d p.a. Warranty is granted. If the prior and canons at any time fail to provide this candle, the grantor and her heirs may distrain upon this land until satisfaction is made. This agreement is drawn up in the form of a chirograph.

[Mid thirteenth century]

Cartulary no. 76; approx. 178 × 108 + 8 mm; chirograph, indented at top margin; endorsed: Wenham xv, Agnes; seal, vessica, approx. 42 × 27 mm, natural wax varnished light brown, stylised fleur-de-lys, .IGILL AGNETIS . . .CHEP.

Omnibus Cristi fidelibus ad quos presens scriptum pervenerit Agnes quondam uxor Willelmi de Pebenes salutem in Domino. Noverit universitas vestra me in pura et ligia viduitate mea concessisse, dedisse at hoc presenti scripto meo confirmasse, pro salute anime mee et pro salute animarum antecessorum et successorum meorum, prioratui de Dodenes et canonicis ibidem Deo servientibus et servituris unam peciam terre cum pertinentiis in villa de Wenham Combusta iacentem inter terram dictorum canonicorum versus occidentem et terram Roberti fabri versus orientem, unde unum capud abutat super iter quod se extendit de Cherchesford versus Selfleye et aliud capud abutat versus domum Roberti fabri, ita tamen quod prior et canonici invenient et sustinebunt unum cereum ardentem quolibet die ad magnam missam coram ymagine beate Marie ad magnum altare inperpetuum, habendam et tenendam predictam terram cum pertinentiis predicto prioratui et canonicis ibidem Deo servientibus libere, quiete, bene et in pace, in feodo inperpetuum, salvo michi et heredibus meis magno fraxino super predictam terram stante, reddendo inde annuatim michi et heredibus meis unum obolum, scilicet ad Pascha, pro omnibus servitiis, consuetudinibus, sectis curie et demandis secularibus. Et ego predicta Agnes et heredes mei warantizabimus, adquietabimus et defendemus predictam peciam terre cum pertinentiis predicto prioratui et canonicis ibidem Deo servientibus contra omnes gentes per predictum servitium inperpetuum. Et si ita contingat quod prior et canonici dicte domus aliquo tempore inventionem vel sustentationem predicti cerei in dicto prioratu ardentis cesserint vel deficiant sicut predictum est, liceat michi vel heredibus meis sine contradictione vel impedimento dictorum prioris et canonicorum qui tunc temporis fuerint predictum tenementum distringere quousque michi vel heredibus meis pro transgressione cerei non inventi nec sustenti*ᵃ* secundum formam

127

predictam plenarie fuerit satisfactio. In cuius rei testimonium presentibus scriptis in modum cyrograffi confectis tam dicta Agnes quam dicti prior et canonici alternatim sigilla sua apposuerunt, cuius una pars signata sigillo dicte Agnetis remanet penes dictos priorem et canonicos et altera pars signata sigillo dictorum prioris et canonicorum remanet penes dictam Agnetem. Hiis testibus: domino Hugone Thalemache milite, Galfrido de Dodenes, Rogero de Braham, Roberto de Waudingefeud, Roberto de Boyt(on), Ricardo Glaunvill, Angoto de Seltun', Roberto de Braham, Gilberto fabro, Roberto Clarice et aliis.

> *a* MS: sustentati

> After Easter 1251, when a fine was made between Walkelin de Visdelou and William son of Ralph of Pebmarsh and Agnes his wife concerning the advowson of a mediety of Capel St Mary church (*Shotley Parish Records*, 5, no. 6). For Robert of Boyton, see no. 135n. Geoffrey of Dodnash occurs 1252 × 57, and as late as 1285 (27, 42); a Roger of Brantham occurs mid century and 1276 (21, 48).

ESTATE OF WILLIAM CHARLES

Note: for discussion of nos 137–54, see Introduction, 20–23.

137. Royal licence to the prior and convent to acquire in mortmain land and rent, not held in chief, to an annual value of £10. Westminster, 23 January 1331.

> Cal., *CPR 1330–34*, 45.

138. Recognition by Edmund Gauge that he and his heirs are in perpetuity obligated to the prior and canons for an annual rent of £20, payable in equal instalments at Easter and the Nativity of St John the Baptist, for all the lands and tenements which he purchased from William Charles in Bentley, Tattingstone, Capel St Mary, Stutton and Brantham in the county of Suffolk, and also from all his lands in the county of Essex, into whosesoever hands these lands may pass in future. To this annual payment, without diminution and in perpetuity, he pledges himself, his heirs and all his goods and chattels, lands and tenements in the counties of Suffolk and Essex, into whosesoever hands they may pass, so that if the rent should be in arrears, in whole or in part, at any term, the prior and canons or their assigns may distrain upon these lands and tenements and retain those things distrained until full satisfaction shall be made for rent and arrears. He has paid to the canons £20 for seisin. Sealed in testimony.

Hiis testibus: domino Iohanne de Goldingham clerico, Nicholao Bonde, Rogero de Godelisforde, Stephano de Braunforde, Iohanne Gobioun, Ricardo le Spencer et aliis.   Dodnash, 7 February 1331

> Ipswich, SR0, q s 271 (Fitch's *Monasticon*) at p. 186; approx. 248 × 141 + 13 mm; endorsed: Memorandum si heredes Edmundi Gauge periunt, aliquid iuris vel clamei versus priorem et canonicos de Dodenasch pro terris et tenementis

que quondam fuerunt Willelmi Charles in Bentleye, Tatingeston', Capele, Stutton et Braham in comitatu Suff' extunc scriptum annui redditus stet in vigore, si non pro nichillo habeatur; xxiii; tag and seal missing.

139. Royal licence to John of Goldingham to alienate to the prior and convent in mortmain, in part satisfaction of land and rent to the annual value of £10 which they have the king's licence to acquire, a messuage, 150 acres of land, seven acres of meadow, twenty acres of pasture, ten acres of alderwood, 120 acres of heath and 15s rent in Bentley, Capel St Mary, Brantham, East Bergholt and Tattingstone, the said messuage and lands being of an annual value of £5, as appears by inquisition. Eltham, 2 April 1331.

Cal., *CPR 1330–34*, 96.

140. Notification by John of Goldingham, clerk, that he has conceded and by this present charter confirmed to the prior and canons and their successors in perpetuity all the manor of Dodnash, and also all the lands and tenements which were once held by William Charles in the vills of Bentley, Capel St Mary, Tattingstone and Brantham, with all appurtenances, revenues and rights thereto pertaining, all of which they shall have of him for a term of years (*ad terminum annorum*), to have and to hold of the capital lords of the fee freely, wholly, well and in peace, in fee and perpetuity by the due and accustomed services. He has also conceded, remitted, relaxed and utterly quitclaimed, for himself and his heirs in perpetuity, all right and claim which he had, has or in any way might have in the foresaid manor, lands and tenements with their appurtenances, without retention, so that neither he, his heirs nor anyone in his name may henceforth make any claim therein, but rather they are barred in perpetuity from any action thereto pertaining. Sealed in testimony.
Hiis testibus: dominis Willelmo de Visdelou, Willelmo de Braham militibus, Benedicto de Braham, Willelmo de Boyton, Stephano de Braunford, Iohanne Gobyon, Ricardo le Despenser et aliis. Dodnash, Sunday 5 May 1331.

Cartulary no. 118; approx. 255 × 130+ mm; endorsed: Carta domini I. de Goldingham de tenemento de Charl', xxv; tag and seal missing.

141. Quitclaim by Nicholas Bonde to the prior and canons and their successors of all right and claim which he has or in any way may have in all lands and tenements once held by the lord Edward Charles in the vills of Bentley, Tattingstone, Capel [St Mary] and [East] Bergholt, with no retention, so that neither he nor his heirs may henceforth in perpetuity claim any right in any way in these lands and tenements. Sealed in testimony.
Hiis testibus: domino Iohanne de Furneaux milite, Rogero de Godelesford, Stephano de Branford, Thoma de Wolferton, Iohanne Andreu, Iohanne Gobyon et aliis. Dodnash, Thursday 9 January 1332.

Helmingham, T/Hel/98/11 (A2/84); approx. 245 × 90 + 18 mm; endorsed: Relaxatio Nicholai Bond' de tenemento de Charlis, xv; parchment tag, seal in linen bag, seal approx. 28 × 20 mm.

142. Quitclaim by Roger of Gusford (*Godelisford*) in terms identical to no. 138. Hiis testibus: domino Iohanne de Furneaux milite, Nicholao Bonde, Stephano de Bramford, Thoma de Wlferton, Iohanne Andreu et aliis.

Dodnash, Thursday 9 January 1332

Helmingham, T/Hel/98/12 (A2/85); approx. 232 × 80 + 14 mm; endorsed: Relaxatio Rogeri de Gudliss' de tenemento de Charl', xiii; parchment tag, seal in linen bag, seal approx. 30 × 20 mm.

143. Notification by John of Goldingham, clerk, that he has granted and by this present charter confirmed to the prior and canons and their successors in perpetuity a messuage, 150 acres of land, seven acres of meadow, twenty acres of pasture, ten acres of aldergrove, 120 acres of heath and 15s rent, with appurtenances, which were once held by William Charles in the vills of Bentley, Capel St Mary, Tattingstone, [East] Bergholt and Brantham, and all other appurtenances and rights in any way pertaining to the said messuage, lands and tenements, which he lately purchased from Sarah, widow of Geoffrey Gauge, to have and to hold of the capital lords of the fees freely, wholly, well and in peace, in fee and in perpetuity, by the accustomed services due by law therefrom. He has also remitted, relaxed and utterly quitclaimed in perpetuity to the prior and canons, for himself and his heirs, all right and claim which he had, has or in any way might in the future have in the foresaid messuage, lands and tenements with their appurtenances, without retention, so that neither he, his heirs nor anyone in their name may henceforth make any claim therein, but rather they are barred in perpetuity from any action thereto pertaining. Sealed in testimony.
Hiis testibus: dominis Willelmo de Visdelou, Willelmo de Braham militibus, Benedicto de Braham, Willelmo de Boytone, Stephano de Braunford, Iohanne Gobyoun, Ricardo le Spenser et aliis. Dodnash, 7 July 1332.

Helmingham, T/Hel/98/13 (A2/88); approx. 304 × 119 + 19 mm; endorsed: Carta domini I. de Goldyngham, xxvi; parchment tag, seal in linen bag, seal approx. 30 × 14 mm.

144. Notification by Richard de la Pole, citizen of London, that whereas the prior and canons of Dodnash have and hold the manor of Dodnash and other lands and tenements in the vills of Bentley, Tattingstone, Capel St Mary and Brantham once held by William Charles, and whereas the same William was bound to him in various debts acknowledged by various recognitions made in the king's court and also according to the terms of the recent Statute of Merchants,[1] he has remitted and relaxed for himself, his heirs and executors to the said prior and canons all right and claim which he had or in any way might have had or may

have in the said manor of Dodnash and the said lands and tenements, and has re-nounced also all actions and enforcement of the recognisances relating to the rents due to him in any manner from the manor of Dodnash or the said lands and tenements; so that neither he nor anyone in his name may henceforth and in per-petuity make any claim or initiate any action or the execution of any contract made with him by William Charles or any other person concerning the said manor, lands and tenements. Sealed in testimony.

Hiis testibus: Iohanne de Pulteney tunc maiore London', Nicholao Pik et Iohanne Husbonde tunc vicecomitibus London', Benedicto de Braham, Willelmo de Bra-ham, Nicholao Bonde, Ricardo de Bergholt et aliis.

London, Monday 28 September 1332.

Cartulary no. 119; approx. 262 × 135 mm; endorsed: Relaxatio Ricardi de la Pole civis Lond' super manerium de Dodenessh, xxxiii; seal, round, approx. 25 mm (*Catalogue of Seals, PRO, Personal Seals* ii, P1890).

[1] This must be a reference to the Statute of Merchants of 1285, despite the strange use of 'lately' (*in statuto nuper de mercatoribus edito*). There was no major change in the process for recovery of merchant debts between 1285 and the date of this document. The statute's 'most daring innovation' was that 'all the debtor's land shall be delivered to the creditor to hold until the debt is discharged out of the issues from them' (T.F.T. Plucknett, *Legislation of Edward I*, Oxford 1949, 141).

145. Further notification by John of Goldingham, clerk, of his grant to the prior and convent, in terms similar to no. 143.

Hiis testibus: dominis Willelmo de Vysdelou, Willelmo de Braham militibus, Thoma de Holebrok, Iohanne Talmache, Iohanne de Prestone, Willelmo de Boy-ton, Iohanne de Gobioun, Ricardo le Spenser et aliis.

Dodnash, 12 March 1333.

Helmingham, T/Hel/98/14 (A2/91); approx. 250 × 119 + 19 mm; endorsed: Carta domini I. de Goldingham, xxvi; parchment tag cut from discarded docu-ment, on which is written 'Bernard de Cottone diaconum lat''; seal in linen bag, approx. 35 × 20 mm.

146. Notification by John Talemache of Bentley, in association with Hugh Tale-mache, his son and heir, that he has conceded, remitted, relaxed and utterly quit-claimed in perpetuity, for himself, his heirs and assigns, to the prior and canons all right which he had, has or in any way might have, by hereditary right or other-wise, in the manor of Dodnash with its appurtenances, in the county of Suffolk, which the prior and canons hold at this time in the vills of Bentley, Capel St Mary, Tattingstone and Brantham, and in other adjacent vills, without retention, so that neither he, his heirs or assigns nor anyone in their name may henceforth make any claim therein, but rather are debarred in perpetuity from any action. Sealed in testimony.

Hiis testibus: Iohanne de Goldyngham clerico, Thoma de Holebrok, Willelmo de

Boytone, Iohanne de Frestone, Stephano de Bramford, Thoma de Wholfrestone, Nicholao Bonde, Ricardo le Despencer, Iohanne Gobioun et aliis.

Dodnash, Thursday 20 May 1333.

Helmingham, T/Hel/98/15 (A2/92); approx. 240 × 105 + 23 mm; endorsed: inrotulat' in banco, rotulo placitorum xli a termino Trinitatis anno regni regis E. tertii a conquestu septimo; parchment tag, seal, round, approx. 39 mm, deep red wax, impression very faint, angled shield, legend indecipherable.

147. Pleas at Westminster before W[illiam] de Herle and his fellow justices of the Bench, octaves of Holy Trinity 7 Edward III (6 June 1333), rot. xli. John son of Hugh Talemache, represented by Roger of Burgate his attorney, sought against the prior of Dodnash, Nicholas Bonde and Roger of Gusford (*Guldesford*) a messuage, two hundred acres of land, ten acres of meadow, ten acres of pasture 16s rent, with appurtenances, in Bentley, Tattingstone, Stutton and Capel St Mary as his right and inheritance, and he stated that the prior and Nicholas and Roger did not have entry (*ingressum*) until after the disseisin which John Carbonel unjustly and without judgement made from Hugh Talemache, great-grandfather of John son of Hugh, who is his heir.[1] He stated that Hugh his great-grandfather was seised of the said tenement in demesne as of fee and right in time of peace in the reign of King Henry, great-grandfather of the present king, and he took therefrom revenues (*expleta*) to the value etc. From this Hugh the right etc. descended to a certain Hugh, his son and heir, and from this Hugh to another Hugh as son and heir, and from this Hugh to John, the present petitioner, as son and heir etc. *Et onus que etc. Et inde predictam sectam etc.*

The prior, Nicholas and Roger appeared and defended their right, represented by John of Burgh (*Bergh*) their attorney, and stated that the foresaid John Carbonel had not disseised the said Hugh Talemache, as alleged by John, and on this matter they placed themselves on the county, and John likewise. A writ of *venire facias* was despatched to the sheriff to have twelve jurors appear at York on 2 November. There the foresaid prior, Nicholas and Roger stated that after they had pleaded, the said John had in writing remitted and quitclaimed for himself and his heirs all claim which he had or in any way might have in the foresaid tenement, to the prior and his successors in perpetuity, and they presented the said writing in John's name bearing testimony to this; therefore they sought etc. John did not deny this. The prior and the others departed *sine die*, and John received nothing by his writ, but should be amerced for a false claim.

Cartulary no. 120; approx. 204 × 270 mm; endorsed: Quiet' Iohannis Thalemach, xxx.

[1] In 1275 John Carbonel brought a case against Hugh Tollemache concerning these lands (PRO, C66(Patent Rolls)/94, m. 20 dorse). See Introduction, p. 20.

It is likely that there is some confusion here, and that the Hugh Tollemache who was allegedly disseised was John's grandfather rather than his great-grandfather. The great-grandfather had died 1252 × 57, leaving a minor as his heir (see 42n.). The grandfather first occurs around Trinity 1269 (BL Add. ch. 9487) and suffered the alleged disseisin in 1275. He was married to Hillaria, and he died shortly before 21 December 1296 (*CIPM* iii, no. 389). The father was married to Katherine, and both were still alive in September 1328 (Rye, *Fines*, 126 no. 39; SRO, HD 1047/1/47).

148. Quitclaim by William Charles, son and heir of William Charles, son and heir of the late Edward Charles, to the canons of all lands and tenements which the prior and canons hold in the vills of Bentley, Tattingstone, Stutton, Brantham, and Capel St Mary or in any other vill in Suffolk, with appurtenances, formerly held by Edward Charles his grandfather, so that neither he, his heirs nor anyone in their name may henceforth in perpetuity make any claim therein. Warranty is granted against all persons in perpetuity.

Testibus: Willelmo de Boytone, Stephano de Braunford, Ricardo de Bergholt, magistro Willelmo de Braunford rectore ecclesie de Moose, Iohanne de Brok, Iohanne de Mochillefeld, Willelmo le Cok, Iohanne de Boyton et aliis.

Monday 13 September 1333.

Ipswich, SRO, HD 1538/204/3; approx. 271 × 136 + 14 mm; endorsed: v, Charles; tag and seal missing.

148A. Quitclaim by William Charles in terms identical to no. 148, except that the prior is named as John of Gusford (*Godellesford*). Identical witness list. Because he does not have a seal, he has borrowed that of William Boyton and appended it hereto.[1]

Helmingham, T/Hel/98/16 (A2/94); approx. 245 × 150 + 24 mm; endorsed: Relaxatio W. Charles, xxxii; parchment tag, seal in linen bag, seal approx. 30 × 24 mm.

[1] Compare the seal, with strange design, of no. 149.

149. Notification by William Charles that he has remitted, relaxed and utterly pardoned (*condonavi*) to John of Gusford (*Godelesford*), prior of Dodnash, and the canons all actions, both real and personal, both relating to a certain writing concerning an annual rent, and otherwise to any matter whatsoever, so that he, his heirs and executors are debarred hereby from any real or personal action against them. Sealed in testimony.   Dodnash, Monday 13 September 1333.

Cartulary no. 122; approx. 225 × 72+ mm; endorsed: Relaxatio W. Charles, xxxii; seal, round, approx. 25 mm, red wax; device appears to be crude human figure, with arms and legs outstretched, legend indecipherable.

150. Notification by William Charles, son and heir of William Charles, son and heir of the late Edward Charles, that whereas the prior of Dodnash is bound to him by a bond dated at Dodnash on 3 October 1333 in the sum of £15 sterling, to

be paid at Dodnash church on 21 September next, as is more fully contained in that writing, he wills and concedes that, if he has not utterly discharged a recognisance for £80 (*quat' viginti*) made by him to Richard de la Pole, citizen of London, according to the form of the Statute of Merchants, so that the prior and convent should in no way be obligated by this recognisance and their lands and tenements which they have in their own hands and which by the said recognisance were to be delivered to the foresaid Richard are not utterly discharged (*dishonerentur*) before 15 August next, then the said obligation should be of no moment or effect. If, however, William has annulled the said recognisance so that the prior and canons and their lands in their own hands are discharged, then the said obligation shall remain with effect and force. Sealed in testimony.

Hiis testibus: Willelmo de Boyton, Nicholao de Branford, Iohanne de Brok', Willelmo de Bramford clerico, Iohanne de Boyton.

Dodnash, Sunday 3 October 1333.

Cartulary no. 123; approx. 290 × 80+ mm; no endorsement; tag and seal missing.

151. Notification by William Charles, son and heir of William Charles, son and heir of the late Edward Charles, that he has remitted, relaxed and utterly and in perpetuity quitclaimed, for himself and his heirs, to Prior John of Gusford (*Gudlisforde*) and the canons, present and future, all right and claim which he had or in any way might have had in all the lands and tenements which they hold in the vills of Bentley, Tattingstone, Stutton, Brantham and Capel St Mary or in any other vills in the county of Suffolk, with all appurtenances, which lands and tenements were once held by the lord Edward Charles his grandfather, so that neither he, his heirs nor anyone on their behalf may henceforth in perpetuity claim any right therein. Warranty is granted against all persons in perpetuity. Sealed in testimony with the seal of Roger Bullok, since he does not have his own seal.

Hiis testibus: Willelmo de Boyton, Ricardo de Bergholt, Iohanne Gobioun, Thoma de Wulferston, Alexandro de Freston, Iohanne Argent', Simone de Creppingg', Iohanne de Boyton et aliis. Dodnash, 9 May 1335.

Cartulary no. 126; approx 264 × 124+ mm; endorsed: Quieta clamatio W. Charles, xxxii; seal: round, approx. 20 mm, red-brown wax, rough cross within square surrounded by tracery.

152. Notification by Edward, son of Sir Edward Charles, kt., that he has remitted, relaxed and utterly quitclaimed, for himself and his heirs in perpetuity, to Prior John of Gusford (*Gudelisford*) and the canons and their successors, all right and claim which he had or in any way might have in all the lands and tenements with appurtenances which were once held by Sir Edward, his father, in the vills of Bentley, Tattingstone, Brantham and Capel St Mary, so that neither he, his heirs nor anyone in their name may henceforth make any claim therein against the prior and canons and their successors, but rather are debarred from all actions. Warranty is granted against all persons in perpetuity. Sealed in testimony.

Hiis testibus: dominis Willelmo Giffard, Thoma de Holebrok, Willelmo de Holebrok militibus, Thoma de Visdelou, Roberto de Wachesham, Iohanne de Freston, Willelmo de Boyton, Iohanne Talemach, Nicholao Bonde, Ricardo le Spenser et aliis.   Ipswich, 9 April 1336.

> Helmingham, T/Hel/98/17 (A2/101); approx. 257 × 133 + 22 mm; endorsed: Edwardus filius Edwardi Charles, xxxii; parchment tag, seal in linen bag, seal approx. 30 × 20 mm.

152A. Quitclaim by Edmund, son of Edward Charles, kt., for himself and his heirs, to Prior John of Gusford (*Gudlesford*) and the canons and their successors, of all right and claim which he has or in any way might have had in all the lands and tenements once held by Edward his father in the vills of Bentley, Tattingstone, Brantham and Capel [St Mary], so that neither he, his heirs nor anyone in his name may henceforth make any claim therein against the prior and canons in perpetuity, but rather are excluded therefrom. Warranty is granted against all persons in perpetuity. Sealed in testimony.
Hiis testibus: dominis Willelmo Giffard, Thoma de Holebrok, Willelmo de Holebrok militibus, Thoma de Visdelou, Roberto de Wachesham, Iohanne de Freston, Willelmo de Boyton, Iohanne Talemache, Nicholao Bonde, Willelmo Payn, Ricardo le Spenser et aliis.   Dodnash, 5 April 1336.

> BL Add. ch. 9602; approx. 252 × 140 + 15 mm; endorsed: Quietaclamatio Edmund Charles; xvii; seal: round, approx. 32 mm, red wax, shield of arms, ermine, on a chief five lozenges, CHARLES, between three escallops within a pointed gothic quatrefoil, ornamented into small ball flowers along inner edge, *SIGILLUM * EDMUNDI * CHARLIS.

153. Notification by Edmund Charles, son of Sir Edward Charles, kt., that he has received from the prior of Dodnash all manner of debts in which he was bound to him, for any reason and by any contract, from the beginning of the world to this day. In testimony whereof he has appended his seal.
Hiis testibus: Iohanne Hastede, Ricardo de Leyham, Iohanne Love, Willelmo de Kenebroc, Thoma le Mayster, Benedicto le Jaye, Iohanne de Akenham et aliis.
                                          Ipswich, Wednesday 17 April 1336.

> Helmingham, T/Hel/98/18 (A3/1); approx. 220 × 45 mm; endorsed: xviii; tongue cut from left, round seal in linen bag, approx. 26 mm.

154. Notification by Matilda, widow of Edmund Gauge, that in her pure widowhood and liege power she has remitted, relaxed and utterly and in perpetuity quitclaimed to the prior and canons and their successors all right and claim which she had, has or might in future have, by reason of her dower or otherwise, in all lands and tenements with appurtenances which were once held by Edmund Gauge her husband in Bentley, Tattingstone, Capel St Mary, Stutton and Brantham, so that

neither she nor anyone on her behalf or in her name may henceforth claim any right therein. Sealed in testimony.

Hiis testibus: Iohanne de Staundon, Iohanne Bonchivaler, Rogero le Neuman, Willelmo Marigon, Iohanne Underwode et aliis. Bentley, Tuesday 21 May 1342.

> Helmingham, T/Hel/98/20 (A2/118); approx. 260 × 116 + 19 mm; endorsed: xxxiiii; parchment tag, seal in split linen bag, approx. 30 × 24 mm, red wax, porpoise, legend indecipherable.

MISCELLANEOUS ROYAL AND ECCLESIASTICAL DOCUMENTS

155. Letters patent of King Edward III. Whereas the king lately by letters patent conceded and granted licence, for himself and for his heirs as far as in him lay, to his beloved sons the prior and convent of Dodnash (*Dodenassh*) that they might acquire lands, tenements and rents to the value of £10 *p.a.* according to their true value, either of their own fee or of another's, excepting such as are held of the crown in chief, to have and to hold in perpetuity, the Statute of Mortmain notwithstanding, as is contained more fully in the said letters; willing that this concession may be put into effect, he has conceded and granted licence for himself etc. to John Wynch, lately parson of Wenham, Philip Deneys and William Gerard that they may grant and assign to the prior and convent two messuages, seventy acres and a rood of land, four acres of meadow, twelve acres of pasture, seven acres of woodland, seventy acres of heathland, twelve acres and a rood of aldergrove and rent of 7s 4d with appurtenances in Tattingstone (*Tatyngston*), Bentley (*Bentleye*), Brantham and Capel St Mary (*Capele*), to John Haucoun and William Marigon that they may likewise grant and assign four acres of land and rent of 4s with appurtenances in the said vills, and to Joice Breton and Thomas Bonde that they may likewise grant and assign a messuage and half an acre of land with appurtenances in Ipswich (*Gippewico*), which are not held of the crown in chief and which, over and above the rents and services rendered therefrom and apart from the foresaid rent, are valued at a true annual value of 53s 5½d, according to the inquisition made and returned to Chancery, by the king's command by Roger of Woolverstone (*Wolferston*), the king's escheator in Suffolk, to have and to hold to the prior and convent and their successors in perpetuity in full satisfaction for the said lands *etc.* to the value of £10. Special licence is simultaneously granted to the prior and convent to receive and hold these lands *etc.* in perpetuity, the Statute of Mortmain notwithstanding, so that none of the foresaid persons should be harassed by the king, his successors or ministers by reason of the said statute; saving to the capital lords of the fee the due and accustomed services. Witnessed by the king himself. Westminster, 12 July 1366.

> Helmingham, T/Hel/98/30 (A2/180); approx. 355 × 225 + 50 mm; no medieval endorsement; royal great seal on blue cords, in linen seal bag.

> These letters patent are not enrolled. For a grant to the priory by William Marigon, see no. 69, and by Thomas Bonde and Lora Bretun, no. 116.

156. Notification by Prior Adam le Neuman and the canons that whereas lately Prior John of Gusford (*Gudelesforde*) and the canons by the unanimous consent and will of the chapter conceded and obligated themselves and their successors by a certain writing dated Thursday 24 April 1343 to John of Stanton, for a certain sum in cash which he gave them, to provide him for the duration of his life with a corrody, that is baked white bread weighing 50 *solidi*, a gallon of best beer, two dishes of cooked food, with drink-money and pittance when such occur (that is on a meat day two dishes of meat and on a fish day two dishes of fish), in all things aforesaid as a canon of the house of Dodnash receives, to be taken and received each and every day by him or his attorney from the prior and canons and their successors, that is the bread and beer at the door of the pantry or buttery, the plates of meat or fish at the kitchen door; they had also obliged themselves and their successors to provide John with a chamber with *garderobe*, to be repaired and maintained at the charge of the convent, with free entry and exit through the gates of the priory thereto, and to provide each year for his lifetime two candlesticks and two pounds of wax candles and sufficient straw for his bedding for the year; and they had also conceded that if the prior and canons were to be ordered or constrained by the lord bishop, either with their assent or for the utility of their house, to take wages, then the said John should receive each day the same wages as a canon; for the provision of all these things for John for his lifetime, the prior and canons had pledged themselves and their successors, all their lands and tenements and all their goods, both temporal and spiritual, in the county of Suffolk, into whosesoever hands they may come, to distraint by the said John, so that for his lifetime he might distrain in person or by his bailiff for all the foresaid and for arrears, and remove and retain those things distrained until full satisfaction should be made; afterwards, however, John relaxed and utterly quitclaimed all right and claim which he had in the foresaid corrody by his deed addressed to the prior and canons, and he humbly petitioned that they should concede the corrody in its entirety to John de Lewalle, chaplain of Tattingstone (*Tatingiston*). The prior and canons, therefore, through their good will and by the common will and assent of the chapter, have made fuller concessions to the foresaid John the chaplain in the following form:

Notification by Prior Adam and the canons that by the unanimous consent of their chapter they have conceded and granted and are bound and obligated to John de le Walle, chaplain of Tattingstone, for the duration of his life to provide him with a corrody, that is, to provide for his lifetime reasonable upkeep in food and drink; for as long as John lives among them in their community, they will and concede that he should sit and eat at their table, that is to say at the prior's table, and that he should be served reasonably with food and drink, just as one of the canons of the house, at least twice a day. If it should happen that John, because of serious illness, should be confined to his chamber, then they concede that he should have every day during such confinement a white wheat loaf weighing 50 *solidi*, a gallon of best beer, two meat dishes on meat days or two fish dishes on fish days as the canons themselves receive, with drink money and pittances when they occur, the bread and beer to be received at the door of the pantry or buttery, the dishes of meat or fish and the drink-money or pittance at the kitchen door.

They are bound to provide for him for his lifetime an honourable chamber and *garderobe*, that is to say, the chamber by the gate, to be repaired and maintained at their charge, with free entry and exit through their gates at any reasonable time he pleases, without contradiction by them or by any of their successors. They are bound also to provide him each year with two pounds of wax candles, and sufficient straw for his bedding twice a year. If John should abide elsewhere than with them in the company of the convent, they will that they and their successors should be bound and obligated to pay to John or his attorney for each whole year that he is absent 25s in good and legal money, in equal instalments at Easter and Michaelmas, and if he abides elsewhere for less than a year, then he should have, in person or through his attorney, the due proportion of the annual sum, that is 6d for each week he is away. John wills and concedes that when he resides elsewhere and receives the said money from the prior and canons as his corrody and maintenance, or has declined to receive it, then he should receive nothing else for his corrody, except his chamber. To the payment and warranty of this corrody the prior and convent pledge themselves and their successors, all their lands and tenements and all their goods, temporal and spiritual, in the hundred of Samford (*Saunforde*), into whosesover hands they may come, so that John or his bailiff may distrain upon them or any part of them until full satisfaction is made for the corrody and any arrears. In testimony whereof the parties have sealed each other's copy of this agreement.

Dodnash, in the chapterhouse, Tuesday 25 November 1348.

Cartulary no. 134; approx. 450 × 300 mm; chirograph indented at top margin; no endorsement; fragment of seal, vessica, red wax, priory seal.

157. Indenture made between William le Newman, rector of Erwarton (*Everwarton*) on the one part and the prior and canons of St Mary of Dodnash in Norwich diocese on the other, whereby the prior and canons, in consideration of the many benefits which *dominus* William has conferred upon them and does not cease to confer, and indeed strives daily to confer or have conferred upon them, most especially in that he has remitted £100 of silver owed to him by them and has relaxed all actions which he had against them by reason of any debt, injury or dispute from the beginning of the world to the making of these presents, as is clearly stated in an acquittance sealed by him and held by them, which debts amount to a not inconsiderable sum of money, have conceded and promised for themselves and their successors that they will in perpetuity find each week, from day to day, a canon from the collegiality of the priory to celebrate each day divine office, both during William's lifetime and after his death, for his soul and for the souls of John le Newman and Avelina, his father and mother, of Sayer Sulliard, lately rector of Rendlesham (*Rendlisham*), of Edmund brother of Robert of Ufford, earl of Suffolk, and Alice his wife, of Adam le Newman, late prior of St Mary of Dodnash, and of Roger, Geoffrey and Hugh, brothers of William le Newman, and also to the souls of those to whom William and Adam are obligated and for the souls of all the faithful departed. The prior and canons shall remember the foresaid souls in all their fasts, vigils and all the benefits performed by them

in the priory, and these souls shall be participators in all the spiritual benefits of the priory in perpetuity. The first Monday of Lent shall be the anniversary of the said William and the others forenamed, and if they are dead by that day, the names of William and the others shall be inserted in the martyrology of the house to be recited at chapter, and on that Monday each of the canons shall include these souls in their *memento* in the masses which they celebrate, and each canon in lesser orders shall say the penitential psalms and other customary prayers, including the names of William and the others foresaid with the names of deceased canons. The names of William and the others foresaid shall be declared in all the chapters of England in the mortuary roll of the canons of Dodnash. On the vigil of that first Monday of Lent the prior and canons shall specially and solemnly recite the office of the dead, that is *Placebo* and *Dirige*, for the souls of *dominus* William and the others named, and each year they shall have six pennyworth of bell-ringing (*sex denarios pulsantur campanis*), and they shall distribute 40d to forty poor persons. The prior shall in perpetuity on that day distribute 40d to his brethren as a pittance. The prior and canons also promise and concede for themselves and their successors that if, God forbid, they should fail in the payment of 6d for bell-ringing, 40d to the poor and 40d in pittances for the brethren, or do not perform the exsequies or maintain the anniversary, or fail in part or in whole to celebrate or have celebrated mass on any day without reasonable cause, for each day they shall pay to the almoner of the lord bishop of Norwich 6d and to the almoner of Holy Trinity, Ipswich, 6d, as a penalty. For the faithful observance and conduct of all this from year to year and from day to day, the prior and canons have conceded for themselves and their successors that it should be enquired each year by the ministers of the bishop whether such monies had been paid, and if it should be proved that they had not, then the prior and convent might be compelled by ecclesiastical censure to make such payment; and they submitted themselves to distraint by *dominus* William, his heirs and assigns in all the lands and tenements of the priory until the full discharge of all the above obligations. For greater security the prior and canons have submitted themselves, their priory, their successors and all their goods, movable and immovable, spiritual and temporal, wherever they may be found, to the distraint and coercion of any ecclesiastical or secular judge. In testimony whereof the prior and canons and William have sealed each other's copy of this indenture.

Dodnash, 27 November 1351.

Cartulary no. 137; approx. 420 × 330 mm; chirograph indented at top margin; no medieval endorsement.

For a lease in Bentley to William le Newman's parents granted in 1316, see no. 163. Adam le Newman had been appointed prior of Dodnash in May 1346, but had been replaced, probably because of his death, in June 1349. He may have been the brother, or possibly the cousin, of William the rector and his three known brothers Geoffrey, Hugh and Roger; for charters relating to the family, see BL Add. chs. 9528, 9531, 9598, 9610–13, 9645. For a subsequent loan to the canons by William see no. 213. He had been parson of Tattingstone in 1336–37 (Rye, *Fines*, 181 no. 28), and of Bucklesham in 1345 (Helmingham, T/Hel/52/5).

158. Notification by Thomas Fyncham, gentleman. By an indenture dated 27 November 1351 made between William le Newman, sometime parson of the church of Erwarton (*Everwardton*) and the prior and canons of Dodnash, whereby the prior and canons have agreed that they shall in perpetuity every day of the year find one of the canons of their house to sing for the soul of William and for divers other of his friends whose names appear more plainly in the said deed, and also by the same deed the prior and canons undertook to keep the first Monday in Lent as the year-day of the foresaid parson and his named friends, and that they should have the said parson and his friends in their *memento* at their mass every day, and also on the said Monday the prior and his successors should give to forty poor men 40d, and also the prior and his successors should pay on that Monday to his brother canons 40d, and moreover the prior and canons on the vigil of the said Monday should solemnly recite *Placebo* and *Dirige* for the souls of the parson and his named friends, and the prior and his successors should cause the bells of the house to be rung for the deceased souls and should pay the bell-ringers 6d, and the prior conceded for himself and his successors that should they fail in any of these obligations, then it should be lawful for William, his heirs and assigns to distrain upon all the lands of the priory and to withhold the things distrained until these obligations had been fulfilled, as is more plainly stated in the said deed. The present prior has failed in the fulfilment of these obligations, wherefore he, Thomas Fyncham, cousin and heir of the said William le Newman has ordained, deputed and attorned John Talemach, esquire, of Helmingham (*Helmyngham*) in the county of Suffolk and has given him full power in his name and stead to distrain upon the lands and tenements of the prior and to withhold those things distrained until the obligations be fulfilled. He has also ordained, deputed and attorned the said John Talmach, his heirs and assigns and given them full power in his name and the name of his heirs, that if the prior or his successors should in future fail in these obligations, they may distrain *etc.* Sealed in testimony. 25 March 1506.

Cartulary no. 156; approx. 392 × 120 + 22 mm; no endorsement.

159. Mandate of Thomas [Percy], bishop of Norwich, to the Officials of the archdeacons of Norfolk and Suffolk and to all deans, rectors, vicars and parochial chaplains in the said archdeaconries. The prior and convent of Dodnash have complained that certain persons, moved by the spirit of evil, unmindful of their own salvation and with God far removed from their eyes, have at the present time unjustly invaded, subtracted, stolen and occupied the rents, possessions, customs, services and other rights and goods granted, conceded and assigned of old to the prior and convent in pure and perpetual alms, to the peril of their own souls, setting a dangerous example to others and to the grave danger and prejudice and the manifest disinheritance of the canons. Lest therefore he should allow such evil deeds to pass under the veil of dissimulation, the bishop orders each of the recipients of these presents, in virtue of obedience and under threat of major excommunication, that they should warn each and every one of these invaders, thieves and occupiers that, within fifteen days of delivery of this monition (that is five days

for the first, five days for the second and five days for the third and peremptory warning), they should fully restore to the prior and convent the foresaid rents, possessions, customs, services, rights and goods, or should make satisfaction for them, otherwise the recipients of these presents shall legitimately fulminate against them and each of them general sentence of major excommunication with canonical monition, and shall promulgate this sentence every Sunday and feast-day at Mass when a multitude of people are assembled, with cross held aloft, bells ringing and candles lit and all other due solemnity, continuing thus from day to day until full satisfaction is made in this matter to the prior and convent. They are to certify the bishop by their sealed letters patent of action taken in this matter, when so required by the prior and convent.

South Elmham, 3 October 1358.

Helmingham, T/Hel/98/24 (A3/2); approx. 365 × 125 mm; endorsed: Sententia lata contra malefactores et invasores ecclesie sive ecclesiarum; tongue cut from left, now missing.

BENTLEY

160. Grant in fee and heredity by Prior Richard and the canons, by unanimous consent, to John son of Andrew of a parcel of land in Dodnash on which the house of St Mary of Dodnash was once sited, with the embankments and hedges with which it is enclosed and with other appurtenances, to have and to hold to him, his heirs or assigns or to whomsoever to whom he may wish to grant it in any way, rendering to the canons and their successors 4d *p.a.* for all services etc. Warranty is granted. For this grant John has given them 5s and has rendered homage to them, John and his successors may not build upon this land without the consent of the prior and convent.   [Mid thirteenth century]

Cartulary no. 99; approx. 188 × 120+ mm; no endorsement.

Omnibus Cristi fidelibus ad quos presens scriptum pervenerit Ricardus prior de Dodenes et eiusdem loci canonici salutem. Noveritis nos unanimi consensu et assensu concessisse, dedisse et hac presenti carta confirmasse Iohanni filio Andree unam peciam terre nostre in Dodenesse, scilicet illam peciam in qua domus Marie de Dodenes quondam sita fuit, cum fossatis et haiis quibus includitur et cum aliis pertinentiis, habendam et tenendam predictam peciam terre cum omnibus suis pertinentiis ut supra predictum est predicto Iohanni et heredibus suis vel suis assignatis de nobis et successoribus nostris, vel cuicumque et quandocumque predictam peciam terre cum pertinentiis dare, vendere, legare vel aliquo modo assignare voluerit, libere, quiete, bene, in pace, in feodo et hereditate, reddendo inde annuatim nobis et successoribus nostris quatuor denarios ad quatuor terminos anni, scilicet ad festum sancti Michaelis unum denarium et ad festum sancti Andree unum denarium et ad Pascha unum denarium et ad nativitatem sancti Iohannis Baptiste unum denarium, pro omnibus servitiis, consuetudinibus, exactionibus, donis, auxiliis, sectis curie et demandis secularibus. Et nos predicti prior et canonici et successores nostri warantizabimus, acquietabimus et defendemus predictam peciam terre cum fossatis et haiis quibus includitur et suis omnibus aliis pertinentiis ut supra dicitur predicto Iohanni et heredibus suis vel suis assignatis per predictum servitium sicut predictum est contra omnes gentes Cristianos et Iudeos. Et pro hac autem concessione, donatione et huius presentis carte nostre confirmatione dedit nobis predictus Iohannes quinque solidos argenti et fecit nobis inde homagium. Et sciendum est quod predictus Iohannes nec heredes vel assignati sui possunt nec debent edificare in predicta pecia terre sine assensu et voluntate nostra vel successorum nostrorum. Et ut hec omnia predicta sicut predicta sunt perpetuam optineant stabilitatem, presenti scripto sigillum capituli nostri apposuimus. Testibus hiis: domino Hugone Talemache milite, Galfrido de Dodenes, Rogero de Braham, Aubri de Braham, Radulfo de Braham, Roberto de Boytune, Galfrido de Mara, Mauricio filio Rogeri, Alexandro de Stuttune et aliis.

The dating of this significant charter, which confirms that there was a site change, is very problematic. The only other occurrence of Prior Richard is in no. 194, which is of little help. Similarly, a Hugh Tollemache occurs at the turn of the twelfth and thirteenth centuries, and three others from the mid thirteenth to the early fourteenth century. Most attestations by Ralph of Brantham are late thirteenth-century, probably 1270s or 1280s, but an earlier Ralph does attest before 1221 (14). There are at least two Rogers of Brantham, one witnessing charters from before 1196, one in the late thirteenth century, with one of these (or a third) attesting in mid century. Geoffrey de la Mare occurs 1252 × 57 (42), but was still alive in 1283 (BL Add. ch. 9519). The attestations of a Robert of Boyton range from before 1196 to mid thirteenth century. The other attestations of Alexander (son of Osbert) of Stutton are all early to mid thirteenth-century, some of them at least probably late 1220s or early 1230s (44, 60–1, 110). Maurice son of Roger attests early to mid century (79–80) and mid century (84), and Aubrey of Brantham mid century (21, 24). This charter can, therefore, almost certainly be located in the mid thirteenth century, and the balance of probability is that Prior Richard preceded Prior Robert, who occurs 1252 × 57 (42).

161. Grant in perpetuity by Prior Robert and the convent to Robert of Falkenham, clerk, his heirs and assigns, for their homage and for an entry-fine of 2s, of a parcel of land in the parish of Bentley between the embankments of Jordan Skileman and the canons' land, through which runs a green path leading from Jordan's house to Wayte's house, and of which one headland is enclosed by Jordan's embankment and the same green path to the south, to be held for an annual rent of half a pound of wax. Warranty is granted. [Mid thirteenth century]

A1 = Cartulary no. 90; approx. 212 × 78+ mm; no medieval endorsement.

A2 = Cartulary no. 91; approx. 226 × 98+ mm; no medieval endorsement; small fragment of priory seal, natural wax varnished green.

Omnibus Cristi fidelibus presentibus et futuris frater Robertus prior de Dodenes et eiusdem loci conventus salutem in Domino. Noveritis nos communi consilio et assensu concessisse, dedisse et hac presenti carta nostra confirmasse Roberto de Faucenham clerico, pro homagio et servitio suo et pro duobus solidis quos nobis dedit in gersumam, unam peciam terre in parochia de Benethleye iacentem inter fossata Iordani Skileman et terram nostram, mediante viride itinere quod se extendit de domo dicti Iordani versus domum Wayte, cuius unum capud se concludit inter predictam fossam Iordani et dictum viride iter versus austrum, tenendam et habendam de nobis et successoribus nostris illi et heredibus suis vel suis assignatis inperpetuum libere, quiete et hereditarie, bene et in pace, reddendo inde nobis et successoribus nostris annuatim unam dimidiam libram cere ad unum terminum, scilicet ad annuntiationem beate Marie Virginis, pro omnibus servitiis, consuetudinibus, curie sectis, querelis et demandis. Et nos et successores nostri warantizabimus, acquietabimus et defendemus predicto Roberto et heredibus suis vel suis assignatis predictam terram cum pertinentiis per predictum servitium contra omnes gentes inperpetuum. In huius autem rei testimonium presenti scripto commune sigillum nostrum apposuimus. Hiis testibus: domino Ricardo de Braham, domino Waltero de Braham, Hugone de Doden(es), Galfrido de Doden(es) fratre suo, Roberto de Waudingfeud, Roberto de Boytun', Ricardo de Boitun, Iurdano filio Henrici, Ricardo de Bruario, Roberto de Capele, Willelmo le Mikeleboy, Roberto de Hulneye et multis aliis.

> Prior Robert occurs 1252 × 57 (42), as does Jordan Skileman. Robert of Boyton occurs from 1223–24 (16) to 1243–44 (Rye, *Fines*, 47 no. 16). Robert of Hulney occurs 1223–24 (16), and Sir Richard of Brantham and Jordan son of Henry (Bloman) in 1250 (25).

162. Notification by Prior John and the convent that, whereas Elena la Wayte has conceded and sold to Thomas Berte of Bentley, to whom she has granted a charter, a house with an adjacent plot of land as it is enclosed, with appurtenances, in the vill of Bentley (*Bentleye*) by the path leading from the house of William le Clerck to Thomas's own house, which house so granted is of the canons' fee and is held of them by various customs and services, so the prior and convent, by the common consent of their chapter, have conceded and by this indenture confirmed in perpetuity to the said Thomas Berte and his heirs the foresaid house and Elena's enfeoffment, to have and to hold of them with all appurtenances for an annual rent of 7d in equal instalments at Michaelmas, the feast of St Andrew, Easter and the feast of St John the Baptist and suit of court at Dodnash for all other annual services. The prior and convent and Thomas have sealed each other's copy of this indenture.
Testibus: Willelmo de Braham, Willelmo de Crepping', Rogero Argent', Roberto de Botesham, Edmundo de Chatisham, Roberto le Wyte, Roberto Daniel et aliis.

Dodnash, 9 February 1309.

> Helmingham, T/Hel/98/8 (A2/40); approx. 222 × 121 + 9 mm; chirograph, indented at top margin; endorsed: Carta indentata inter nos et Thomam Barte super .i. domum cum .i. pecia terre adiacente, tenend' sibi et heredibus suis per servitium .vii. d. et sectas curie; carta Thome Berte de Bentleye, xxxvi; parchment tag, fragment of seal, brown wax, device indecipherable.

163. Agreement (*ita convenit*) whereby Prior John and the convent have granted, conceded and demised at fee farm to John le Neuman and Avelina his wife and to John's heirs a parcel of their land, 30 yards in length and 2½ yards wide, lying between John's messuage to the south and the canons' land to the north, of which one headland abuts on the land once held by William le Neuman and the other on the canons' land, to have and to hold in fee farm, in fee and in perpetuity, rendering annually to the prior and canons and their successors 8d in silver as fee farm in equal instalments at Michaelmas, the feast of St Andrew, Easter and the Nativity of St John the Baptist for all other services and secular demands. Warranty is granted to John and Avelina and John's heirs and assigns in perpetuity. John[a]

pledges his land and tenement in Bentley (*Benetheleya*), which is of the fee of the prior and convent, to distraint by them in case of non-payment of the said fee farm. The parts of this indenture were sealed alternately by the parties.

Wednesday 4 February 1316.

a Much damaged from this point.

Helmingham, T/Hel/98/9 (A2/56); approx. 195 × 150 + 7 mm; chirograph, indented at top margin; descriptive endorsement, xxxvii; parchment tag, fragment of seal, brown wax, device indecipherable.

John and Avelina were the parents of William le Neuman, rector of Erwarton, who made substantial loans to the priory, in which a chantry was established for him and nominated beneficiaries in 1351 (157).

164. Agreement between Prior John and the canons of Dodnash on the one part and William Schereve of Tattingstone (*Tatingeton*), Florence his wife and William his son, a minor, on the other, whereby the prior and canons have conceded to them at fee farm a parcel of pasture called 'Gilbesacer' with appurtenances in the vill of Bentley, lying between the heathland of the prior and canons called 'Buggesdoun' to the east and the stream flowing to the mill of Henry le W(*illeg.*) to the west, of which one headland to the north abuts on the land of Gilbert le Shepherde and the other to the south on the pasture of the prior and canons, to have and to hold with all appurtenances and with free entry and exit from Martinmas next [11 November] for the duration of their lives, rendering annually 2s in equal instalments at the four usual terms for all services and secular demands. William, Florence and William concede that if the rent should be in arrears, the prior and canons may distrain upon and reoccupy the pasture in perpetuity, without any claim by them. Warranty is granted against all persons. Sealed alternately by the parties.
Hiis testibus: Iohanne de Schatesham, Radulfo le Clerk, Thoma Rauff, (*illeg.*), Willelmo Finisford de Tatingston et aliis.   Sunday, 9 November 1343.

Cartulary no. 132; approx. 260 × 130 mm; badly stained; no medieval endorsement.

165. Notification by Prior John and the convent that they have conceded, granted and by this present charter confirmed to Margery, widow of Edmund Cobat of Bentley (*Benetheleye*), all lands and tenements which Edmund held of them in Bentley, to have and to hold for the duration of her life, rendering annually to them and their successors 20d in silver in equal instalments at Michaelmas, the feast of St Andrew, Easter and the feast of St John the Baptist, and rendering suit of court to the prior and convent at Dodnash every three weeks, for all other annual services and demands. Warranty is granted for the term of her life against all persons. After her death all the lands with appurtenances shall remain to Roger, son and heir of Edmund Cobat, and his heirs in perpetuity, to be held of the prior

and canons and their successors in perpetuity [*last two and a half lines totally illegible*].

> Cartulary no. 133; approx. 226 × 128 mm; chirograph indented at top margin; no medieval endorsement.

166. Notification by Prior Henry and the canons that they have conceded and leased at farm to Thomas del Waldoune all the lands and tenements of John le Shepherd held of them in Bentley (*Bentleye*) and Tattingstone (*Tatingeston*), to be held until the attainment of majority by John's heir, and all the pasture which John Rodlond lately held of them, to have and to hold of the prior and canons from Easter next until the majority of the said heir, rendering annually to the prior and canons and their successors 4s in equal instalments at Easter, the feast of St John the Baptist, Michaelmas and the feast of St Andrew, for all other services. Thomas del Waldoune wills and concedes for himself and his successors that should the said rent be in arrears in part or in whole, which God forbid, then the prior and canons may distrain upon all his lands and tenements in Bentley and Tattingstone and may retain those things distrained until full satisfaction is made. In testimony whereof the parties have sealed each other's copy of this indenture. Hiis testibus: Hugone le Neuman, Ricardo Baroun, Edmundo Bereman, Iohanne Tapin, Iohanne Ingelond et aliis.   Dodnash, 16 April 1356.

> Cartulary no. 139; approx. 260 × 130 + 25 mm; endorsed: Indentura T. Waldon; fragment of seal, round, approx. 28 mm, bird facing left, + S. . . . . .DONE.

167. Notification that an agreement was reached between Prior Henry and the canons on the one part and Randulf Luthare and Margery his wife on the other, whereby the prior and canons have conceded and demised at fee farm to Randulf, Margery and Randulf's heirs a parcel of land containing three acres, lying between the canons' land to the west and the road from Dodnash to Ipswich to the east, of which one headland to the south abuts on the canons' land and the other to the north on that of Ralph the clerk, rendering therefrom 18d *p.a.* in four equal instalments at the feast of St Andrew, Easter, the feast of St John the Baptist and Michaelmas, and also in autumn, when so notified, the work of one man for one day, for all other services. Warranty is granted against all persons. Randulf and Margery concede that should the fee farm ever be in arrears, which God forbid, then the prior and canons may distrain upon the land and their chattels thereon without contradiction. In testimony whereof the parties have sealed each other's copy of this indenture.
Hiis testibus: Hugone le Neuman, Radulfo clerico, Iohanne Topin, Ricardo Curtays, Edmundo de Liteman et aliis.   Monday 7 November 1356.

> Cartulary no. 140; approx. 255 × 158 mm; chirograph, indented at top margin; descriptive endorsement, xxxix.

168. Indenture between Prior Henry and the canons on the one part and Thomas dil Waldoune and Isabelle his wife on the other, whereby the prior and canons have conceded and demised at fee farm to Thomas and Isabelle a parcel of pasture in the vill of Bentley (*Bentleye*), lying between the land of Sir Thomas of Holbrook (*Holbrok'*), kt, to the west and the canons' land to the east, of which one headland abuts on the canons' land and the other on that of the late Gilbert the shepherd. They have also conceded to them the profits from the land of the late Gilbert the shepherd purchased from John Helis, son and heir of the said Gilbert, to have and to hold to Thomas, Isabelle and their heirs in perpetuity, rendering therefrom an annual rent of 12d for the pasture and the late Gilbert's tenement. Warranty is granted. In testimony whereof the parties have sealed each other's copy of this indenture.

Hiis testibus: Willelmo Livermere, Hugone le Neuman, Galfrido le Neuman fratre suo, Edmundo Liteman, Ricardo Baroun et aliis. Sunday 5 June 1362.

> Cartulary no. 143; approx. 265 × 115+ mm; badly faded; endorsed: Carta indentata inter nos et Thomam de Waldoun super pecia pasture apud Bukysdoune et terra Gilberti bercarii tenenda sibi et heredibus suis per servitium et .ii. s. et sectam curie, xl; Thomas Waldon de terra in Benteley.

> In the early thirteenth century Hugh Tollemache had confirmed the grant by the abbey and convent of Tilty to Thomas of Dodnash and his heirs of land at Buxton (*Buggesdoune*) (Helmingham, T/Hel/49/1).

169. Indenture whereby Prior Roger and the canons have for themselves and their successors conceded to Edmund dil Heyt of Bentley (*Bentleye*), his heirs and assigns, license for and right of pasturage and commoning in their grassy track in the vill of Bentley between their land on one side and Edmund's on the other, with its headlands abutting on the lands of the prior and canons, for all his beasts, with free entry and exit to the said path with his beasts, rendering therefrom to them and their successors 2d of silver *p.a.* in equal instalments at Michaelmas and Easter. If it should happen that Edmund, his heirs or assigns should default in payment at any term, in whole or in part, then the canons may distrain upon the said grassy track and may remove and retain those things distrained until full satisfaction is made for the rent and arrears. The copies were sealed alternately by the parties, by the prior and convent with their seal *ad causas*.

Dodnash, Sunday 24 September 1363.

> Helmingham, T/Hel/98/27 (A2/171); approx. 200 × 140 + 20 mm; chirograph, indented at left hand margin; endorsed: Beyngteley; parchment tag, seal missing.

170. Agreement (*ita convenit*) whereby Prior Roger and the canons have conceded and leased at farm to Peter le Clerk and Joanna his wife, of Stutton, a parcel of land at 'Constables Bregge', lying between the canons' land to the west, Peter's meadow to the east, the meadow of John of Holbrook (*Holbrock*) to the south and the prior's meadow to the north, to have and to hold with appurte-

nances from the day of the making of these presents for a term of twenty years, rendering therefrom to the prior and canons or their attorneys 16d in silver *p.a.* in equal instalments at the Nativity of St John the Baptist and Christmas for all services and secular demands. Warranty is granted for this term of twenty years against all. Sealed alternately by the parties. 29 September 1363.

Helmingham, T/Hel/98/29 (A2/173); approx. 245 × 120 + 26 mm; chirograph, indented at top margin; endorsed: Petrus Clerk de Stutton, de prato de Bentelee; parchment tag, seal missing.

170A. Memorandum of a grant by Prior Roger and the canons to Peter le Clerk, John his younger son and John's heirs of parcels of land in Bentley, Brantham and Tattingstone, and a parcel next to the land of Walter Douce, for an annual rent of 7s 8d. [c.1363 × 1383]

BL Add. ch. 9551, on dorse of grant by William of Crepping (*de Creppynges*) of Stutton to William the smith of Stutton and Amable his wife of land there, for 2s *p.a.*, 10 June 1303.

The dates are those of Prior Roger, and although the memorandum is on the dorse of a charter of 1303, the beneficiary occurs in 1363 (170) and there is no evidence of a Prior Roger in the early fourteenth century.

171. Indenture whereby Prior Roger and the canons have, for themselves and their successors, conceded to John Drivere of Bentley (*Bentelegh*), his heirs and assigns, license for and right to pasturage and commoning in their grassy track in the vill of Bentley, between their land on one side and John's messuage on the other, abutting at both headlands on the lands of the prior and canons, for all his beasts, with free entry and exit to the said path with his beasts, rendering therefrom to them and their successors 2d *p.a.* in silver in equal instalments at Michaelmas and Easter. If it should happen that John, his heirs or assigns should default in payment at any term, then the canons may distrain upon the said grassy track and may remove and retain those things distrained until full satisfaction is made for rent and arrears. Sealed alternately by the parties.

Bentley, Sunday 24 September 1363.

Helmingham, T/Hel/98/28 (A2/172); approx. 192 × 114 + 9 mm; chirograph, indented at top margin; endorsed: Pro victu de Benethl'; parchment tag, seal missing.

172. Indenture whereby Prior Roger and the canons have, for themselves and their successors, conceded to Thomas Skout and Isabelle his wife, their heirs and assigns, licence for and right to pasturage and commoning in their grassy track in the vill of Bentley (*Bentleghe*), between their land on one side and the messuage of Thomas and Isabelle on the other, abutting at both headlands on the lands of the prior and canons, for all their beasts, with free entry and exit to the said path

with their beasts, rendering therefrom to them and their successors 2d *p.a.* in silver in equal instalments at Michaelmas and Easter. If it should happen that John and Isabelle, their heirs and assigns should default in payment at any term, then the canons may distrain upon the said grassy track and may remove and retain those things distrained until full satisfaction is made for rent and arrears. Sealed alternately by the parties. Bentley, Monday 6 February 1369.

Helmingham, T/Hel/98/31 (A2/186); approx. 285 × 115 + 17 mm; endorsed: De past' in Benetlye; two parchment tags, fragments of seals, natural wax; right hand, round, approx. 28 mm, device indecipherable; left, round, approx. 25 mm, eagle displayed.

173. Indenture whereby Prior Roger and the canons have leased at farm to John Cubbut senior and John Cubbut junior of Brantham two crofts enclosed by banks and ditches in the vills of Tattingstone (*Tatyngstone*), Bentley (*Benteleye*) and (*illeg.*, *probably* Brantham), of which one croft is called 'Potterissacre' and the other 'le Rodyng', and their headlands abut on the wood called 'le B. . .nemedywe' and on the land called 'Hodilond', to have and to hold to them, their heirs and assigns for the next nine years, rendering annually 6s 8d at the four usual terms in equal instalments for all services and secular demands. The canons shall have right of distraint should the rent fall into arrears. Sealed alternately in the form of an indenture.
Witnessed (*among others illeg.*) by William Bewlyn, Matthew Hoberd, John Roger and Richard Baron. Monday 28 September 1377.

Bodley, Suff. ch. 196; approx. 210 × 135 + 21 mm; badly damaged.

174. Indenture whereby Prior Walter Baa and the canons have conceded and leased at farm to Semeine Thacher of East Bergholt (*Estbergholte*) a tile-kiln (*unum tylkelne*) with an adjoining close (*clauso*) and a messuage built thereon, with appurtenances, as they are enclosed in the vill of Bentley (*Benteleye*), from Christmas last for a term of five years, rendering therefrom annually to the prior and canons 8000 tiles in two equal instalments on 24 June and 15 August; if at any term the said tiles should be in arrears in part or in whole, the prior and canons may reenter this messuage with appurtenances and retain those things there distrained until full satisfaction is made for the tiles and for the damages of the prior and convent. Semeine shall have his clay, water and sand (*argillam, sudum et sand*) from the prior's land as may best be done without damage, with no contradiction from the prior and convent. In witness whereof the parties have appended their seals to the parts of this indenture. Thursday, 5 April 1397.

Helmingham, T/Hel/98/34 (A2/215); approx. 215 × 140 + 10 mm; chirograph, indented at left margin; no medieval endorsement; parchment tag, seal missing.

175. Indenture whereby Prior John and the canons have conceded, leased and granted at farm to Thomas atte Heth of Bentley (*Benteleighe*) three parcels of land and one green way with appurtenances in Bentley; of which one parcel is called 'Russellfeld' and lies next to the land of John Newman to the south and that lately held by John Baroun to the north, of which one headland to the east abuts on the land of John Newman and Richard Rolf and the other to the west on the land of the prior and canons; the second parcel is called 'Bonchevalersage' and lies opposite the gate of the messuage lately held by John Baroun to the east and the land of the prior and canons to the west, of which one headland to the south abuts on the land of the prior and canons and the other to the north on Thomas's own land; the third parcel was lately held by John Dryvere and lies next to the land of the prior and canons to the south, and one headland to the east abuts on Thomas's land and the other to the west on the common road; and the green way lies opposite Thomas's messuage, and one headland to the north abuts on the land once held by Richard att Heg and the other to the south on Thomas's land; to have and to hold with their appurtenances and with a certain common opposite 'Skylmanesfeld' to Thomas atte Heth, his heirs and assigns from Christmas next until the completion of a full term of one hundred years, rendering therefrom annually to the prior and canons 10s 4d in equal instalments at Easter, the Nativity of St John the Baptist, Michaelmas and Christmas. If it should happen that the said rent should at any term be in arrears in whole or in part, then the prior and canons and their successors and their attornies may distrain upon the three parcels with the green path, or any part thereof, and retain those things distrained until full satisfaction is made for the farm with arrears, together with damages and expenses. Warranty is granted for the duration of this term against all persons. In testimony whereof the parties have sealed each other's copy of this indenture. Dodnash, in the chapterhouse, Sunday 13 December 1411.

Cartulary no. 151; approx. 230 × 175+ mm; endorsed: Thomas atte Heth, Benteley; large fragment of (? a new) priory seal, vessica, red wax, the Virgin and Child standing, in base a shield of arms, three leopards (Brotherton).

176. Indenture whereby Prior Robert and the convent have demised and leased at farm to Edmund Warde, fuller, and Walter Wytch of Bentley a fulling mill (*molendinum fullereticum*) called 'Charlismelle', with the pasture pertaining of old to the mill and with an alderwood adjacent to the mill to the east, to have and to hold with the mill-pond and the current of water, and with all commodities and appurtenances, to them and their heirs and assigns for a full term of sixteen years, doing no manner of waste or destruction in the said mill, pasture and alderwood for the duration of the said term, rendering annually to the prior and canons and their successors 40s in silver of the good and usual money of England in equal instalments at Christmas, Easter, the Nativity of St John the Baptist and Michaelmas. Edmund, Walter and their executors and assigns shall maintain the millbank in reasonable repair and shall also maintain the flow of water into the stream up to the end of the pasture, as is necessary. The prior and canons shall maintain the upkeep of the mill well and competently at their own cost for the

duration of the term, except for 'furryng, toppyng, luggyng and dagcheyng', and for those purposes shall when necessary provide Edmund, Walter and their attornies sufficient timber and planks, with carriage thereto, providing that they are given reasonable notice by Edmund and Walter. If Edmund and Walter or their attornies are molested or aggravated or suffer any impediment in the mill by the default of the prior and canons, then they may detain and recoup from the said farm in proportion to the length of time (*quantitatem temporis*) and by the view and acknowledgement of both parties.

The prior and convent have also granted and leased at farm to Edmund and Walter a meadow called 'Whetecroftpastur', with free entry and exit in 'Whitisleye' to carry hay from the said meadow to 'Whetiseroc', and with free entry and exit with their carts and horses in 'Marleye' from the said pasture to 'Sandric'.

The prior and convent have also granted and leased at farm to Edmund and Walter and their attornies a parcel of land in the vill of Bentley (*Bentleye*) lying between the land of the prior of Holy Trinity, Ipswich, and the land of 'Bentley-howsis', of which one headland abuts on the wood called 'Ingerethwode', to have and to hold the said meadow, pasture and parcel of land with all commodities and appurtenances to them, their executors and attornies from the feast of the Purification of BVM next (2 February) for a full term of sixteen years, rendering annually 22s of the good and legal money of England in equal instalments without delay at the Nativity of St John the Baptist and the Purification.

If it should happen that Edmund and William or their attornies are in arrears by more than four weeks in payment of the said farm of 62s *p.a.*, in part or in whole, at any term, then the prior and convent and their successors may distrain upon the mill, alderwood, meadow, pasture, lands and their appurtenances, and may remove and retain those things distrained until full satisfaction is made for the said farm with arrears, and if this is not sufficient, they may reenter the said mill, *etc.*, and hold them in their former state until full satisfaction is made for the farm, with damages. Warranty is granted for the duration of the term against the king and all other persons, for the foresaid service. In witness whereof the parties have sealed each other's copy of this indenture. Dodnash, in the chapterhouse, 8 September 1427.

Helmingham, T/Hel/98/36; approx. 316 × 218 + 20 mm; chirograph, indented at top margin; no medieval endorsement; tag and seal missing.

177. Indenture whereby Richard Whityng, prior of Dodnash, and the convent have conceded and leased at farm to Thomas Whityng of Tattingstone (*Tatyngston*) all their land called 'Potters' with adjacent meadow, as it lies enclosed with hedges and ditches between the land of John Fyncham called 'Conwalle' to the west and the meadow of John Fastolf, John Fyncham and others to the east, of which one headland to the north abuts on the path leading from 'Charles' to 'Constablesbregge' and the other to the south on the current of water running from Dodnash to Woodbridge (*Wodebregge*); they have also leased to him two parcels of land containing three acres, be there more or less, with all appurte-

nances, of which the first is called 'Breadlingispigtell' and the second 'Constablisfeld', which lands and meadow lie in Bentley, Tattingstone and Brantham, to have and to hold for the duration of his life, rendering therefrom annually to the prior and canons and their successors or their attorneys one penny, in equal instalments at Michaelmas and Easter. If the rent shall fall into arrears, in whole or in part, by fifteen days, distraint may be made on the said lands until full satisfaction is made for the annual farm, with damages and expenses. In testimony whereof the parties have sealed each other's copy of this indenture. Dodnash, in the chapterhouse, 20 March 1460.

> Cartulary no. 154; approx. 305 × 170 + 32 mm; endorsed: Potters; fragment of priory seal, red wax.

178. Indenture [*in English*] whereby Robert Kaar, prior, and the convent, that is Alexander Booll and Matthew Houte, have leased at farm to John Thurston of Bentley and his assigns a field called 'Russell Feld' containing sixteen acres, more or less, for a term of three years, to have and to hold from Christmas next. The said John is to have sufficient 'stuf' from the great field to hedge the said field for three years. For the first year he has paid in full. In testimony whereof the parties have sealed each other's copy of this indenture. 12 December 1492.

> Cartulary no. 155; approx. 190 × 100+ mm; chirograph, indented at top margin; no endorsement.

178A. Indenture [*in English*] whereby Prior John Brydgewater and the canons have by their common consent leased at farm to Edmund Cukhowe of Tattingstone (*Tatyngeston*) a piece of land, which is a parcel of 'Charles', called 'Cardeneymylfelde', with all appurtenances, which abuts at one headland on the lane leading from Bergholt (*Barkolt*) to Dodnash, and at the other to the east on 'Poplere Medowe', lying between 'Potteres' on one side and the path leading from Dodnash to 'Cardeneymyll' on the other, to have and to hold to him, his heirs, executors and assigns from the date of this present indenture for a full term of seven years, rendering annually to the prior and canons and their successors 23s 4d in equal instalments at Easter and Michaelmas. It is agreed between the parties that the tenant of the field to the south of 'Cardenemylfeld' should keep, maintain and hold the hedge dividing them. In testimony whereof the parties have sealed each other's copy of this indenture. Dodnash, in the chapterhouse, 20 March 1523.

> Helmingham, T/Hel/98/41 (A2/353); approx. 345 × 110 + 20 mm; chirograph, indented at top margin; no medieval endorsement; parchment tag, seal missing.

EAST BERGHOLT

179. Grant by Prior John and the convent to John le Cok, junior, of [East] Bergholt, for his service and for half a mark which he gave as an entry-fine (*in gersumam*), of a parcel of enclosed land, with a parcel of meadow adjacent, as marked by their boundaries, lying lengthwise between the land of Hubert de la Walne on one side and his own aldergrove on the other in [East] Bergholt, to have and to hold to him, his heirs and assigns in fee and heredity in perpetuity, rendering to the canons 12d *p.a.* in equal instalments at the four usual terms for all services *etc.* Warranty is granted against all persons in perpetuity. Drawn up in the form of a chirograph sealed alternately by the parties.
Hiis testibus: Hugone Talemache, Rogero Argent, Roberto de Botingham, Roberto le Whyte, Iohanne le Schyp, Roberto de Sprouton, Waltero atte Schawe, Roberto Daniel et multis aliis.   [Early fourteenth century]

> Helmingham, T/Hel/98/5 (A2/16); approx. 220 × 108 + 18 mm; chirograph indented at top margin; endorsed: xx; parchment tag, fragment of seal, natural wax, device indecipherable.

> John of 'Botingham' attests in 1304 and 1343 (185, 195); Robert le Whyte, in 1304 and 1309 (162, 195); Robert Daniel in 1309 (162). Prior John occurs from 25 October 1304 to 2 February 1316, and was immediately succeeded by John of Gusford, who had resigned by 10 May 1346.

180. Agreement (*ita convenit*) between Prior Henry and the canons on the one part and Richard Ade (*Ad'*) of East Bergholt (*Estbergholte*) on the other, whereby the prior and canons have conceded and leased at farm to Richard and his heirs, for a term of one hundred years, a parcel of their land in East Bergholt lying between Richard's land on one side and that of William le Sponere on the other, of which one headland to the west abuts on 'Schaddislane' and the other to the east on Richard's land, to have and to hold of the prior and canons and their successors, rendering annually 28s in equal instalments at the four usual terms for all other services and secular demands pertaining to the prior and canons, and rendering on their behalf to the capital lords of the fee the due and legally accustomed services. To the payment of this rent Richard pledged himself and his heirs and the foresaid parcel of land, into whosesoever hands it may fall, to distraint by the prior and canons and their bailiffs, so that they may distrain, remove and retain those things distrained until full satisfaction shall have been made for the annual rent of 28s and for arrears. In testimony whereof the parties have sealed each other's copy of this chirograph.
Hiis testibus: Willelmo atte Heȝe, Henrico atte Brokes, Iohanne Thoft, Willelmo Luve, Willelmo Marigon et aliis.   Dodnash, Sunday 20 June 1350.

> Cartulary no. 135; approx. 218 × 190 mm; endorsed: Carta Ricardi Ade de Estbergholt, xxiiii.

181. Indenture whereby Prior Roger and the canons have conceded and demised at farm to William del Heyt of [East] Bergholt (*Bergholte*) a parcel of the meadow of 'Mosemedwe' in the vill of Bergholt, lying between the canons' meadow on one side and that of William on the other, to have and to hold of them to William, his heirs and assigns, rendering annually a penny at Easter for all services and secular demands. Warranty is granted against all persons in perpetuity. William has conceded, for himself and his heirs, that should the rent be in arrears by two years, then the prior and canons may distrain both upon William's own meadow and the foresaid meadow, into whosesoever hands they may have come, and may remove and retain those things distrained, with no complaint or contradiction by him or his heirs, until full satisfaction is made. In testimony whereof the parties have affixed their seals to each other's copy of this indenture. Hiis testibus: Willelmo Marigon, Ricardo Wynne, Willelmo Hacun, Iohanne Cristemasse, Nicholao Dekeman et aliis.   Dodnash, 30 September 1370.

Cartulary no. 146; approx. 250 × 92+ mm; chirograph, indented at top margin; descriptive endorsement, xxi; seal, round, approx. 28 mm, eagle displayed, legend indecipherable.

182. Indenture whereby the prior and canons have leased at farm to William Marigon all those lands and tenements which they lately have by his gift and enfeoffment in the vill of [East] Bergholt, to be held by him for his lifetime for an annual rent of 16d; after his death they are to remain to Joan his wife for her lifetime for an annual rent of 8s, payable at the usual terms; and after her death to John their son for his lifetime, for an annual rent of 10s. After John's death, the lands and tenements, with pasture and all other appurtenances, shall revert and remain in perpetuity to the canons and their successors, with no contradiction or impediment whatsoever. If it should happen that Joan or John cause any waste or destruction therein, the prior and convent may distrain upon all those tenements, re-enter therein and reseise, until full satisfaction is made for arrears of the farm and for damages. Warranty is granted in the form aforesaid against all persons. Hiis testibus: Rogero de Wlferston, Waltero Cosyn, Willelmo Haucoun, Willelmo fabro, Ricardo Wynne et aliis.   East Bergholt, Monday 25 April 1373.

Ipswich, SRO, q s 271 (Fitch's *Monasticon*), vol. ii, at p. 178; approx. 240 × 114 + 16 mm; endorsed: Indentura, de terris et tenementis Willelmi Marigon, xxii; slits for three tags, tags and seals missing.

A further memorandum on the dorse notes that William's ancestors held this messuage in villeinage, concerning which the canons had a charter of the lady Ada de Thoni relating thereto.

For the license to Marigon to alienate land to the priory, see no. 155, and for his grant, no. 69. For a further lease to him, see no. 190.

BRANTHAM

183. Notification to all Christ's faithful by Roger of 'Stronde' and Joan his wife that they are bound to the prior and canons for an annual rent of 16d payable in four equal instalments for a parcel of land in Brantham called 'Cotebregedune', of which one headland abuts to the east on the road leading from the house of Peter Lays towards Brantham church, and the other to the west on the land of Roger Munjoye and of Roger of 'Strond', and which lies lengthwise between the land of Robert le Chuttere to the north and that of Richard the clerk to the south. If they or their heirs default in the payment of rent, either the convent's bailiff or the king's, at the canons' choice, may distrain until full satisfaction is made. Sealed in testimony.

Hiis testibus: domino Hugone Thalemach, domino Iohanne de Wenham, Willelmo de Crepping, Andrea Helte, Radulfo de Braham, Willelmo Maupetit, Willelmo de Bruario de Capel, Radulfo clerico de Benetley et aliis.   [Late thirteenth century]

> Cartulary no. 101; approx. 225 × 75 + 11 mm; endorsed: Carta Rogeri de Strond et Iohanne uxoris sue, v.
>
> Seven of the witnesses attest nos 85–6, and three nos 26, 46, 50.

184. Notification by Nicholas Brente of Brantham (*Braham*) that he is bound to the prior and canons for an annual rent of 18d and half a measure of refined salt (*dimidium quart' salis albi*) for the length of his life for a certain parcel of land and a salt-house (*salina*) in the vill of Brantham, with a lead-pan (*plumbo*) weighing 100 lb in the salt-house. If he should default in the payment of the fore-said rent or salt, in part or in whole, he obligates himself to the prior and convent to the payment of a penalty of half a mark, and grants that they may distrain through their bailiffs until full satisfaction is made. Moreover, he submits himself to the coercion of the sheriff or of the bailiff of Samford (*Saunford*), who may distrain upon all his goods for payment, and for any such distraint shall receive half a mark. If it should happen that he surrenders the said land or salt-house, he wills and concedes that the land should be seised and the salt-house delivered in good estate, the latter with timber walls and doors and with the lead-pan therein. He wills and concedes that when he dies, neither his heirs nor his executors should have the administration of his goods until full satisfaction is rendered to the prior and canons for all that is due for the unsown land and for deterioration in the salt-house and the 100 lb lead-pan. Sealed in testimony.

Dodnash, Tuesday 25 March 1326.

> Cartulary no. 117/2; approx. 234 × 71+ mm; no endorsement.
>
> For the earlier grant and quitclaim, see nos 71–3.

185. Notification by John le Passh of Brantham (*Braham*), chaplain, that a certain Nicholas de le Brok of Brantham once purchased from the prior and canons a

messuage and certain tenements in the vill of Brantham, to hold of them for the annual service of 20d, as is more fully contained in a certain old charter granted by the canons to him; and long afterwards, a certain Robert le Passh and Sarah his wife purchased from Adam de le Brok, kinsman and heir of Nicholas, a part of the said tenements, that is, a messuage with flax-ground in the croft called 'le Merefeld' and a parcel of land on 'Ysemeredoune', with marsh and certain commons in a common marsh, to have and to hold to Robert le Passh, Sarah his wife and Robert's heirs in perpetuity for the said service of 20d and in addition another 10d as specified in the charter thereto relating. He, John, has purchased from Robert le Passh his father these lands, and he now acknowledges that he is obligated to the prior and canons for the service of 20d and the additional 10d each year, to the payment of which he pledges himself, his heirs and all the said tenements which he has by the grant and enfeoffment of Robert le Passh in Brantham, by whatever means they came to him. Sealed.

Testibus: Roberto de Botingham, Willelmo Danyel, Iohanne de Wogate, Willelmo Maggs, Roberto Maupetit, Nicholao de Cattiwade et aliis.

Brantham, 29 July 1343

> Ipswich, SRO, HD 1538/204/4; approx. 245 × 130 + 20 mm; endorsed: Braham, carta domini Iohannis Passh capellani de redditu .xxx. d., iii; tag and seal missing.

> For the grant of this land to the canons by John de la Mare, see no. 79; for Nicholas del Broc, see no. 81.

CAPEL ST MARY

186. Indenture whereby Prior Henry and the canons have leased at farm to John Lityll and Agnes his wife a parcel of arable land in the vill of Capel St Mary (*Capele*) lying between the lands of Philip Greneslade of Saxham, of which one headland abuts on the land of the late Sir William Gernun, kt, and the other on that of John of Breckles (*Breklis*), to have and to hold to them and their assigns from Michaelmas 1361 for a term of seven years for an annual rent of 9d in equal instalments at the four usual terms. Warranty is granted. John and Agnes concede right of distraint and reoccupation should this rent fall into arrears in whole or in part.

Hiis testibus: Willelmo de Waldingfeld, Roberto Oldhawe, Petro Bole et aliis.

> Cartulary no. 141; approx. 245 × 152+ mm; chirograph, indented at top margin; badly faded; descriptive endorsement; seal (not illustrated), small vessica, approx. 35 × 26 mm, red wax, Virgin and Child.

187. Notification by John le Tailur of Bentley (*Bentleye*) that he has granted, relaxed and utterly quitclaimed, for himself and his heirs in perpetuity, to Prior Henry and the convent all right and claim which he had or in any wise may or

might have in a parcel of pasture with appurtenances which he held at farm by the lease granted to him and his successors by Prior Henry, which lies in Capel St Mary (*Capele*) between the heath on one side and the wood called 'Hulnei' on the other, so that neither he nor his heirs nor anyone in their name may henceforth make any claim therein. Sealed in testimony.

Hiis testibus: Roberto fabro, Ricardo Barun, Iohanne Coiner et aliis.

Bentley, Monday 10 January 1362.

Helmingham, T/Hel/98/25 (A2/168); approx. 235 × 80 + 14 mm; no medieval endorsement; tag and seal missing.

188. Indenture between Prior Henry and the canons on the one part and Robert the smith (*fabro*) of Bentley (*Benteleye*), Alice his wife and Edmund their son on the other, whereby the prior and canons have conceded and leased at farm to Robert, Alice and Edmund a parcel of pasture once held of the convent by Hubert le Peyntour in the vill of Capel St Mary (*Capele*), lying between the wood called 'Hulney' to the south and the heath of Capel to the north, together with a way, assigned by the prior and canons or their attorneys, with chase of beasts where it can best be done without damage, from Robert's house to the said parcel of pasture, to have and to hold to them for the duration of their lives from Easter 1362, rendering therefrom annually to the prior and canons and their successors 3s in silver in equal instalments at Easter, the feast of St John the Baptist, Michaelmas and the feast of St Andrew for all services. Warranty is granted against all persons. Should they default in payment of this farm in part or in whole, then the prior and canons and their successors may distrain upon that parcel of pasture and on all the lands of Robert, Alice and Edmund, into whosesoever hands they have come, and may without contradiction retain those things distrained until full satisfaction is made for arrears and damages. In testimony whereof the seals[a] of Robert, Alice and Edmund are appended.

Hiis testibus: Ricardo Talmach' de Benteleye, Iohanne Ormer de eadem, Edmundo atte Het3 de eadem, Ricardo Baroun de eadem, Thoma Casnel de eadem et aliis.   Bentley, Wednesday 20 April 1362.

[a] There is only one slit for a single tag.

Cartulary no. 142; approx. 248 × 122+ mm; chirograph, indented at top margin; endorsed: Dodnash.

189. Indenture whereby Prior Roger and the canons have conceded and leased at farm to John Cardenal of Capel St Mary (*Capel*) five parcels of land in various places in the vill of Capel, of which one is called 'Dovelond', another 'Wrangecroft', the third 'Grimslond', the fourth was once leased to John Litil and the fifth is a parcel of pasture lying next to the wood of 'Hulney', to have and to hold to him, his executors and assigns from Michaelmas next for a full term of thirty years, rendering annually 17s 11d of good and legal money in equal instalments at the four usual terms. Should this rent fall into arrears by one whole year, then the

157

prior and canons and their successors may re-enter and reseise the four parcels of land and one of meadow with all goods and chattels thereon, until full satisfaction is made for rent and arrears. Warranty is granted against all persons for the term of thirty years. In witness whereof John's seal is appended to this indenture. Hiis testibus: Thoma Standone, Iohanne Breklis, Iohanne Samson, Rogero Gylebert, Iohanne Boytone et aliis.

Dodnash/ Capel St Mary,[a] Monday 27 November 1368.

[a] At beginning of text Dodnash, in dating clause at end Capel St Mary.

Cartulary no. 145; approx. 222 × 145 mm; endorsed: Wenham, Grimslond iacen' in Capel.

190. Indenture whereby Prior Roger and the convent have conceded and leased for life to William Marigon of East Bergholt (*Bergwolte*) a piece of meadow in Capel St Mary lying between his meadow and their pasture, of which one headland abuts on their meadow and on the path leading from 'Olbregge' to the wood of 'Hulnei', to hold for his lifetime for an annual rent of 3s 4d payable in four equal instalments. Warranty is granted against all persons for his lifetime. If there should be failure of payment in part or in whole, the canons may enter and reseise until full satisfaction is made. After his death the meadow is to revert to the canons and to remain to them without contradiction. Sealed alternately by the parties.

Hiis testibus: Willelmo Hacun, Iohanne Cristemasse, Nicholao Dekeman et aliis.

Dodnash, 30 April 1375

Ipswich, SRO, HD 1538/204/6; approx. 222 × 116 + 20 mm; chirograph, indented at top margin; endorsed: Willelm' Marygon de prato apud Holbrigge iacente yn Capell'.

For other references to William Marigon, see nos 69, 155, 182.

191. Indenture whereby Prior Robert and the convent have by their unanimous consent granted and leased at farm to Gilbert Debenham, esquire (*armiger*), two parcels of land with appurtenances called 'Prioris Londe' in the vills of Capel St Mary (*Capell'*) and Copdock (*Coppedok*), which parcels of land William Byrd of Copdock leased from the prior and canons, to have and to hold to Gilbert and his executors from the date of these presents until the completion of a full term of one hundred years, rendering therefrom annually to the prior and canons and their successors a rose at the Nativity of St John the Baptist at Gilbert's manor of Little Wenham (*Wenham Parva*), if it is sought there by the prior or his successors, for all services, exactions and demands. For this concession and lease Gilbert has paid the prior and canons £20 in cash. In testimony whereof the parties have sealed each other's copy of this indenture.

Dodnash, in the chapterhouse, 17 December 1436.

Cartulary nos 152–3; two parts of chirograph; 152: approx. 335 × 58 + 12 mm; 153: approx. 335 × 46+ mm; no endorsements.

For Debenham, see W.I. Haward, 'Gilbert Debenham: a Medieval Rascal in Real Life', *History* xiii, 1928–9, 300–14; also J.G. Wedgwood, *History of Parliament: Biographies of the Members of the Commons House, 1439–1509*, London 1936, 264–5, and for his connection with the duke of Norfolk, patron of Dodnash, C. Richmond, *The Paston Family in the Fifteenth Century: the First Phase*, Cambridge 1990, 135, 138, 237, 248–9.

192. Indenture whereby Prior Robert Newbourne and the convent have leased and granted at farm to William Dekyth and Mary his wife, of Capel St Mary (*Capell'*), three parcels of land with appurtenances in Capel St Mary, of which the first is called 'Doveland', the second 'Grymeslond' and the third 'Marlepetfeld', to have and to hold to them, their executors and attorneys from Michaelmas next for a full term of sixty years, rendering annually to the prior and convent and their successors 12s in silver of the good and legal money of England in equal instalments at Easter and Michaelmas, and acquitting the said three parcels of land with appurtenances against the king, the capital lords of the fee and anyone else for all burdens and payments incumbent thereupon for the duration of the said term. The prior and the convent shall cause to be dug and shall have the clay called 'marll', in the parcel of land called 'Marlepetfeld' whenever necessary for their own stock (*stauro*) thereof throughout the foresaid term, with no contradiction by William and Mary or their attorneys. If the said farm of 12s should be in arrears, in part or in whole, at any term, then the prior and convent may distrain not only upon the said three parcels, but also on all other tenements of William and Mary, and may remove and retain those things distrained until full satisfaction is made for the farm and for arrears. In testimony whereof the parties have sealed each other's copy of this indenture. Dodnash, in the chapterhouse, 10 October 1436.

Helmingham, T/Hel/98/37 (A2/272); approx. 286 × 140 + 25 mm; chirograph indented at top margin; no medieval endorsement; parchment tag, fragment of seal, round, approx. 24 mm; device very indistinct, shield in circle.

FALKENHAM

193. Indenture [*in English*] made between Robert Carre, prior of Dodnash (*Dodnyche*) on the one part and Richard Martyn of [Long] Melford on the other, that whereas the prior has demised and let at farm to Thomas Walden of Falkenham (*Falcanham*) and to Richard Marget of the same town all the lands and tenements, meadows, 'fedyngs' and pastures, together with all other issues and profits with their appurtenances which pertain to the said prior by reason of his priory of Dodnash from the feast of the Annunciation [25 March] before the date of these writings for a full term of five years therefrom, rendering annually to the prior and his assigns £10 of the good and lawful money of England in equal instalments at All Saints and the Annunciation, as is more plainly stated in several

writings made between them; the foresaid prior has granted to the said Richard and Roger Martyn, their executors and assigns, the foresaid yearly service of £10, to be received from the said Thomas and Richard at the said terms, without any payment being made to the prior for the term of five years. For this Richard and Roger Martyn have paid to the prior at the making of this indenture a certain sum of money agreed between them, with which the prior declares himself fully content and paid for the said services for the term of five years. In testimony whereof the parties have set their seals to each other's copy.   18 May 1493.

> Helmingham, T/Hel/98/39 (A14/3); approx. 290 × 165 mm; no medieval endorsement; tongue cut from left, seal missing.

> Richard and Roger Martyn are commemorated in the lower windows of the south aisle, or Martyn aisle, of Long Melford church, dated 1484. This gentry family had lived there since the fourteenth century, and a later Roger Martyn (*c.* 1527–1615) compiled an account of the pre-Reformation church (D. Dymond and G. Paine, *The Spoil of Melford Church: The Reformation in a Suffolk Parish*, Ipswich 1989).

SHIPMEADOW

194. Grant by Prior Richard and the canons to Adam son of John of Walpole, his heirs and assigns in fee and heredity, of the whole marsh of 'Westfen' in Shipmeadow (*Scipmedwe*) with appurtenances, for their homage and the annual rent of 16d payable in two instalments at Easter and Michaelmas for all services, customs, suit of court and demands. Warranty is granted against all persons in perpetuity. Sealed in testimony.

Hiis testibus: Rogero de Colevil', Hervico de Vallibus, Iacobo de Ilketelesham, Rogero filio Osberti, Warino de Barsham, Rogero de Metingham, Willelmo filio Ede, Reginaldo Curming et aliis.   [Mid thirteenth century]

> Ipswich, SRO, HD 1538/278/3; approx. 182 × 100 mm; no turn-up; descriptive endorsement; tag and seal missing.

> Of the witnesses, only Roger of Mettingham occurs elsewhere in this collection, in a charter (119) before 1242. Adam of Walpole occurs 1274–75 (Rye, *Fines*, 77 no. 46). It is impossible to date Prior Richard precisely, but it seems probable that he precedes rather than succeeds Prior Robert, who occurs 1252 × 57 (see 160n.).

STUTTON

195. Notification by Prior John and the canons that they have conceded and granted to Roger Argent of Stutton and Margery his wife, for the duration of their lives, all the tenement which they have in the vill of Stutton with buildings, arable lands, woods, pastures, waters, roads, paths, hedges, ditches and with all other appendages, which tenement was once held of the prior and canons by Ralph de

le Brege, son of Thomas de le Brege chaplain, to have and to hold to Roger and Margery for their lifetimes freely, quit, well and in peace, rendering annually to the prior and canons and their successors 7s in silver, in equal instalments at Easter and Michaelmas, for all other services and secular demands. Warranty is granted in return for the foresaid service against all persons for their lifetimes. Right of distraint is reserved should the rent be in arrears, in whole or in part. After the deaths of Roger and Margery the tenement with its appurtenances shall revert to the prior and canons and their successors in perpetuity. This is drawn up in the form of an indenture sealed alternately by the parties.

Testibus: Willelmo de Crepping, Roberto de Botingham, Willelmo Everard, Roberto le Whyte, Roberto Layss', R. . .*a* Wakelin, Roberto clerico et aliis.

Dodnash, 25 October 1304.

a hole in MS.

Cartulary no. 115; approx. 190 × 120+ mm; chirograph, indented at top margin; no endorsement.

For the release by Margery, see no. 210; for a subsequent grant to John Argent and the legitimate heirs of his body, see no. 197.

196. Notification that when there was dissension between the prior and canons on the one part and Sir William Visdelou, kt, on the other concerning the embankment (*fossati*) of a certain wood of the prior and canons in the vill of Stutton called 'Breggewode', and concerning also a certain annual rent from a tenement which Sir William holds of the canons in Stutton, which was once held by *dominus* Robert of Shelton, eventually on this day an agreement was reached (*ita convenit*) whereby Sir William conceded and utterly quitclaimed for himself and his heirs in perpetuity to the prior and canons and their successors all rights and claim which he had or in any wise might have in the foresaid embankment with appurtenances; and he acknowledged also that he held a certain tenement called 'Monelond', which had been held of the canons by *dominus* Robert of Shelton, of the said prior and canons and their successors by the service of 7s 6d *p.a.* paid at the three usual terms for all service. For this concession and quitclaim the prior and canons have conceded and granted to Sir William a parcel of woodland lying below his woodland in the wood of Stutton, which parcel had come to them as an escheat from Robert dil Lound, their tenant, who was hanged for a felony he had committed, to have and to hold in perpetuity to Sir William and his heirs by the service due therefrom. Drawn up in the form of an indenture to which Sir William's seal was appended.   Sunday, 31 May 1321.

Helmingham, T/Hel/98/10 (A2/69); approx. 217 × 125 + 10 mm; chirograph indented at top margin; endorsement: Carta domini W. de Visdelu de tenemento de Schelton; vi; parchment tag, linen seal bag, seal missing.

The manor which became known as 'Stutton Hall' was held in the earlier thirteenth century by the Pavilly family (cf. 62), but passed in 1311 to William Visdelou and Rose his wife by the terms of a final concord which concluded a case brought against them by Reginald son of Walter de Pavilly and Alice his wife (Copinger, *Manors* vi, 98; Rye, *Fines*, 126 no. 41). For the Visdelou family, see *Shotley Parish Records*, *passim*, and beyond Suffolk, Farrer, *Honours and Knights' Fees* i, 54–60.

197. Notification by Prior John of Gusford (*Godelesford*) and the canons that they have conceded, granted and by this present charter confirmed to John Argent of Stutton (*Stuttone*) all their tenement in the vill of Stutton which was once held by Ralph del Bregg', son of Thomas del Bregge the chaplain, with all arable land, meadows, pastures, woods, as they are enclosed by hedges and embankments, waters, roads and paths, and all other profits and appurtenances in any way pertaining to the said tenement, without any retention, to have and to hold to him and the legitimate heirs of his body of the prior and canons and their successors in perpetuity, rendering therefrom annually to the prior and canons and their successors 4s in equal instalments at Michaelmas and Easter for all other services, customs, suit of court and secular demands. Warranty is granted against all persons. If it should happen that John dies without legitimate heirs of his body, then all the tenement with its appurtenances shall revert to the prior and convent and their successors in perpetuity. In testimony whereof the parties have appended their seals to each other's copy of this agreement.
Testibus: Nicholao Bonde, Ricardo le Spenser, Symone de Creppingg', Willelmo de Finesford, Roberto Petit, Iohanne de Boytone et aliis.

Dodnash, Sunday 4 July 1333.

Cartulary no. 121; approx. 260 × 158+ mm; chirograph, indented at top margin; endorsed: Terra ista veniet retro ad domum de Dodenasch pro defectu sanguinis; ista terra dimissa est Iohanni Argent et Matilde Breggs; seal, round, approx. 20 mm, red-brown wax, squirrel facing to right, legend indecipherable.

For a previous grant of this land to Roger Argent and Margery his wife for their lifetimes in 1304, see no. 195; for the release by Margery, see no. 210. The endorsement noting that this land reverted to the priory through default of heirs conceals the murder by John of his sons, in a fit of madness, for which he received a royal pardon in 1344 (*CPR 1343–45*, 15).

TATTINGSTONE

198. Indenture whereby Prior John of Gusford (*Gudelesforde*) and the canons have conceded and leased at farm to John of Cretingham and his heirs two parcels of land in the vill of Tattingstone (*Tatingeston*), of which one parcel lies between the land of John Mandewile on both sides, one headland to the north abuts on the land of the same John Mandewile and the other to the south on the road leading from the house of John Swalue towards 'Scherevis Grene'; and the other parcel lies between the land of Alexander of Freston and of John Redlond, one headland to the east abuts on the king's highway leading from the bridge called 'Newebregg' towards Ipswich, and the other to the west on the land of William Douce; to have and to hold with all appurtenances of the prior and canons and

their successors to John, his heirs and assigns in perpetuity, rendering therefrom annually to the prior and canons 8d in four equal instalments at Michaelmas, the feast of St Andrew, Easter and the feast of St John the Baptist for all services. Warranty is granted against all persons in perpetuity. The said John shall build on the said land one or two adequate houses. For greater security, John of Cretingham has bound himself to distraint by the prior and canons, their successors and their bailiffs upon the two parcels of land and the house or houses thereupon in the event of non-payment of the rent, until full satisfaction is made for the rent and arrears. In testimony whereof the parties have alternately sealed each other's copy of this indenture. Dodnash, 8 August 1341.

> Cartulary no. 131; approx. 290 × 187 mm; chirograph, indented at top margin; endorsed: Indentura de .ii. peciis terre domini Iohannis Cretyngham in Tatyngston, .viii. d.

199. Indenture whereby Adam son and heir of Hugh le Webber of Tattingstone (*Tatiston*) has remitted and quitclaimed for himself and his heirs in perpetuity to the prior and canons and their successors all right and claim which he has, had or might in the future have in a parcel of pasture with appurtenances in the vill of Bentley (*Bentleye*), lying between the land of the prior and canons on both sides, of which one headland to the west abuts on the canons' stream running towards 'Neubregge' and the other to the east on the land of the prior and canons, so that neither Adam, his heirs nor anyone in their name may henceforth in perpetuity claim any right therein. In return the prior and canons have remitted and quitclaimed, for them and their successors in perpetuity to the said Adam, his heirs and assigns all right and claim which they had, have or might have in the future in a parcel of pasture with appurtenances in Tattingstone (*Tatingston*) between the pasture of the prior and canons to the north and that of William Douce to the south, of which one headland to the west abuts on the foresaid stream and the other to the east on the lands of the prior and canons and of Adam, saving to the prior and canons the lordship of the said pasture, that is of Adam and his heirs, and other services, that is an annual rent of 4d to be received from the pasture. They have moreover granted to Adam, his heirs and assigns in perpetuity a path (*viam*) six feet in breadth in the field called 'Smyriefeld' in the vill of Tattingstone, lying between Adam's ditch (*fossatum*) and the land of the prior and canons, to hunt and chase freely from Adam's house (*mansione*) in the said vill towards the said pasture, but without any further damage being done to the prior and canons in that chase, rendering therefrom ½d *p.a.* to the prior and canons and their successors in perpetuity; so that neither the prior and canons nor their successors may henceforth in perpetuity make any claim to the foresaid parcel of pasture or path, except for the fealty of the said Adam, his heirs and assigns and an annual rent of 4½d as foresaid. Adam conceded for himself, his heirs and assigns that should the fealty or the rent ever in future happen to fall in arrears, then the prior and canons and their successors might distrain upon the pasture with appurtenances and retain those things distrained until full satisfaction was made for fealty and rent. In testimony whereof the parties have sealed each other's copy of this indenture.

Hiis testibus: Willelmo de Finisford, Stephano Attemer, Roberto de Finisford, Henrico Snou, Iohanne de Boyton et aliis.   Dodnash, Sunday 30 March 1337.

Cartulary no. 129; approx. 265 × 185 mm; chirograph, indented at top margin; endorsed: Carta Ade le Webber, ii; seal, shield-shaped, approx. 40 × 28 mm, brown wax, bird walking to right, under indecipherable letters.

200. Indenture whereby Prior Roger and the canons have conceded and leased at farm to John Ingelond of Bentley (*Bentlegh*) and Joan his wife a messuage with a house built thereupon, together with arable lands, woods, meadows and alder-groves adjacent, as divided by its limits and bounds, ditches and embankments between them at south, east, north, and at the west from the tenement called 'Cockis' by the water running from that tenement to the pasture called 'Mellepas-tur', together with a croft called 'Melleleye' and a pasture called 'Oyepasture', lying in the vill of Tattingstone (*Tatyngston*), to have and to hold of the prior and canons for the term of John' and Joan's lives, rendering annually therefrom 20s 8d in equal instalments at the four terms of the year for all services and secular demands. After their deaths the messuage with the house thereon and all appurte-nances shall remain to Adam and John, their sons, for the term of their lives by the foresaid service; after the deaths of Adam and John (junior), it shall remain to Isabelle and Juliana, daughters of John (senior) and Joan and to Robert son of Nicholas Wykeman of [East] Bergholt (*Bergholte*) for the term of their lives by the foresaid service. After the deaths of Isabelle, Juliana and Robert, the mes-suage shall revert and remain in perpetuity to the prior and canons and their suc-cessors, with contradiction by no person. If it happens that the farm should be in arrears at any term, in whole or in part, the prior and canons may re-enter, reseise and distrain the said messuage with all goods and chattels therein, and may re-move and retain those things distrained without contradiction until full satisfac-tion shall have been made for the farm with arrears. They shall hold the messuage in such a way that neither John and Joan nor anyone above named may cause waste or destruction to the house, woods and trees except by the will and deliver-ance of the prior and canons and their successors; saving to the prior and canons and their attorneys a reasonable path for going, driving and carrying to the mill and to the lands, meadows and pastures with their horses and animals, and saving to them also the right of felling trees on the foresaid lands and carrying them away with their horses and carts whensoever and wheresoever it may please them, in such a way that the stumps of the felled trees shall remain to the profit of John and Joan and the others named above. Warranty is granted against all per-sons in the form aforesaid. In testimony whereof the parties have sealed each other's part of this indenture.

Hiis testibus: Rogero Payn, Iohanne Swalwe, Augustino Stone, Roberto Reed-lond, Iohanne Cheseman et aliis.

Dodnash/Tattingstone,[a] Monday 6 October 1371.

[a] At beginning of text Dodnash, in dating clause at end Tattingstone.

Helmingham, T/Hel/98/32 (A2/189); approx. 225 × 135 + 7 mm; chirograph, indented at top margin; descriptive endorsement; three parchment tags, to left-hand tag is attached fragment of seal, natural wax.

201. Indenture whereby Prior Roger and the canons have conceded and leased at farm to Roger Payn of Tattingstone (*Tatyngston*), Joan his wife and John their son two parcels of land, of which one lies in the vill of Tattingstone between Roger's land on one side and that of William dil Mer' on the other, of which one headland to the west abuts on the land of the prior and canons and the other to the east on the road, and the other lies in the vill of Bentley (*Benteleye*) between the lands of the prior and canons on both sides, of which one headland to the south abuts on the road from Tattingstone to Bentley and the other to the north on the land of William dil Mer, to have and to hold with appurtenances for the term of their lives, rendering annually to the prior and canons 3s 4d in equal instalments at the four terms of the year for all services and secular demands. Warranty is granted by this service for the term of their lives against all persons. Roger, Joan and John have conceded that should the said rent be in arrears, in whole or in part, at any term, the prior and canons may reseise and re-enter upon these two parcels, with all the chattels found thereon, and may retain them without contradiction until full satisfaction is made for the rent and arrears. After their deaths these parcels shall revert to the prior and canons and their successors in perpetuity without contradiction. In testimony whereof the parties have sealed each other's copy of this indenture.
Hiis testibus: Arthur Keen, Roberto Clerc, Rogero Seasun, Roberto Rodelond, Iohanne (*illeg.*) et aliis. 4 October 1372

Helmingham, T/Hel/98/33 (A2/192); approx. 277 × 100 + 15 mm; chirograph, indented at top margin; descriptive endorsement; parchment tag, seal missing.

202. Indenture whereby the prior and convent have leased at farm to John Inge-lond and Joan his wife of Bentley (*Bentlya*) a meadow called 'Thwytysmedwe' in Tattingstone, lying to the west of the fulling mill called 'Thwytys melle', and also a croft of land called 'Cawfeld', and a wood with a piece of heathland in the same vill of Tattingstone lying between the canons' heathland to the north and the road leading from the house of the late Henry Thwytis to Tattingstone church to the south, of which the headlands abut on the wood of John of Holbrook (*Holbroke*) to the east and the canons' road leading from Robert Rodelond's house to the heath of 'Bouperdon' to the west, to have and to hold of the canons for their lifetimes for an annual rent of 12s at the four terms of the year in equal portions for all services and secular demands. After their deaths these lands shall remain to Adam their son for his lifetime by the same service, and after Adam's death they shall revert to John, Isabelle and Juliana, son and daughters of the foresaid John and Joan, and after the deaths of John, Isabelle and Juliana they shall revert and remain in perpetuity to the prior and canons. Warranty is granted on the above terms against all persons. John, Joan and their children have conceded that if the rent should be in arrears, in whole or in part, at any term, the canons may re-enter

these properties and reseise them without contradiction, until full satisfaction is made for rent and arrears. Sealed by the parties alternately in the form of an indenture.

Hiis testibus: Iohanne Card, Thoma Petit, Rogero Scard, Roberto Rodeland, Iohanne Cheseman et aliis.   Dodnash, Monday 2 October 1373

Ipswich, SRO, q s 271 (Fitch's *Monasticon*), vol. ii, at p. 178; approx. 225 × 126 + 12 mm; chirograph, indented at top margin; descriptive endorsement; slits for four seals, tags and seals missing.

203. Indenture whereby Prior Roger and the canons have conceded and leased at farm to Peter le Maydyn of Stutton, Joan his wife and Peter their son a parcel of land called 'Clackysland' in the vill of Tattingstone (*Tatinggistun*), lying between the land once held by William Duce on one side and the land called 'le Hoo' on the other, of which one headland abuts on the meadow of John of Holbrook (*Holbrok*) and the other on the land called 'Gardenislond' to the north, to have and to hold with appurtenances of the prior and canons to Peter, Joan and Peter and the legitimate heirs of the body of Peter the son, rendering annually to the prior and canons 3s 5d in equal instalments at the four usual terms of the year for all services and secular demands. If the said farm of 3s 5d should fall into arrears in part or in whole, the prior and canons may distrain upon the said parcel of land and the goods and chattels found thereupon, and may retain those things distrained until full satisfaction is made for the farm and its arrears. Warranty is granted against all persons in perpetuity. If it should happen that the younger Peter should die without legitimate heirs of his body, then the foresaid parcel of land shall revert to the prior and canons in perpetuity. In testimony whereof the parties have sealed each other's copy of this indenture.

Hiis testibus: Roberto Beri, Henrico Boyry,[a] Rogero Payn, Iohanne Wratere, Iohanne Cole.   Dodnash, Monday 7 May 1375.

[a] Reading uncertain.

Cartulary no. 148; approx. 220 × 104+ mm; chirograph, indented at top margin; endorsed: Petrus Maydyn de Stutton; Clackyslond in Tatinggeston; fragment of seal, round, brown wax, eagle displayed.

204. Notification that Prior John and the canons have conceded, leased and by this indentured charter confirmed to John atte Mere of Tattingstone (*Tatyngston*) a parcel of arable land with appurtenances which lies in the field called 'Asschfeld' in the vill of Tattingstone, between the land of Henry Scard on one side and the lessee's own land on the other, of which one headland to the west abuts on the land of the prior and canons and the other to the east on the lessee's land called 'Wrongeaker', to have and to hold to him, his heirs and assigns from 24 June next for a full term of sixty years, rendering therefrom annually to the prior and canons, their successors or their attorneys for such a number of acres 4d in equal instalments at the four terms of the year for all suits, services and secular demands.

If the foresaid rent should at any term be in arrears and not paid, then the prior and canons and their successors or their attorneys may distrain upon the said parcel of land, and also on all the lands and tenements of the said John atte Mere, wherever they may be, and may remove and retain those things distrained until full satisfaction is made for the rent and for arrears. Warranty is granted for the foresaid term against all persons. In witness whereof the prior and canons have set their seal to this indentured charter.

Hiis testibus: Iohanne Talmache, Roberto Geye, Ricardo Aggor, Ricardo Baldwyne, Roberto Bery et aliis.   Tattingstone, Sunday 22 June 1410.

> Helmingham, T/Hel/98/35 (A2/233); approx. 215 × 132 + 17 mm; chirograph, indented at top margin; descriptive endorsement; parchment tag, fragment of seal, round, dark-brown wax, shield with cross.

205. VACAT – see no. 178A.

GREAT WENHAM

206. Agreement (*conventio*) made between Prior R. and the canons on the one part and William Treysgos of Wenham Combusta on the other, whereby they have leased at farm to him all the land which they hold in Wenham Combusta with its appurtenances from Michaelmas 1284 for a term of twelve years. For this lease William shall render each year at Michaelmas to the prior and canons a seam and a half of pure corn, either in person or by his attorney. He has obligated himself, should he fail in this render in any of the twelve years, to the payment of 12d to the lord archdeacon of Suffolk for the time being, and he shall be compelled to make satisfaction for the foresaid grain by the ecclesiastical tribunal, and he has renounced royal prohibition. For greater security he wills and concedes that the king's bailiff for the time being may compel him to make satisfaction by the distraint of his chattels, movable and immovable, both within and without his house; and as often as the king's bailiff makes such distraint, William shall pay him 12d for his labour. The prior and canons will warrant and defend the said tenement with its appurtenances to William or his certain assigns for these twelve years against all persons. At the end of this period the tenement shall revert to the prior and canons without contradiction by William, his heirs or assigns. In witness whereof this is drawn up in the form of a chirograph sealed alternately by the parties.

Presentibus: Radulfo clerico de Benetley, Richardo de Bruar', Willelmo fratre eius, domino Hosberto de Coppedoc capellano, Willelmo clerico de Wenham Combusta et aliis.

> Cartulary no. 109; approx. 168 × 85 + 10 mm; chirograph, indented at top margin; descriptive endorsements.

> For the origins of the Tresgoz family at Troisgots (Manche, arr. St-Lô, cant.

Tessy-sur-Vire), see Loyd, *Anglo-Norman Families*, 106–7. The main branch of the family was represented *c.* 1200 by Robert, who was bailiff of the Cotentin in 1195 and under John, to whom he adhered and therefore lost his Norman lands. At this time a William, predecessor of the William of this charter, is recorded as holding one and a half fees of the king in Norfolk and Suffolk in 1190–91, and two and a half fees and eight parts of one knight (*sic*) there in 1210 × 12 (*Red Bk Exchq.*, 77, 479); he also held six knights' fees in Essex and Hertfordshire of the honour of Peverel of London (ibid., 173, 591). William de Coleville held half a knight's fee of this earlier William at Aspall by a fine of 1209 (*Fines* ii, no. 505).

207. Indenture whereby Prior Henry and the canons have conceded and leased at farm to Alexander le Clerk of Great Wenham (*Brondewenham*), for a term of twelve years, all their land in the vill of Wenham, with all manner of pasturage (*herbagio, pascua et pastura*) and with all other appurtenances, to have and to hold to him and his assigns from 2 February 1362, rendering annually to the prior and canons and their successors 3s 6d in equal instalments at Easter and the feast of St Margaret [20 July], commencing at Easter next; Alexander shall render to the capital lords of the fee the due and lawfully accustomed services. Warranty is granted for the foresaid service against all persons for the term of twelve years. Alexander conceded for himself and his assigns that should the farm be in arrears at any term by five days, in whole or in part, which God forbid, then the prior and canons and their successors may enter into all this land with its appurtenances and reseise it, with whatever chattels may be found thereon, with no contradiction by Alexander or his assigns. Sealed alternately by the parties.
Hiis testibus: Iohanne le Spenser, Iohanne Waryn de Capele, Willelmo de Waldyngfeld, Stephano de Bramford, Alexandro Andreu et aliis.

Dodnash, 2 February 1362.

Helmingham, T/Hel/98/26 (A2/169); approx. 227 × 116 + 7 mm; chirograph, indented at top margin; endorsed: Alexander Clerk de Wenham Combusta iii^{ta}; parchment tag cut from old document, fragment of seal, round, approx. 22 mm, natural wax, bird walking to left.

208. Indenture whereby Prior John Bryggewater and the convent have leased at farm to Stephen and William Cardynall 5½ acres of land lying in three parcels in Great Wenham (*Magna Wenham*), called 'Aspelond', to have and to hold, be there more or less, to Stephen and William and their assigns from Easter last for a full term of forty-one years from the date of these presents, rendering annually to the prior and canons and their successors or their attorneys 4d sterling at Michaelmas for the duration of the term. If the farm is in arrears at Michaelmas, in part or in whole, the prior and canons and their successors or their attorneys may enter into these parcels or any one of them, distrain upon them and retain those things distrained until full satisfaction is made for the annual farm and arrears. In testimony whereof the parties have sealed each other's copy of this indenture.

30 June 1497.

Helmingham, T/Hel/98/40 (A2/349); approx. 318 × 115 + 18 mm; endorsed: Cerdenall, Wenham; two parchment tags, on left-hand tag fragment of round seal, red wax, device indecipherable.

For the grant and other documents relating to the acquisition of 'Aspelond', see nos 131–5.

MISCELLANEOUS OBLIGATIONS AND ACQUITTANCES
209–15

209. Notification by Prior John and the convent that they have pardoned to John le Neuman, senior, of Bentley, all actions and pleas which they have or in any way might have against him for the breaking of any agreement or for any debt due to them, from the beginning of the world to this day, so that neither they nor their successors may implead him in the future. Sealed in testimony with their common seal.   Dodnash, 23 December 1279.

> Cartulary no. 107; approx. 222 × 66 mm; no endorsement; seal missing.

> For the priory's dealings with later generations of the Newman family, see nos 157, 163, 213.

210. Notification by Margery, widow of the late Roger Argent of Stutton, that she has pardoned to Prior John of Gusford (*Godelesford*) and the canons all manner of actions, both real and personal, from the beginning of the world to this day, so that neither she nor anyone in her name may henceforth in perpetuity bring any action against them. Sealed in testimony.
Testibus: Nicholao Bonde, Ricardo le Spenser, Roberto Petit et aliis.
                                      Stutton, Thursday 30 September 1333.

> Cartulary no. 124; approx. 212 × 64 mm; endorsed: v; seal, oval, approx. 28 × 24 mm, brown-black wax, human figure on left kneeling at feet of standing figure at right (not illustrated).

> For the lease of land in 1304 for their lifetimes to Roger Argent and Margery, to which this release doubtless refers, see no. 195; for a lease to John Argent, probably their son, on 4 July 1333, see no. 197.

211. Notification by Thomas of Tey (*Ty*) of Milden (*Meldyng*) that he has in perpetuity pardoned to the prior and convent all manner of actions, complaints (*querelas*) and demands which he has or might have against them by reason of any debt, deed (*facti*) or any other contract initiated or concluded between them from the beginning of the world to this day, so that neither he nor anyone in his name may henceforth make any claim against them by reason thereof, but rather are utterly debarred from any real or personal action. Sealed in testimony. London, in the church of St Edmund King and Martyr, Lombard Street, Saturday 24 September 1334.

> Cartulary no. 125; approx. 275 × 97 mm; no endorsement; seal, round, approx. 26 mm, red wax, in a cusped circle, a shield of arms: a chevron (hatched) between three elm trees (as *PRO: Catalogue of Seals: Personal Seals* ii P2120).

For a very brief note on the Tey or Teye family, see *PSIA* viii, 201–2. Robert and William of Tey occur in an Essex context in the 1330s (*A Calendar of the Cartularies of John Pyel and Adam Fraunceys*, ed. S.J. O'Connor, Camden 5th ser. ii, 1993, no. F52). In the 1390s Robert Teye was king's esquire and MP for Essex (Tout, *Chapters* iv, 38).

212. Notification by John of Boyton, son of Richard of Boyton, of Capel St Mary, that he has pardoned to Prior John of Gusford (*Gudlisford*) and the canons of Dodnash all actions, both real and personal, which he might have against them or any one of them for any reason whatsoever. Sealed in testimony.

Dodnash, Sunday 21 June 1338.

Helmingham, T/Hel/98/19 (A2/104); approx. 227 × 78 mm; endorsed: I. de Boyton; tongue cut from left, fragment of seal, round, approx. 20 mm; natural wax varnished brown; lily in ornate surround, legend indecipherable.

213. Indenture recording that whereas Prior Henry and the canons have acknowledged that they are bound to *dominus* William le Newman, rector of Erwarton (*Everwarton*) in the sum of forty marks of silver by reason of a loan to be repaid to William, his executors or attorneys at the church of St Mary of Dodnash within ten years of the date of these presents, at the rate of four marks every Easter until full satisfaction is made, as is more fully contained in letters obligatory, William has conceded that when the prior and canons shall have paid twenty marks of silver within ten years at the rate of two marks every Easter, until full satisfaction is made for the said twenty marks, then the said letters obligatory for forty marks shall lack effect and be held at naught. In testimony whereof this indenture is sealed alternately by the parties.   Dodnash, 11 July 1352.

Cartulary no. 138; approx. 306 × 47 mm; endorsed: domini Willelmi; seal missing.

For earlier loans to the priory, and for the establishment of his chantry in Nov. 1351, see no. 157.

214. Notification that Andrew of Bures, kt, and William of Bures his brother have quitclaimed to Prior Henry and the canons all right and claim which they have or in any way might have in all lands, tenements, rents, services and customs which they have held at any time by concession and enfeoffment of the prior and convent or their predecessors, and have pardoned to them all manner of action, both real and personal, which they have or might have against them, for all times past, by reason of legal transgression or otherwise. Sealed in testimony.

Saturday, 14 February 1355.

Helmingham, T/Hel/98/23 (A6/6); approx. 205 × 122 + 20 mm; endorsed: dominus And' de Bures et dominus Willelmus; two parchment tags, on the left of which round seal, approx. 26 mm, red wax, shield in cusped circle, device indecipherable.

Sir Andrew of Bures, d. 12 April 1360, held *inter alia* the manor of Raydon, land at Hintleshan and other extensive estates in Suffolk and Essex, in which he had been granted free warren in October 1335 (*CIPM* x, no. 638, p. 522; *C Ch R 1327–41*, 341). William of Bures, his brother, was probably the parson of Wickhambrook in 1355 (Rye, *Fines*, 192 no. 22).

215. Notification by John Beneyt of Chattisham (*Chatesham*) that he has remitted, relaxed and utterly quitclaimed, for himself and his heirs, to Prior Roger and the canons, the sum of £8 13s 4d, for which they are indebted to him. This he has done for the sustenance of his body and the salvation of his soul, so that neither he, his heirs nor anyone in his name may henceforth make any claim thereto. Sealed in testimony.   Dodnash, Monday 15 December 1382.

Cartulary no. 149; approx. 247 × 77 mm; no endorsement; seal missing.

ADDENDUM

When this volume was in proof, Dr Nicholas Vincent discovered and kindly communicated to me a reference to Dodnash priory in PRO, E13/82A (Exchequer Plea Roll, 32–3 Edward III), m. 89–d. This is a case brought by the crown in 1359, alleging that in 1340–41 the prior and canons had not paid the tenth on those lands acquired in 1331 from John Goldingham, clerk (nos 137–54 above), as they were not included in the *Taxatio* of 1291.

INDEX OF PERSONS AND PLACES

Numbers given first, in Roman type, are those of charters in this edition; W indicates that the person concerned occurs as a witness. There follow, in italic type, references to pages in the introduction.

Places are in Suffolk, unless otherwise indicated; e.g. Cambs., Cambridgeshire; Ess., Essex; Gloucs., Gloucestershire; Hants, Hampshire; Herts., Hertfordshire; Leics., Leicestershire, Middx., Middlesex; Norf., Norfolk, Sx, Sussex.

181

INDEX OF SUBJECTS